Praise for *Recovery Writing*

"Deftly weaving together his own recovery journey, the stories of other addicts, and ways of 'writing through recovery,' James Ryan, in *Recovery Writing: Discovery and Healing in the Twelve Steps* provides a useful and breathtakingly poignant set of observations on how the act of writing is integral to healthy recovery. Part memoir, part how-to book, Ryan's book is a must-read for anyone interested in understanding the power of writing in overcoming the cunning, baffling, and powerful pull of addiction."—**Michael Bernard-Donals**, Professor of English at the University of Wisconsin-Madison and author of *Forgetful Memory: Representation and Remembrance After Auschwitz* and other titles.

"If writing connects us with energies and powers beyond ourselves, how does writing contribute to the mysterious process of healing from addiction? Drawing from extensive research, the stories of other addicts, and deep reflection on his own experience, Ryan explores the power of writing to help people in the Twelve Step program move from selfishness to compassion, from isolation to relationship, and from resentment to serenity. Because of its honesty, thoughtful analysis, and imaginative sweep, his book is often thrilling to read and makes a real contribution to the literature of addiction and recovery."—**Margaret Bullitt-Jonas**, author, *Holy Hunger: A Woman's Journey from Food Addiction to Spiritual Fulfillment;* co-editor, *Rooted and Rising: Voices of Courage in a Time of Climate Crisis*

"A brilliantly humane, authentic contribution to the writing and wellbeing movement that will resonate with readers struggling with addiction, working with those who have addiction, or anyone seeking a practical, self-determined way to reach their full potential in life."
—**Dr. Stacey Cochran**, the University of Arizona

"Over the last few years, I've read every book on recovery I could get my hands on. None has been more enlightening than James Ryan's *Recovery Writing*. Ryan succeeds in communicating the essence of recovery through the voices of people who use language to transmute the gift of desperation into a new way of life. The book is a must read for anyone who wants to understand the promises of recovery, and how to claim them for one's own."—**Stephen R. Haynes**, Author of *Why Can't Church Be More Like an AA Meeting?: And Other Questions Christians Ask about Recovery*

"Finally, a book that brings fresh insight to one of the most well-traveled paths of recovery. James Ryan shows that for many people, written self-examination is not the onerous chore it is often imagined to be, but is actually one of the most powerful (and mystical) aspects of Twelve Step spirituality. This is less a book about recovery than it is a deep dive into the little explored practice of spiritual writing."—**Piers Kaniuka**, MA, MTS author of *Real People, Real Recovery* and curator of the *Resistance Recovery* podcast and FB group

"For those who are hungry for relief from their suffering, this book is a feast that satisfies on every level. Interwoven within these pages are stories of hope that highlight the value of connection and revel in the mystery of faith while offering practical and specific suggestions for writing our way into recovery. For desperate people looking for a pathway through their pain—this book is a must read."—**Teresa J. McBean**, former Director of the National Association of Christian Recovery and co-pastor at Northstar Community

"Dr. James Ryan combines personal experience and his doctoral research in writing studies to examine what many popular self-help books take for granted: writing's potential to heal. Ryan shares the stories of people in recovery with respect, love, and humility. In doing so, he teaches readers about the power of expression to help us see ourselves more clearly and grow in community with others. I read it with my journal and pencil by my side."—**Kate Vieira**, author of *American by Paper* and *Writing for Love and Money*

"*Recovery Writing* shines new light on the key role writing plays in addiction recovery. From the serious research of science to Bill Wilson's seances and Ouija boards, Ryan blends his own writing experiences with motivating stories from an array of addicts who dared pick up pencil or pen and found a doorway to their souls. His book may give more addicts the courage to do the same."—**Fr. Bill W.**, Episcopal priest, and researcher on Two Way Prayer

Recovery Writing

Writing

*Discovery and Healing
in the Twelve Steps*

JAMES RYAN

Lantern Publishing & Media ● Woodstock and Brooklyn, NY

2023
Lantern Publishing & Media
PO Box 1350
Woodstock, NY 12498
www.lanternpm.org

Printed in the United States of America

Library of Congress Cataloging-in-Publication Data

Names: Ryan, James (James William), author.
Title: Recovery writing : discovery and healing in the twelve steps / James Ryan.
Description: Woodstock, NY : Lantern Publishing & Media, 2023. | Includes bibliographic references.
Identifiers: LCCN 2022033976 (print) | LCCN 2022033977 (ebook) | ISBN 9781590566909 (paperback) | ISBN 9781590566916 (epub)
Subjects: LCSH: Substance abuse—Treatment. | Creative writing—Therapeutic use. | Diaries—Therapeutic use.
Classification: LCC RC564 .R93 2023 (print) | LCC RC564 (ebook) | DDC 616.86/06—dc23/eng/20221114
LC record available at https://lccn.loc.gov/2022033976
LC ebook record available at https://lccn.loc.gov/2022033977

For the addict still suffering, sober or not,
and anyone else who finds help in these pages

TABLE OF CONTENTS

Acknowledgments

Many thanks are due to many people, including:
My parents, who suffered much and supported me anyway
My brother, who had to see the worst of it
Piers Kaniuka, who showed me how to recover
Kate Vieira, who helped me see my need to do this research
Michael Bernard-Donals, who guided me through
Heidi Weston, who made it all possible and worthwhile
And each addict I interviewed, for sharing their story with me

INTRODUCTION

Bad ideas about writing can ruin your life.

Not in most circumstances, of course. Many people have mistaken ideas about what writing is and how it works, and they can still put together a grocery list just fine. But if you're an addict trying to recover in a Twelve-Step fellowship, then, at some point, your sponsor will probably ask you to write. If your ideas about writing interfere with your ability to do the kinds of writing your sponsor asks you to do, you could be in real trouble.

The writing exercises your sponsor assigns won't be like school work. Your sponsor won't care if your grammar is any good or if your spelling is correct. They will want you to discover something about yourself, and—even more than that—they will want you to change. Recovery writing is meant to be *transformative*. It reveals hard truths about us so that we can let go of old thinking and old behavior and live new lives. Unfortunately, bad ideas about writing can get in the way of this process.

For example, if you worry too much about your spelling and grammar, you might miss the point of an exercise completely. Equally, if you worry about getting the "correct" answers instead of honest ones, you could end up being "right" instead of changed. Other problems can arise if you write in order to impress your sponsor (or somebody else). If you write with those motives, you can really wreck yourself emotionally and might end up thinking that recovery doesn't "work" for you. By focusing on superficial goals—following grammar and style, producing the "correct" content, pleasing an audience—we miss the deeper, spiritual point of this kind of writing, and we jeopardize our recovery from addiction.

While superficial distractions can do real harm, there is another kind of bad idea about writing that lurks further below the surface: the notion that we can use writing as a form of self-control. I worked at a treatment center for two years before entering grad school, and I watched many of our guests produce what they thought was effective recovery writing, only to relapse soon after exiting treatment. Many of them made the mistake of thinking they could use writing as a tool to control their mood and behavior. Sometimes, this took the form of magical thinking: "If I do a good job on this writing project, then I will feel good and stay sober!" Other times, the belief was more psychological: "If I gain good insight into myself, I'll be able to change my behavior." Whatever the case, they wanted to use recovery writing as a tool to get a desired result. But recovery writing is not like a tool. It doesn't give you control. Instead, it asks you to stop striving for control. It asks you to *surrender*.

As we will see, the most profoundly transformative and healing experiences that result from recovery writing happen not when addicts produce "good" or "effective" writing, but when they ask something more powerful than themselves to change their lives and then use writing as a means to let that "something" in. This book is about *that* kind of writing, the kind that gives us *contact* with something beyond ourselves, something that has the power to save our lives.

I became interested in transformative, spiritual writing practices through my own experience recovering from addiction. When I was first introduced to Twelve-Step fellowships, I flopped around in meetings for five years before landing in a group of addicts who emphasized the *program* part of the Twelve-Step program, meaning that they saw the Steps not as a set of ideas but as a series of actions to take. These actions were largely *literate*, involving a good amount of reading and writing. When I read and wrote the way my sponsor suggested, my life radically changed for the better. I became sane and sober, and I gained a new understanding of the world and my place within it. Later, as I completed my master's degree and moved on into my PhD, I became deeply curious about recovery writing practices. I wanted to know how something as commonplace as writing could facilitate profound and sweeping changes for a person, especially an addict, so badly tangled up in self-destructive behavior like I had been.

For my PhD research, I interviewed thirty-one addicts about their writing practices. As a rule, I spoke with only addicts who a) had at least one year of recovery, b) had experience in one or more Twelve-Step fellowship (e.g., Alcoholics Anonymous, Narcotics Anonymous, Al-Anon), and c) felt that writing was an important part of their recovery. These selection criteria ensured that the addicts I spoke with were more or less stable in their sobriety and had first-hand experience of recovery writing. The questions I asked these addicts focused on a core set of interests: I wanted to know what kinds of writing they did, how it felt to do those kinds of writing, and how they thought about the relationship between their writing and their recovery. During our conversations, I attempted to set aside my own prejudices and adopt the position of a curious but understanding outsider. I did this because I didn't want the addicts I interviewed to skip over important details, assuming I would know how to fill in the blanks. I also wanted to make sure I was listening with fresh ears. Both as a researcher and as a person in recovery, I needed to learn something new about recovery writing. I had to discover techniques, experiences, and perspectives different from my own in order to complete a dissertation and in order to grow spiritually. As a result, this book is full of ideas about how to write in recovery that never would have occurred to me on my own.

When my interviews were complete, I transcribed the recordings and combed through the data. Once again, I attempted to set aside my own history as much as possible to discover new patterns and themes. Certain commonalities emerged immediately. For example, because I interviewed only addicts who felt that writing was important to their recovery, my interviewees all spoke highly of writing and its value to addicts. Other important themes became apparent only after significant work with this material and equally significant work in overcoming my own inherited biases. For example, addiction is commonly spoken of as a "disease" of some kind, located in each addict's body or mind. Further, recovery often involves profoundly transformative *personal* experiences. As a result, many people think of addiction as a private affair, with both the problem and its solution residing in the individual addict. But the story collectively told by my interviews revealed a highly *social* form of healing. Whatever the origins of addiction might be, it was clear that—for these addicts and their writing practices at least—recovery meant discovering oneself inside a network of new and restored relationships. What recovery writing changed for these addicts (and for me, I see now) was not an individual physical or mental disorder, but their fundamental way of relating to other people and to life itself. As a result, this book is about *that* kind of recovery—the kind that changes you not just as an individual but also as a social being.

Throughout this book, I have interlaced my main chapters with "story" and "how-to" chapters. For each story chapter, I've taken the transcript from my interview with an addict and arranged some of their responses into a narrative of their recovery writing process. How-to chapters offer concrete instructions for some of the writing exercises mentioned by the addicts I interviewed. These stories and how-to guides represent the experiences of real addicts in recovery, along with the directions they used to have those experiences. I've also introduced pieces of my own story into this book, with memoir-ish chapters sprinkled throughout.

The next chapter features Jen's story, which captures a number of important themes that will be developed throughout the book. Recovery writing facilitates a process by which addicts move from *desperation* to *surrender*, from *surrender* to *contact*, and from *contact* into *action*. In Jen's story, you'll see the basic movement of this process, which begins with a moment of desperation for Jen, followed by her surrender and a series of ever-deepening experiences of contact.

One final note before we begin: the stories and exercises related in these pages are meant to be helpful to anyone, no matter what struggles they may face in life. If, in these pages, you find anything useful to you personally, feel free to give it a try, even if you do not identify as an addict or as a member of any Twelve-Step fellowship. Trust me when I say that none of us addicts will mind.

"In the act of writing, I made room"

JEN M.'S STORY

The following is an edited transcript of some of the things Jen told me during our interview. When we talked, Jen shared stories about how her writing practices put her in contact with both herself and her higher power.

Jen's story contains references to healing from a history of sexual violence. Similar references appear throughout this book.

I had started writing a list of my resentments, and I went to a meeting. I was newly sober, so I wasn't numb to my feelings anymore. In my memory of that night, I see this guy there who is well known, went to meetings regularly—a really nice, friendly guy who would talk to all the newcomers. I'm talking to him outside the meeting, and at this point I'm like 118 pounds. I'm skinny as a rail. I'm a hot mess. But this guy is talking like: "You're a beautiful person. Don't worry, your husband is not going to leave you. Any man would be happy to have you." He's trying to be encouraging, but I start to have a dissociative experience because of my trauma history. I'm having a panic attack. My hands are shaking and my palms are sweating. There's also a part of me watching myself, going: "What is your body doing? You are completely overreacting to what this person is doing. He is not a threat to you."

Later that night, I'm in my room. I find myself in the bathroom with the door locked, sitting on the floor, sobbing, and I'm like,

"What is wrong with me?" But I know. And I know I have to do this shit or else I'm either gonna drink again or I'm going to have to live like this for the rest of my life. So, I go to get my notebook and go back into the bathroom. I have the door locked to the room, and I lock the door to the bathroom. I sit on the bathroom floor and I write inventory until three in the morning. I didn't finish it, but that was a moment of finally saying to myself: "This is going to help. I have to do this."

And yet, even after that experience—even after feeling like I had to grab onto this shit like a lifesaver—I left something off my inventory. And then, when I read it, I got to a couple of things toward the end, and I skipped over them too. After that, I started making amends. Two weeks later, things are going fine. I get up in the morning, I get in my car, driving down to Starbucks where I was working, and all of a sudden I am having a flashback of the sexual assault from when I was seventeen. I can't even remember what happened to trigger it. It might have been a little conflict with somebody in the sober house where I was living. Nothing major. Something happened where I felt mildly ashamed of myself around my actions, so now I'm vulnerable, and, man, out of that shame and vulnerability is where a flashback comes from. I immediately think: "Jen, you fucked up on your inventory. If you hadn't done that, you wouldn't be feeling this way." In other words, not doing an honest inventory for me meant that I was going to be vulnerable to feelings of shame. I wasn't free of what shame could do, and so I'm like: "I have to talk to my sponsor and I have to tell my sponsor. I have to tell her I lied about my inventory."

I call her up. I'm like: "I gotta talk to you about something. Here's the deal: when I was writing my inventory, I left this thing off on purpose, and then, when I was reading, I skipped these two things. This is the thing I left off, and these are the things that I skipped." When I finally let her get a word in edgewise, she goes: "Jen, that's really huge. Thanks for telling me." I'm like,

Wow, that's why we do this stuff. Even after not doing an honest inventory—and then noticing that my suffering came back—I was still able to come back to these principles, like, "Get me to a phone, I'm going to be honest this time," and there you go. This shit works. Not that I advocate lying on your inventory. Don't do that! [laughs]

The way I think inventory works is that writing it down— the pen in my hand putting the words on the paper—is literally letting go of the thing. My image of a higher power is a stream, and if there are a lot of sticks blocking the stream, it impedes the flow of water. If I'm walking through the stream, they're tripping me up. But if I pick up those sticks and get them out of the way, it smooths the flow of water. That's it. It's that simple. Words on a paper are getting those thoughts out of my head onto the paper, and that's what unblocks the stream and makes room for a spiritual healing power to move in.

At the same time, I think the Steps can be a bit of a blunt instrument when it comes to past trauma or even a kind of experience, like, "Wow, this person was really awful to me, and it hurt me deeply." I absolutely have a right to those feelings. Those feelings are okay. They're normal. For something like that, I might journal. I can write a piece of resentment inventory and actually see what part of self it's about, but that part of self is still suffering, and that's okay. If I'm writing it down, then I'm not using my suffering to lash out at anybody else, I'm not wallowing in it, and I'm not complaining to other people or yelling at that person. So, that's what journaling is for—to find a more productive outlet for those feelings. I'm not throwing my feelings at somebody else, but I'm also not stuffing them down. I get to feel them, acknowledge them, and then maybe that will turn into inventory later, or maybe not. Maybe it just helps to write it out, and to feel heard and validated by myself.

In the early days of AA, they talked about beginning your day by putting pen to paper. You would begin your day in prayer, put pen to paper, and see what inspiration comes through God. Dr. Bob* would spend time in a group, just sitting quietly and seeing what came out. I don't know what you would call that kind of writing, but sometimes—specifically if I have a problem or something I have to tackle—I will write like that.

The idea first came to me in the first summer of my sobriety, when I was praying from a squirrel-brained place about what to do about childcare for my kids. At the time, my head was all over the place. But I was like: "Okay, I need to figure out what I have to know first, what I need to know next, and what I need to know after that. I'm going to sit down and get quiet with a pen and a piece of paper, and I'm going to see what God has come out of me." I wasn't looking for the next Scripture or anything; it was just, "Help me organize my thoughts and let me see what comes out of this pen as I tackle this problem." I was newly sober. I was newly working part-time, and I just prayed: "I don't know how to do this. I've never done it before. Help me write my to-do list, God."

And, of course, the answers came. I thought to myself, "Oh, this is what Dr. Bob and the others did this for—to begin their day with guidance from God." Again, I'm not sure how I'd describe that kind of writing, but maybe a couple times a year, if I'm struggling with something for a few days in a row, I'll sit down and it's like: "What the hell is on my mind? Let me just get that out of the way."

Honestly, I think that writing cuts a bit deeper than talking for me. Even if I'm chewing something over—like figuring out childcare or what to do about a coworker who's bugging me, or what direction I need to go with a client—if I'm puzzled enough to talk to someone about it, it might look like I'm asking for help, but at my core, I can't get away from the egotism of thinking I already know what the answer is. There's a sense in which—even when I'm stumped—I think I've already got the answer inside me, and I just have to get to it. So, in setting the intention that I am writing

---

*   Dr. Bob is one of the co-founders of Alcoholics Anonymous.

specifically because I want to connect with a spiritual power, I'm also admitting at a deep level that I really *don't* have the answer. For me, the writing is a concrete admission of, "I don't know what the hell to do."

For me, that admission is a big deal because I struggle with what my belief in God is, and how to believe in a higher power, and what that even looks like. It is in the writing that I really say, "Okay, let me just make space and see what happens." It's not me asking for anything. I'm just looking at whatever the situation is, and then something—and this is just crazy—something comes to me later in the day or something shifts, and I think to myself: "*I* didn't just think that thought. That's not *my* thought. That's a brand-new thing. It has nothing to do with what direction I was going two days ago. It has nothing to do with how I felt about that person."

For example, I had a resentment against someone at work that was stuck in my craw. I'd known them for two years, and I kept writing the same resentment inventory about them. In all that time, I didn't learn anything that gave me a new level of compassion for them, but all of a sudden—*WHOOF*—I felt differently. It was gone! I didn't get any new data. I didn't have some new heart-to-heart with that person. They didn't just tell me some sob story about their life so that I went, "Oh my God, now I have compassion for them." No. Something else changed me, and the only part I played was that, in the act of writing, I made room for it to come in.

HOW TO WRITE
Nightly "Ten Questions" Inventory

The first type of writing Jen mentions in her story is a "moral inventory," which is the most common form of recovery writing. When I asked the addicts I interviewed what kinds of writing they did to recover from addiction, almost all of them named moral inventory first, and they told me that inventory played a unique and vital role in their recovery. However, they did not all agree on exactly what a moral inventory should look like on the page. This disagreement arises from the fact that the term "inventory" covers a wide range of writing practices in Twelve-Step fellowships, which can focus on different aspects of an addict's life and can be written at different stages in their progress through the Twelve Steps. What these various forms of moral inventory have in common is that they all use writing for the purpose of self-examination and reflection.

One way to get a sense of what this kind of writing is like is to try out the "Ten Questions" inventory, which requires only a few minutes at the end of each day. This method was introduced to me by Jeff H., who used an iPhone app each night to answer a set of questions taken from the AA Big Book. The questions in the app are a little different from the ones I provide here,[1] but the method is the same.

To do this exercise, set aside some time to be alone in the evening. Read each question and sit with it quietly until answers come. Write down your answers before moving to the next question. To get the most benefit from this inventory, don't dismiss any of these questions too quickly. Assume that each one has something to show you about your day. And like any recovery writing practice, this one benefits from an initial period of meditation or prayer to help you get quiet on the inside before you begin:

1. Was I resentful? (If so, how?)
2. Was I selfish? (If so, how?)
3. Was I dishonest? (If so, how?)
4. Was I afraid? (If so, why? Of what?)
5. Do I owe an apology? (If so, to whom? For what reason?)
6. Have I kept something to myself which should be discussed with another person? (If so, what? Who should I tell? And when can I tell them?)
7. Was I kind and loving toward all? (If not, where did I fall short?)
8. What could I have done better?
9. Was I thinking of myself most of the time?
10. What can I do for others?[2]

1

How I Became Desperate

On my twenty-fifth birthday, my girlfriend of two weeks told me I was too crazy to date and hung up the phone. I stared at the receiver in my hand, listening to the dial tone like maybe she'd come back on and say it was a joke. But it wasn't a joke. *I* was the joke. I really was too crazy to date. I'd been more or less sober (sometimes more, sometimes less) for five whole years, and I was just as nuts as ever. I was needy, restless, depressed, immature, anxious, hungry, and lost. And, yeah, I was hearing voices again. Just like when I used to get high. They scratched on my walls at night and whispered to me from down the hall. For months, something had been boiling up inside me. I felt like I was going to burst. This girl was my only friend in town, and I'd been holding on to her for dear life.

I found myself lying on my crappy linoleum kitchen floor and sobbing because I didn't have what it takes to be a person in this world. I couldn't make human relationships work—not with a girlfriend, not with a friend, and not with anyone else either. I just felt useless. And tired. And alone. And that is how I became desperate.

I know. Losing a two-week girlfriend is pretty soft for a rock bottom. But that's how it happened for me. I could see with great clarity at that moment that everything I'd thought and done up to that point in my life was a complete loss, and I had no clue how to live.

I want to be clear: becoming desperate means more than just losing your marbles or having a crap day. And it means more than hitting a wall of consequences and realizing you've got no one else to blame. When addicts say we "hit rock bottom," it means—or it ought to mean—that we've had a flash of insight, a full realization of the extent to which our own intellect, ingenuity, character, and willpower have utterly failed us in life. All the powers of the ego combined fall to pieces before the cold face of reality, and we are broken by the realization that we will never be able to put together a way of living that works. It's the *clarity* of that realization—that, on our own, by our own power, we're completely helpless—that constitutes desperation, *not* the severity of the pain we are in or the extent of the consequences we're facing.

As a case in point, my dad once had to commit me to the psych ward because I was threatening violence at home. After three days of goofballs and weird encounters, the doctor told me I was allergic to THC, meaning that in this case, every time I smoked weed, I'd be back in the nuthouse again. I thought he was full of shit. Got stoned right away.

Another time, I was fried out of my mind in downtown LA, believing I was a demon in heaven, scared to death of all the old ladies dropping pennies at me while the mustached guys in unmarked sedans plotted my demise on their walkie-talkies. I slept it off. The next morning, I thought it was funny.

Eventually, my family told me that I could either be homeless, get my act together, or go to rehab. I went on a final tour of bong hits and said my goodbyes. But I wasn't under any illusions that I had a drug problem. Not me. It was just that my parents were a couple of squares and I had to play along. For now.

It's not pain or consequences that get you to desperation. It's the insight, whenever it happens, that your life is broken and you can't fix it, no matter what you do. For me, it happened five years after rehab, following a string of moves around the country—from college to college, job to job, relationship to relationship—sometimes experimenting with alcohol and other times stone-cold sober, until, finally, someone broke up with me and called me crazy and somehow, it all just suddenly came to light. It didn't matter if I was clean or high, boozy or sober, I just didn't fit in this world. Never had, never would. And there was nothing I could do to fix it.

Simply put, I was broken.

Or the world was.

Or both. Any which way, I was screwed.

But that realization wasn't enough to do me any good, not on its own. The mere acknowledgment of brokenness, or of *powerlessness* as they call it in the Twelve-Step fellowships, is not enough to get anybody to a point of desperation. Feeling sorry for myself was more or less a normal state of affairs for me, and this experience, this breakup, could easily have become just more *despair*—a giving up on life—rather than *desperation*, a powerful, motivating force for change.

After that phone call, I took a walk. It was spring in New England. Sunny little college town. I shuffled down Main Street and considered my options. I could try to "keep on keeping on," but . . . no, actually, I couldn't do that. The idea gave me the shivers. Now that I'd seen how broken I was, I couldn't pretend anymore. At the very least, I would need something to take the edge off, something to block me from the consciousness of my fundamental ineptitude and ill-fittedness for life, meaning I would need to get high again. But no. That wouldn't work either. If I got high, I'd just end up all spun out and loopy and itchy and paranoid, then I'd open my damn mouth around somebody and land myself right back in the psych ward. In short, there were no good options left. If I couldn't stay dry, and I couldn't get high, then the only thing left was to die.

I had a bridge in mind, with a long drop into rough waters.

And then I remembered Piers. Bald guy. Big round belly. Kinda looked like Bruce Willis if you squinted, but his gaze was sharp enough to cut right through you. I'd met him just a couple days ago through his girlfriend. She and I volunteered at the same place and would take smoke breaks together. I'd talk all crazy at her, and she'd say, "You should really meet my boyfriend," so we set it up to all go see a movie together. Me and Piers hit it off. He used to get high, like I did. And he used to be crazy, like I was. But there was something different about him. He seemed *okay* somehow. I had this rat running circles around my head all day and all night long, making me bonkers. Piers *should have had a rat like that*. Everyone I knew in recovery had one. We all did. We all itched and scratched our way through each day. Even when we were years past jonesing for a hit, we were still consumed by anxious energy. The meetings I went to were full of people getting up and down for no reason, full of nervous laughter and chit-chat, distracted libidos roaming listlessly around the room looking for something to bite. Gabor Mate called us "hungry ghosts," which summed it up pretty well. We were out of our bodies and out of our minds but still hungry as hell and we didn't even know what for. Nothing was as good as drugs, so we just had to hurt, and be itchy, and distract ourselves however we could, slowly piecing some time together and trying to have a life. I couldn't even do that anymore.

But Piers was *okay*.

He told me about a meeting he went to where "things got a little spiritual sometimes" and "an energy went around the room." I got curious about that—about Piers being okay and the energy going around the room—when I was thinking about jumping off a bridge. If Piers was really alright, and his alrightness was really related to some spooky spirit stuff, then maybe I should check that out. After all, the meeting was only a few days away. So I circled back home and stuck it out a little while longer.

And *that* is why I say I was in a state of desperation rather than despair: desperation requires contact with a messenger, a guide, someone or something able to show you the way out of the mess you are in. Without Piers, my best option was to break a bunch of bones and then drown while wishing I'd picked a gentler exit from life. With Piers, a spark of curiosity drew me forward—a dancing light in the dark forest. I wanted to press on and see if whatever magical thing had happened to him could also happen to me.

2

THE "GIFT" OF DESPERATION

Desperation is a highly valued state of being in Twelve-Step cultures, where it is commonly referred to as a "gift." For example, in an AA meeting, you might hear an old-timer say something like, "I came into this program with the gift of desperation." And then go on to explain how crappy their drinking life was and how much they wanted to change. The value they are emphasizing with this kind of talk—the "gift" part of being desperate—is, of course, *not* the way desperation feels. For me, desperation felt distinctly ungiftlike, as if my whole life fell apart and I would probably die if Piers's spooky spirit thing didn't work out. It feels that way for most of us. Desperation is a hungry, scary, painful feeling. So when an old timer says, "You gotta get that gift," you, the newcomer—if you are not already desperate—just might feel like taking a pass.

But in their praise of desperation, the old-timer means only to persuade you to eat your vegetables. It might not be pleasant, but it is good for you. Desperation comes from a realization of brokenness, along with an encounter that gives you reason to believe your life can change for the better. In this sense, desperation is radically motivating. It gets you off your ass and into action. You'll go to the meeting, listen to other addicts talk, maybe even say something yourself. You may even ask someone to sponsor you (that is, to take you through the Twelve Steps) and follow their suggestions. Thus, the "gift" part of the "gift of desperation" lies in the way it enables you to do things you would never otherwise do, and thereby to change in ways that would be impossible if you were even a smidge less desperate.

But this state of being is also a gift in another sense: we *receive* desperation rather than make it for ourselves. You can't get desperate by flexing a mental muscle or focusing really hard. There is no discipline or practice that can produce this result. The only way to get desperate is for life to kick your ass and for you to wake up to how hopeless you are. Then, some flicker of new possibility appears on your horizon—some last gasp of hope that something beyond yourself just might have an answer.

Because we have to receive rather than perform or create desperation, it is a gift in yet a third sense: *not everyone gets it.* Plenty of people arrive in the rooms of AA or some other Twelve-Step fellowship with no idea how hopeless they are. Some go to please another person, some to please the courts, and others to satisfy their own curiosity. Whatever the situation, people come to the meeting and see recovery happening all around them, but they don't know how badly and deeply they need it, nor do they feel any real urge to pursue it for themselves.

I did that too. For years. I went to rehab, then to a youth-at-risk wilderness program, then I was in sober living for a year. I was in and out of meetings after that, sometimes trying to hang on and other times giving up. I once went to an AA meeting in a new town and introduced myself as a drug addict who was currently dabbling in alcohol. "I don't need your help at the moment," I said, "but it's good to know you're here." Those poor drunks. They really tried hard to persuade me to keep coming back. They all told stories about how they used to think things were fine until they weren't, hoping that I'd see myself in their stories and recognize the dangers that lay ahead for me. But I didn't pay them any mind. And I never went back to that meeting.

I wasn't ready. I hadn't yet received the gift of a phone call on my birthday to tell me I was too crazy to date.

Desperation is good for you even if it feels bad, it is received rather than performed, and not everybody gets to experience it. There is one final aspect of desperation's giftlikeness that I'd like to cover: *when it happens, it comes as a surprise.* Again, I'll use myself as a case in point:

The first time I ever went to any Twelve-Step meeting was after I'd been discharged from the psych ward. My parents made me go. It was a meeting of Marijuana Anonymous. Whether by design or by pure chance, I do not know, but this meeting was also on the grounds of a hospital, and patients from *its* psych ward were allowed to attend. Just before the chairperson got things started, a bunch of white robes and gray sweatpants shuffled in. I recognized one of the guys from my stay in the other hospital. He must have been pill-chasing, or ward-hopping, or something. I remembered how he'd once told us in group that wearing his Walkman gave him all the powers of the Starship Enterprise. I liked that guy. He gave off a "five-year mission into deep space" kinda vibe. But he didn't seem to recognize me. He was too busy chewing his tee-shirt.

In any case, I came prepared. I had a backpack full of comic books and an egg timer. I set the timer for one hour and read my comics while everybody talked. *Tick-tick-tick-tick-tick*—all through the hour. When the alarm finally rang, I put my comics away and told everyone that the meeting was over. It was time for me to go.

I got up, walked outside, and that was that. First meeting done.

Now, I want to ask you a serious question: What kind of odds would you have placed on a guy like that recovering? A guy who was obviously a complete disaster but couldn't see it for himself, a guy who set an egg timer to make sure he didn't have to sit in a meeting one second longer than necessary and who paid zero attention to the recovery happening around him—would you have bet on him getting well? Or, many years later, when he was a blubbering mess after a phone call and decided he needed—like, really, deeply *needed*—to go to an AA meeting, would you have been surprised?

For the record, I would not have bet on me.

And I was as surprised as anyone to find myself desperately waiting for the night of Piers's meeting to come.

3

WRITING TO GET DESPERATE

In spite of desperation's *giftlikeness*—that is, in spite of our inability to produce it at will for ourselves or for anybody else—old-timers in recovery do still try to help newcomers enter this state of being. In fact, most of the activities in Twelve-Step fellowships are structured, one way or another, around efforts to help struggling addicts realize a) that they are in bad need of help, and b) that there is hope of their recovery. The meetings and small talk, the sharing and storytelling, the pamphlets and books—in other words, all of a fellowship's persuasive power—are intended to help newcomers identify as addicts and accept the fellowship's help. The idea is that addicts will hear the stories, laugh at the jokes, check out the literature, and be "persuaded to say," as the Big Book puts it, "Yes, I am one of them too; I must have this thing."[3]

Of course, these efforts do not always work. Addicts tend to be fairly well defended against the possibility of getting clean and sober—the same way non-addicts are defended against the possibility of stopping breathing—which is to say that these defenses are *instinctual*, and the addictive substance or behavior is *vital* to the addict. For addicts, addiction is (or at least *feels*) necessary for life.

Many a drunk has sat through an AA meeting and thought, "Yeah I've got a problem, but I'm not as bad as these creeps," or, inversely, "I'm in such rough shape, their solution could never work for me." Just below the consciousness of protests like these lurks the notion that if they were to fully identify with the folks in the meeting, the alcoholic would have to give up drinking (think: breathing) for good. The idea is frightening, repulsive, nonsensical. And so, the addict must keep themself from entering a state of desperation by refusing to admit either a) that their problem is real or bad enough to warrant any action, or b) that their own recovery is possible.

Because active addicts almost always experience some degree of resistance to identification with recovering addicts, sponsors normally start their work with a new sponsee by introducing some kind of activity meant to uncover and resolve this resistance. Often, this takes the form of one or more conversations, the goal of which is to help the sponsee arrive at what we might call the "minimum viable level of desperation"—also called the admission of powerlessness. By admitting that they are powerless over alcohol, an alcoholic confesses that they cannot control their drinking and are ready to accept help. Such an admission does not cover every aspect of their life, just the drinking part. And so, the admission of powerlessness represents an alcoholic's recognition that they are just broken enough to know they need help in the drinking department. To paraphrase the psychiatrist and early AA board member Harry Tiebout, admitting powerlessness in Alcoholics Anonymous means surrendering to alcohol as an alcoholic, not to life as a person. I call this the *minimum* viable degree of desperation because, in many cases, it is enough to get the addict off their ass and into recovery, while at the same time saving for later many inevitable confrontations with life. AA's sharp focus on alcohol (just like NA's sharp focus on drugs, for example) kicks this particular can down the road.

Even so, some addicts do show up in the rooms, like I did, with a certain "deflation at depth," as Bill Wilson used to call it. We come bruised and busted—as addicts, unable to make our addictions work and, as people, unable to create a meaningful life. Those of us who show up in a fellowship already desperate come by that state of mind "naturally," that is, without any formal intervention by family or a sponsor or anybody else. It's just that life is painful, and we suffer it long enough to finally get *tired*, in the fullest sense of that word. We lose our ability to try at life. We can't even fight on behalf of our addictions anymore.

It's not easy to produce deflation at depth in an addict if they haven't already acquired it naturally. For many of us, storytelling and informative pamphlets are just not going to cut it. We need something that hits deeper than all that meeting stuff. For me, it was several agonizing years of on-again, off-again abstinence-without-recovery that finally wore me down. But some sponsors, who want to spare their sponsees from any further pain, have found another way to get newcomers from a place of resistance to the minimum viable level of desperation and perhaps beyond: they have their sponsees *write*.

In my research, I found that writing is used in many ways in Twelve-Step fellowships. Writing is produced by the fellowships themselves, both in the form of program literature (that is, all the pamphlets, books, and worksheets produced by a fellowship for its members) and in the form of internal documents (the meeting minutes, letters to central offices, announcements from regional committees, and so on). The AA Big Book, for example, was written by early members of AA and has become an influential piece of program literature, serving as a guide to recovery for alcoholics and many other kinds of addicts.

But it isn't just fellowships that produce writing. On an individual level, I found that addicts use many kinds of writing in hopes of recovering from their addictions. They write to generate desperation and to make a series of other discoveries and changes throughout the Twelve-Step process. They write prayers, moral inventories, amends lists and letters, daily personal reflections, dialogues with the divine, and a wide array of "everyday" genres that they feel inform their growth in recovery. The addicts I interviewed blogged, journaled, moderated Facebook groups, wrote memoirs, drafted song lyrics, and scribbled comments in the margins of their Big Books. They kept collections of quotes, produced personal mission statements, drafted ideals for future conduct, inscribed manifestations, and penned affirmations of their own worth. They wrote morning pages, newsletters, sermons, poems, fairy tales, short stories, and academic essays. All in all, I counted seventy different genres named by these addicts as important to their recoveries. They had different ideas about writing's value and relationship to recovery, but generally agreed that it helped them tell the truth about themselves and connect to a higher power in ways that they couldn't or wouldn't have done without writing's help.

When it came to the writing they did specifically to enter a state of desperation, the addicts I spoke with wrote things like histories of their addictions, lists of times when they felt powerless, goodbye letters to their addictive substances or behaviors, and definitions of key terms like "powerlessness" and "unmanageability," along with reflective writing that applied these definitions to their own lives. In all of these writing exercises, the point was for the addicts to reflect on their lives and see the ways in which their addictions had grown beyond their own control.

For example, Jeff H. told me his sponsor had him write a list of five things he would have in a perfect life. He spent time thinking of the possessions and relationships he most desired—the perfect job, partner, house, and so on—until he had his dream life on the page. When he read the list to his sponsor, the sponsor asked, "If you had all those things, could you stop drinking?" He looked over his list again, and he knew. He would drink himself right out of that job and that partnership. He'd lose the house, crash the boat, wreck the car, drain the bank account. None of it would stop him. "Even in my imagination, where I have no limits," he told me, "even there, I can't even think up a life where I can stop drinking. I'm powerless. If I'm going to stay sober, it's going to take something bigger than me."

HOW TO WRITE
A Timeline of Your Addiction

Many addicts have discovered their desperation by writing about it, which is why sponsors often ask their sponsees to write histories of their addictions. Writing down the facts of your history helps you get honest with yourself about the depth of your problem, and it allows you to share your story truthfully with other addicts.

To write this timeline, you'll want to focus on specific behaviors you've engaged in without getting into the weeds of every detail. This isn't a memoir or a short story. The purpose here is to arrive at a more or less chronological list of the kinds of actions you've taken that are relevant to your addiction. For example, if you used to steal from your family to support a drug addiction, you can put "started stealing from my family" on your timeline and leave it at that. However, if there were significant moments in that history, like "stole my mom's heirloom jewelry" or "stole all the money from my son's piggy bank," make sure those get placed on the timeline too.

Your timeline should include things like:

a) addictive substances and behaviors you've done,

b) harmful things you did while under the influence or in order to support your addiction,

c) previous attempts to control your using or to quit,

d) consequences you suffered because of your using,

e) major promises you've broken and lies you've told,

f) times when you felt out of control.

The goal of this timeline is to put the facts of your behavior on the page so that you can see and reflect on it all at once. A full record of these facts will also enable you to tell the whole truth about yourself, to yourself and to other addicts.

4

THE CHURCH BASEMENT GHOST

The meeting Piers told me about was in the basement of a church on Main Street. A narrow, wobbly stairway dropped at a sharp angle down into a carpeted hall. Through an open door on the left, two guys were hanging out and chatting. When I entered, they were immediately interested. They didn't seem like drunks to me. They weren't all sucked up into their thoughts like all the other addicts I knew. These guys were genuinely attentive to me and my presence. I figured they were church people.

"I'm sorry," I said. "I was looking for the AA meeting."

They laughed. "This *is* the meeting," they said.

Then, they asked me how I was doing.

And they cared.

That's when I noticed that the tables behind them were set up with books in front of every other seat. I recognized the blue covers of the hardbacks. They weren't Bibles. This was a Big Book meeting. I'd never been to one of those before.

When it was time for the meeting to start, the lady who was chairing the meeting banged a gavel. Someone read the Steps. Someone else led a prayer. Then the chair opened her copy of the Big Book and picked up reading where they had left off the previous week. She read about something called "moral inventory."

I was familiar with the Steps. They hung on the wall at a lot of meetings, and the rehab I had gone to was based on them, or said it was. The stuff we had done in rehab—learning to make "I" statements about our feelings, listing positive qualities about ourselves, hitting foam blocks with a baseball bat and screaming—none of that sounded much like what these Big Book folks were talking about. From what I could make out, moral inventory was some kind of writing project where you wrote about whatever pissed you off, but it was really about how you were selfish. Somehow, "God" had a lot to do with it. The details were fuzzy. I had trouble tracking exactly what the book was talking about, but I was able to pay attention to the people. Even if I didn't understand what they were saying, I could see in their eyes how this stuff made them *feel*.

It looked good to me.

The chair would read a portion of the book out loud, and folks would follow along in their own copy or just listen. Sometimes she would read more, sometimes less. Sometimes she'd even stop multiple times in the same paragraph. From what I could tell, she was just reading until something interesting struck her—an idea or detail that gave off a spark—and then she'd talk about how she saw her own life in relation to what she'd just read. After the chair spoke, others would chime in, doing the same thing. They were all interpreting their lives through the words of the Big Book, and interpreting the Big Book through their own life experiences. When everyone who wanted to share was finished, the chair would pick up reading again until another turn of phrase struck a spark.

When these people talked, they spoke about themselves and their problems in a way I hadn't heard before. They were unflinchingly honest about their personal failings and yet still told their stories from a place beyond their struggles. They found their problems funny even. To be clear, most Twelve-Step meetings produce a certain kind of humor. People will share a funny story about drinking or drugging, and we'll all laugh about things that would not be funny to non-addicts, like: "Haha, I stole that guy's wallet and then spent an hour helping him look for it!" I've heard funny stories about armed robbery, extramarital affairs, blackouts, drug smuggling—you name it.

But the sharing at this meeting was different somehow—more personal, more penetrating. These people weren't just making jokes about audacious, chemically induced behavior; they were casually, warmly, and publicly stating their personal flaws and shortcomings. They talked about the harm they caused their families and the pain they needlessly inflicted on themselves due to their own resentments and fears. They just accepted all this without shame and found joy in sharing it with each other. These weren't just war stories from a group of sloppy drunks—they were real confessions.

The result was that some kind of spirit really did move around the room like an energy, warm and light. It surrounded the people telling their stories, filled the space between us as we listened, and seeped into us all, gently touching the deep, dark secrets inside, the things we promised ourselves we'd never tell anyone, as if to say: "It's okay. You can share this here. You are not alone anymore."

You may think I'm describing this spirit as a metaphor for what it feels like to be in a room of people who tell the truth about themselves. I am not. Granted, I've done my share of LSD, but I do mean literally that I experienced a warm and loving presence that seemed to arise from—but also facilitated—the truth telling in that room. It came in waves that would swell as the sharing passed from one addict to the next. When one wave completed its surge and began to wane again—or when its arc was disrupted by the protests of some resistant drunk—the chair would take us gently back into the Big Book, and another wave would start to grow.

The authors of the Big Book said that they had been "rocketed into a fourth dimension of existence of which [they] had not even dreamed."[4] I could see that, and I could see the effect it had on people. It made them feel okay inside, the way that Piers did, and being in their presence only heightened my desire. I desperately wanted to feel the way that these people felt, and they told me that I could have that feeling if I just did a short writing project about things that made me angry. None of this made any sense, but I was on board. Well, almost on board.

It may sound odd given what I've just said about the glowing, loving presence of truth-telling light, but every time the people in this meeting said "God"—and they said it a *lot*—I flinched. I'd grown up in a religious environment that I did not care for, and I had rejected all things related to "God" a long time ago. And so, even as I saw with my own eyes—and felt with my own heart—this weird spooky spirit thing Piers had told me about, I was not about to sit there and let them tell me this was God. Why ruin this feeling with that kind of horseshit? No, thank you. I spent that meeting cycling back and forth between fascination with what I was seeing and disgust at what I perceived to be the religiosity of it all.

Piers came in late and shared during the last couple spirit-waves for the evening. He brought a certain intellectual flavor to his sharings that intrigued me. He also offered me a ride home, and on the way, he told me that if I ever wanted to do any of the things they talked about in that meeting, he would show me how. In other words, he offered to act as my sponsor. I said I wasn't sure yet. I'd think about it. I didn't really like all the God stuff, I said.

But I was holding under my sweatshirt a copy of the Big Book that I'd stolen from the meeting. After Piers dropped me off, I stayed up reading it cover to cover, without a break. I didn't understand a word of it, but I couldn't put it down. Just by reading this book and doing some writing, people were having remarkable, life-changing experiences.

I wanted to have one too.

"What Finally Crushed Me"

MARK A.'S STORY

Mark describes writing moral inventory before and after confronting the full depth of his powerlessness. His experience suggests that the real value of recovery writing can be realized only once we've gained the "gift" of desperation.

I went through the Steps for the first time in rehab. At the time, I still thought I could do an amended version of the program. The Steps were terrific, but I was going to apply them to certain parts of my life and not others. My gross narcissism led me to believe that my method would work for me because I was different and special. I hadn't genuinely surrendered to the idea that I really, really needed this. I hadn't yet died to my own personal powerlessness.

While in treatment, I started to write an inventory of my resentments. I was an incredibly angry guy, but I didn't believe I was angry. Because I was *always* angry and resentful and bitter, I had no context in which to place my anger, thus identifying it. Also, my self-concept was like something between the Big Lebowski and Jeff Spicoli from *Fast Times at Ridgemont High*. I really believed myself to be this super mellow, zen guy who let things roll off his back. It was difficult for me to even contemplate that I might actually be an angry person because that idea was so ego-dystonic. I managed to come up with a list that first time, but I didn't really connect with my resentment. It was just like a dormant volcano. There was this huge magma chamber of resentment and anger, but it was sealed off. I followed instructions, but I was so disconnected from myself that I wrote the list only because other people were doing it and I had nothing else to do.

I left treatment after two weeks and went to a homeless shelter in Boston. Then I wound up in Maine, first near Bar Harbor, then Portland. I kept writing and finished my first inventory. Actually, I don't know if there was any genuine inventory in my notebook. At the time, I thought of inventory writing as a cool parlor trick, like psychoanalyzing yourself or something. Again, that first inventory didn't have any real depth.

I stayed sober for nine months, if you want to call it "sobriety." I was physically sober, but quite insane. After nine months, I went back out for a year and a half, using and drinking, and it was hell on earth. Making a surrender and writing a little inventory will ruin your relapse. Even the little blade of truth that was in my first inventory was enough to expose me to my selfishness, my dishonesty, my insecurity, my sense of inferiority, and my fear so that when I relapsed, I was now conscious of all those behaviors. The mental defense mechanisms I had deployed in the past weren't effective anymore because once you recognize them as defense mechanisms, they stop working.

Eventually, I went back to the same rehab for a couple of weeks, and I was so damaged. I was such a mess. When my time was up, I begged them to let me stay. I said I would live in a tent in the backyard. I'd work for free. You could work and stay on in a position they called "monitor," but there was only one monitor space and another candidate. She ended up getting the spot, and I was terrified. They drove me back to Portland, and I was homeless again. I had been evicted. I had lost my job. I walked around the old port for an hour, desperately trying not to drink. Eventually, I watched myself walk into a bar and start drinking. After that, I moved out to Seattle for a while, then down to San Diego. Then I took a job running a discotheque in Mexico and started smoking meth. At that point, I would do anything you put in front of me. It was like I was just operating on the death instinct. When I learned that the guys I was working for in Mexico were going to kill me, I ran out in the middle of the night and took a bus to La Paz. I had very little money left, so I started buying this rotgut booze in an attempt to drink myself to death. I kept drinking and drinking and drinking, but to my horror and amazement, I kept waking up. That was what finally crushed me. I could deal with dying, because I wanted to extinguish my consciousness—I wanted to turn it off. But it finally hit me that, for whatever reason, that just wasn't going to happen. I was going to have to keep suffering— another year, five years, ten years, twenty years—and that was when I really had a First-Step experience. I came face to face with the depth of my powerlessness.

What happened to me was I got really sick outside the bus station in La Paz. I must have looked so bad that passersby were taking pity on me. These two girls told me I had to get home, and they helped me get on a bus. So, I went to Tijuana and then crossed into San Diego. I went to the hospital because I was sick and homeless and penniless. I actually took a Third Step by myself in a parking lot. I found a public computer and emailed a guy who had sponsored me. I wrote him this long email, apologizing for wasting his time and asking for another chance to take his direction. He sent me a very brief reply. The instructions were: write inventory, stay where you are, and save up money so that you can properly make amends. I really couldn't get in touch with him much during that time, and when I did, I got very little practical information. I was basically left on my own to write a shitload of inventory. As a result, I actually started to write inventory with heart. I finally started to write real inventory because I knew I needed it.

Instead of writing one big inventory, I was writing it piecemeal. I'd write one piece at a time and read it if I could. I didn't have many people to read to, so I would read my inventory to random people at meetings. I had so much stuff going on at the time that I was mostly just writing about things that happened then and there. Sometimes, stuff from the past would bubble up, but it was mostly from the previous two years.

I read the Big Book quite a bit, especially page 67, which is the meat of the instructions for the fourth column. That page has these two really potent sentences in the middle paragraph, saying that even when the other person is to blame, we should disregard them completely. We are not clearing them of wrongdoing, and we are not vilifying them. What they did is now irrelevant. Say, you get run over in the parking lot and your back is broken. The paramedics show up, and you say: "It wasn't my fault! Go get the other guy!" And they say: "We're here to help *you*. Do you want us to save your life or go get the other guy?" You have to choose. That's one of the most challenging concepts in the Steps. It's this radically existential responsibility: if you are disturbed, it's because you are disturbable. What disturbed you is secondary. The fact is that you are disturbable, and that's on you. Yet it's seemingly paradoxical because you're also powerless. "Well, wait, am I powerless or am I accountable?" Both. You're responsible *for your state of powerlessness*. You don't get off the hook at all.

So, I would pray before I wrote. I'd try to get quiet for a few minutes. Writing without prayer doesn't have the same heart. I mean, from the sheer volume of inventory I've written over the years, I can now write "good" inventory without prayer, meaning it's not absurd and it looks intellectually pleasing. But without sufficient payer, inventory lacks any power. It's even possible that the content is the same, but it doesn't hit me on the same level because the prayer tells a very deep part of me: "This is important. I care about this." If that deep part of me isn't engaged, then I don't change, because the part on top—the ego, or the prefrontal cortex, or whatever you want to call it—can't generate any real change. It can *think* about changing—which I do all the time because I intellectualize as a defense—but it doesn't have the depth or the power to actually make a difference.

I've seen this countless times with sponsees when they hit a year or two of sobriety. They're not so desperate anymore, and then they hit a rough spot. So you say, "Write the inventory"; and they say: "I already did, and it didn't work. I wrote, but I don't feel any better." They take it for granted that, because inventory has been cathartic in the past, writing alone is supposed to change the way they feel, and so they misappropriate the exercise and try to use it as a device to feel good. But inventory is supposed to be diagnostic. If it makes you feel good, that's a bonus, like hitting a scratch ticket someone gave you for Christmas, but that's not its purpose. Inventory shows you what needs to change. If you're just writing in an effort to manage your mood, you're not going to see that. You have to want to be different.

5

THE FORMAL FIRST STEP

In conducting my research, I heard several stories about writing that produced a state of desperation in the writer, but none was quite as impressive as that of Nathan, a sex addict from the American South. Nathan introduced himself to me as a pastor, professor, and activist. He serves as minister of a mid-sized congregation in a large Southern city, teaches at a seminary, and works as a community organizer. When Nathan first started working the Twelve Steps in Sex Addicts Anonymous (SAA), his sponsor guided him through an important writing exercise—a Formal First Step—which allowed Nathan to tell the whole truth about his addiction and therefore to recognize his powerlessness.

Nathan's Formal First Step began when his sponsor introduced him to a set of questions from an SAA pamphlet and told him to write out a long-form answer to each of them.[5] These questions cut deep. They asked things like, "What specific activities have been a part of your compulsive sexual behavior?" and "What lies have you told to conceal your sexual activity?" Other questions asked Nathan to list the ways in which his sex addiction affected his education and career, his relationships with family and friends, his physical and mental well-being, his morality and values. Still other questions asked about the ways in which he had been powerless over sex: "Like planning to go to the grocery store," he said, "but finding yourself in a porn shop or cruising."

In short, these questions asked Nathan to perform a comprehensive examination of his addiction, with the aim of discovering the full scope of his addictive behavior, his inability to control his addiction, and its impact on all areas of his life. This would not be a small project for any addict, but for a sex addict, such questions require an extra degree of vulnerability because the behaviors involved are so intimate and often taboo. Nathan told me that writing answers to these questions was "really, really hard," specifically because it worked against his tendency to hide the truth, both from others and from himself:

> The questions were not asking me what I felt. They were asking for data without including my feelings, which have always been an attempt of my psyche to mitigate or to soften the data: "If you just understood that I was really caught up in shame, you would understand." Well, okay. We'll deal with that later. What's the data? Let's talk about the exact nature of how you lived.

Nathan's Formal First Step wanted straight facts, no chaser. No justification, rationalization, obfuscation, minimization, or blame shifting. Just the truth, in black and white.

When Nathan was done, he shared his writing with his sponsor, who then set up a time for him to read his answers out loud to his entire homegroup. The whole meeting would be devoted to Nathan's Formal First Step. He would read for a half-hour or so, and then the other SAA members would have the chance to talk. He would have to tell them everything, and they could say anything in response.

Imagine, for a moment, that you are in the grip of a behavioral addiction well beyond your control, fighting for your life, and the only way forward is to write down every single detail of your sex life, all the quirks, kinks, harm, and trauma—just the facts, mind you, without any hint of embellishment—and to read your list aloud to a room full of people, who then will respond however they like and ask any questions they please. I think you'll agree the idea is discomforting, to put it lightly.

But Nathan showed up for his appointed meeting, sat in the hot seat, and read, verbatim, from his handwritten answers to those questions. The members of Nathan's homegroup were kind to him in their responses. They were sex addicts too, and most of them had gone through the process of a Formal First Step, so they expressed compassion for him and identification with his story. When they were done, Nathan's sponsor posed a final question: "Having heard all of this, Nathan, are you powerless over your addiction?"

Nathan told me this final question "put [his] self-deception in a checkmate position":

> I was exposed. The truth was all out in the open. Was I powerless, or was I gonna continue to bullshit? I couldn't go back on everything I'd said. I had to admit I was powerless. I guarantee you I would not be sober today without writing my First Step. It was the first time in my life I stood in front of a group of men and felt totally vulnerable. There's something about writing and then speaking that writing. Without that, the level of self-deception is massive.

I pressed Nathan on that point, that is, on his experience of the value of writing. I asked whether he really needed to do all that written prep work. Couldn't he have just gotten up there and stated the facts without writing? His response was immediate laughter: "Oh, there's no fucking way you could do it without writing!" Writing was essential to recovery, Nathan told me. "It's the way the self tells the truth about the self. It produces a counternarrative to the vows the self has taken never to say this shit out loud."

How to Write
The Three Circles

This is a second exercise that Nathan described to me. Like the Formal First Step, the Three Circles comes from the program literature of SAA.[6] The purpose of this practice is to help sex addicts define what sexual sobriety means to them. Sex addiction, like all "process" or "behavioral" addictions, is different from substance addictions in this regard. If you are a substance addict (for example, an alcoholic or a drug addict), then it's relatively easy to define sobriety: you are sober if you are not using the substances that you're addicted to. But for a sex addict, a compulsive overeater, or a compulsive spender, it can be harder to draw a clear line around sobriety. The compulsive spender will still need to buy things; the compulsive overeater will still need to eat; and the sex addict will probably still have a sex life. So how can these addicts know when a behavior crosses the line from healthy use to full-blown addiction? The Three Circles exercise is meant to answer exactly that question.

To write the Three Circles, draw three concentric circles on a page: a smallish one in the center, a middle-sized one around it, and finally a large one enclosing both. Each circle should be big enough to write in.

- In the *innermost circle*, write the behavior that, for you, is the very first signal that you have entered a relapse. This is a red-light, point-of-no-return behavior that clearly indicates you have broken your sobriety and are now caught up in a process beyond your control.
- In the *middle circle*, write behaviors that push you toward a relapse. These are yellow-light behaviors that tempt you toward the innermost circle. When you do these things, you can feel yourself slipping back into self-destructive behavior.
- In the *outer circle*, write green-light, healthy, recovery-supportive behaviors that help you avoid the behaviors in both of the other two circles.

Here's how Nathan explained the kinds of things a sex addict might place in the two inner circles. He also underscored the importance of a sponsor's guidance for this practice:

> If pornography is something that is in my inner circle, then if I ever look at pornography, I lose my sobriety. So what about swimsuit magazines or whatever? Maybe if I look at something like that, I'm really headed toward pornography, so that goes in the middle circle. For some guys who were having affairs, taking off their wedding ring would be an inner-circle behavior. To take that off means they'd lose their sobriety. That's the act. That's the beginning of relapse. But for other folks, taking off their wedding ring might be a middle-circle behavior, like: "Hey, listen, you're headed for a relapse. This is a warning light."
>
> You and your sponsor determine those things, so it's really a communal form of writing. Particularly when you first get into the program, there's so much shame that sometimes guys have a tendency to put everything in their inner circle. There's some necessity for wiser addicts to say, "Let's let this be a warning light."

6

FROM DESPERATION TO DISCOVERY

So far, I've been talking mostly about how desperation works in relation to recovery. I defined desperation as motivation to change that is born from two elements: a) awareness of your own brokenness, and b) direct contact with a messenger, someone or something able to show you another way to live. I also described desperation as a "gift" in four senses: it enables you to do things you would not otherwise do; you receive it rather than make it for yourself; not everyone gets it; and when it shows up, it comes as a surprise.

But I also described how some addicts *write* in order to enter a state of desperation. Nathan, for example, became aware of his powerlessness and hopeful of change through his Formal First Step writing. And because he wrote, Nathan took a more active role in attaining his desperation than I did in attaining mine. Whereas I was the hapless object of whatever fates conspired to make sure my girlfriend broke up with me in the same week I met Piers, Nathan pushed through his fear to get words on the page, confronted internal resistance and denial, and read his writing out loud to a room full of people. Scary stuff. But he did it.

Due to this more active role, it may seem that Nathan's story contradicts the notion that desperation is a gift. Specifically, it may look like Nathan *produced* desperation *for himself* rather than received it from some other source. But this is not how Nathan described his experience, and it's not really how writing works either. Nathan did not tell me that he intended to produce desperation when he wrote. He didn't claim to be the sole agent responsible for the outcome of his Formal First Step, and he didn't even say that there was a *causal* relationship between his writing and the resulting desperation, only that writing was a necessary condition for him to tell the whole truth.

Even though it involved writing, Nathan's experience still felt like a gift to him. It was surprising and motivating, and seemed to come from something other than himself. Further, what he gained from his Formal First Step felt like more than just the simple product of his writing, even though he never could have gained it without putting pen to paper.

In fact, almost all of the addicts I interviewed talked this way about their writing. They sometimes reported having spiritual experiences with their notebooks, and they often talked about dramatic changes as a result. But they were also clear that the writing itself, while important and useful, was not directly responsible for their recovery, and *neither were they*. These addicts wrote and they changed, but they didn't claim to be responsible for the changes or, in some cases, even for their own writing. As we will see, some addicts told me stories of recording language and insights that seemed to come from forces beyond themselves. For these addicts, writing was a crucial way to make contact with a higher power.

Over the course of this book, we will see many ways in which recovery writing produces unusual effects, with many folks attributing their writing or its results to a power greater than themselves. At the same time, I will argue that these effects are not really so unusual after all but that instead, the way we normally think about writing—as the intentional product of a writer who is alone responsible for their work—is poorly suited to the task of explaining the actual process of putting words on the page. It can sometimes feel like writing is under our control, but just as often, it feels like writing comes to us as a gift, even though we produce it. Even if we pay really close attention to our thoughts when we write, we often cannot say exactly where an idea came from or just how a turn of phrase occurred to us. This is not to say that there isn't an element of craft to writing, or that authors are not responsible for their words, only that the human mind is mysterious, its connections to other minds and other matters equally so, and that when it is employed in a creative activity like writing, its depths are largely unknown to us.

But before we probe too deeply into the mysteries of the creative mind, we should take a look at two readily apparent features of Nathan's story. First, we can notice that Nathan's story about writing is highly *social*. Nathan did not write alone, and even though the point of his writing was to forward his own recovery, he did not write primarily for himself. Nathan's sponsor and his homegroup provided a social context for his writing that included someone to teach him how to write and an audience for the result. The sponsor's direction, suggestions, and questions, along with the group's attentive and compassionate support, were critical components in Nathan's ability to become motivated to change. The gift of his desperation was shaped for him by a community of other addicts in recovery. They showed him how to realize his powerlessness over compulsive sexual behaviors, and they surrounded him with reasons to believe in the possibility of his own recovery.

Most practices of recovery writing are like this: they require an active fellowship of recovering addicts in order to work, and there is almost always a social end to any writing practice in this context. In other words, addicts in Twelve-Step recovery usually write in preparation for doing something with other people. We write in order to read to our sponsors or our homegroups. We write in order to act differently in our relationships. We write in order to go out and make amends to people we've harmed. And we write in order to enact the principles of recovery in all of our affairs. Only rarely is our writing "private" in the sense that it has no goal other than to affect us as individuals, for even those effects are meant to improve our way of relating to others and to make us more useful to other addicts.

Second, we can see in Nathan's story an example of writing's primary job in this social context. Nathan's Formal First Step, like most recovery writing genres, asked him to reflect on and think differently about his life. It wanted the *facts* of his addiction—the data. This included a list of his past behaviors and also an assessment of how those behaviors harmed others and impacted several areas of his life. To produce and interpret this data, Nathan had to use his memory and his analytical abilities to think in novel ways about his personal history. Complicating matters was the fact that this task ran against his natural tendency as an addict to deny, alter, and minimize the details of his addiction. Hidden from his normal stream of thinking were exactly those things the questions wanted to know—the severity of his addiction and the extent of its negative effects. How had his sexually compulsive behaviors and rituals affected his education? His values? His mental health? The answers to questions like these were not immediately obvious because they required some interpretive work and because they were buried under addictive denial. And so, Nathan had to dig deep.

For writing experts, this process of digging deep and coming up with ideas and insights for a writing project is known as "invention" or "discovery." And this is the work that recovery writing does inside the context of a supportive Twelve-Step community: it helps addicts engage in an ongoing process of discovery.

7

SPOOKY DISCOVERIES

Writing experts have come up with a whole bunch of theories about what discovery is and how it works.[7] Some have argued that things like writing and speechmaking can actually create new knowledge.[8] Others have studied discovery as a cognitive process, that is, as something the human brain does when it thinks through the details of a communication problem.[9] Still others have suggested that discovery is a social process, shaped by a writer's history and culture.[10] In fact, some researchers advocate an extreme version of this social emphasis. They claim that writers don't really discover or write things themselves. Instead, they unknowingly reproduce the stuff of their social environment as they write.[11] There are also researchers who argue that the kind of writing you do determines what you discover as you write. For example, you will (probably) discover different things while writing a grocery list as opposed to a love poem.[12] Some writing experts have proposed specific methods and procedures for making discoveries to help writers see their subject from multiple points of view.[13] Finally, there are a few folks who have suggested that non-rational processes like "chaos"[14] or emotionally expressive writing[15] are the best and truest methods of invention.

These are all good theories, with strong research and argumentation to support them. And we can see how they are all true in their own way when we apply them to Nathan's story. As he wrote his Formal First Step, Nathan created knowledge for himself about his addiction. Of course, he engaged various cognitive processes to arrive at answers to the pamphlet's questions. At the same time, Nathan's sponsor, his homegroup, his fellowship, the recovery movement as a whole, even the history of addiction treatment in the US—all these entities collectively provided a social context for Nathan's thinking and writing. Because he wrote within this context, it is possible to interpret Nathan's Formal First Step—and even his addiction itself—as an expression of larger social forces. Further, the genre Nathan wrote in, as well as the specific discovery method he was using, influenced the ideas and insights that came to his mind as he wrote. Finally, if we were to look closely at Nathan's writing experience, we could probably find "chaotic" moments of sudden insight and identify the ways in which the act of writing itself helped him come up with new ideas for further writing. In short, Nathan made his discoveries by generating new knowledge, by using his brain, by being in a social context, by using a specific set of questions designed to produce a specific range of answers, and by engaging in a writing process.

I didn't present all these theories to Nathan in our interview, so I don't know exactly how he would respond to this analysis. Nathan is an intelligent, educated guy, and would likely see the reasonableness of each scholarly point of view. But my gut tells me he would feel something important is still missing from the picture, something that none of these theories fully grasps. At least, I feel that way. From my perspective, existing research on writing does a decent job of explaining most situations wherein writers are discovering what they have to say about a subject. But what existing research *doesn't* cover is what happens when an addict in a state of desperation uses writing to seek help from a higher power.

Again and again, the addicts who shared their stories with me spoke of "the Universe" and "the Spirit" and "Whatever It Is That's Out There." They said that agents like these shaped their recovery experience and informed their writing in meaningful, material ways. "God" or some other invisible being sometimes wrote *with* these addicts or even *through* them.

Let me tell you a story, so you can see what I mean:

Bailey, a nurse and an alcoholic, told me about an experience she had working through a piece of recovery writing. She was commuting home from work and attempting to think her way through a Twelve-Step writing exercise related to resentment. In "Big Book resentment inventory," addicts name and describe resentments they have, and then look for their own moral failings in relation to those resentments. This inventory is almost always written, but Bailey, an experienced inventory writer, was driving while working through the exercise mentally:

> I'm driving home, and I did the rundown in my head: I'm selfish. I'm self-seeking. I was dishonest. And so on. I'm doing it in my head, and I've got it all figured out. But I'm still going to put it on paper anyways.
>
> I go into the house. I put it on paper, and it's like my hand went across the page and something was written that I would have never, ever, ever come to on my own. And I'm looking at it, like, "Wow, that's exactly the answer!" But where did that come from? It definitely didn't come from me. The Spirit is really here. The Spirit is driving all of this.

Bailey's story describes what might seem like an unusual discovery experience. According to conventional understandings of writing, this is not how discovery is supposed to work. Hands aren't supposed to move on their own, and if they do, they aren't supposed to be able to write intelligent statements all by themselves. Writers are supposed to know what they are writing, even plan it in advance, not find out what "they" have written after the fact. If writing comes through us from an invisible agent, that agent should be something we already know about, like "writing itself" or "social construction" or something similar, not an active, intelligent, non-tangible being. It's spooky. The whole experience is anomalous. And there are no current peer-reviewed theories of discovery that can adequately explain it.

To be clear, any of the theories I mentioned above *could* produce an explanation of Bailey's experience—and some would do a better job than others—but at the end of the day, none of those explanations would be a narrative that she would recognize. All of them would disregard the most important part of Bailey's whole experience, the agent she identifies as primarily responsible for both her insights and her inscription.

They would all throw out the Spirit.

8

SPIRIT BOARDS, DREAM FAERIES, AND PHOTOGRAPHIC ROCKS

In 1955, the poet James Merrill and his longtime partner David Jackson settled in Stonington, Connecticut, and made themselves a tool for communicating with spirits. On a slip of cardboard, they wrote the letters of the alphabet in capitals, along with the numerals zero through nine and the words YES and NO. This set of characters, along with a cup from a local dime store, served as their spirit board. Placing their hands on the cup, they invited otherworldly entities into their home. As the cup moved around, picking out different letters and numbers, Merrill and Jackson recorded messages from beyond.

These seances, which extended at least into the late 1970s, furnished the material for Merrill's most famous work, a trilogy of poetry books about—and at least partially *by*—the spirits they communicated with during those years. The poems feature many lines clearly written by Merrill in the normal sense of "written by," meaning he somehow had the idea for them and then put them on paper himself. But there are also many lines, printed in all capital letters, that are transcriptions of the planchette's eerie movements:

UNHEEDFUL ONE   3 MORE OF YOUR YEARS WE WANT
    WE MUST HAVE

POEMS OF SCIENCE   THE WEORK FINISHT IS BUT A
   PROLOGUE
ABSOLUTES ARE NOW NEEDED   YOU MUST MAKE GOD
   OF SCIENCE
TELL OF POWER MANS IGNORANCE FEARES THE POWER
   WE ARE
THAT FEAR STOPS PARADISE   WE SPEAK FROM WITHIN
   THE ATOM[16]

Such passages are strange, their origins more so, and as the books progress, they become increasingly common, such that there are long sections of simply all-caps ramblings from extradimensional beings, with a few guiding questions from Merrill and Jackson peppered in.

Merrill's discovery practice—the use of a homemade Ouija board to invent material for his poetry—led to some odd results and some equally odd questions related to who exactly wrote those all-caps lines. Merrill edited them into his poems, likely trimming and revising them here and there, and so he is listed as their final author and the owner of their copyright. But Jackson also held the planchette, and he was the one to record the spirits' dictations. Those lines came from his pen, so isn't he their first author? But then, what about the host of characters who revealed themselves to Merrill and Jackson, and whose dictation Jackson supposedly took? What of Ephraim, their trusted guide through the first book, or the bizarre creatures "QUITE LIKE BATS / HUGE SQUEAKING ONES WITH LITTLE HOT RED EYES . . . NOT . . . EXACTLY SEXUAL OBJECTS / BUT BRAINS WITH WINGS" who dictated the lines I quoted above, demanding "POEMS OF SCIENCE"?[17] What are we to make of these beings and their claims to authorship? What are we to make of their description of Jackson—that "HE IS OUR PEN"[18]— or, later, a spirit's insistence that "JM DJ YOU ARE OUR CRYSTAL RECEIVE US   WE ARE / YR LIGHT"?[19] How can we even begin to assess such claims of supernatural, extradimensional authorship?

Similarly, how are we to treat the report of Robert Louis Stevenson, who claimed that the ideas for his major works were given to him by faeries in his dreams?[20] Or science fiction author Richard Shaver's repeated claims that he wrote his stories under the guidance of ancient beings whose voices emanated from inside our hollow Earth?[21] Or Alcoholics Anonymous co-founder Bill Wilson's use of spirit boards and automatic writing during the foundational years of the organization?[22] What about the hundreds of books that claim to be "channeled" literature, that is, literature written by a spirit through the mediumship of the so-called author?

Ouija boards, fairies, automatic hands, denizens of the hollow Earth, and channeled voices may all seem like screwball examples, outliers on the spectrum of acceptable experiences of writerly agency. And it is true that I am picking these examples precisely because they are so strikingly strange. But, in fact, phenomena like these are commonplace among writers and, to a degree, necessary in any practice of writing. In studies of working fiction writers, a majority of them report hearing their characters talk independently of the text. Some even have internal conversations with these characters and experience them as possessing a surprising degree of autonomy.[23] Further, in most acts of writing, we imagine other people—real or unreal—even when we are not writing fiction. Consciously or unconsciously, we summon an inner audience of at least one reader, then draft and revise according to our felt sense of their reactions. In short, writing almost always means that we have to engage with inner voices or imaginary people. In other words, we have to *play*, which involves yielding some of our own agency to imaginal figures, even if, like a child speaking to an invisible tiger, we only do so "for pretend." "Pretending," though, is a serious activity, and imaginal experiences can be powerful ones. They are formative for children, transformative for adults. Sometimes, we encounter in play anomalous effects that are not easy to explain as mere make-believe. Richard Shaver heard weird voices that told him fantastic stories. Robert Louis Stevenson's faeries gave him *Dr. Jekyll and Mr. Hyde*. Bill Wilson's conversations with St. Boniface helped him structure the fellowship of AA as he wrote *Twelve Steps and Twelve Traditions*. And Bailey's hand moved across the page, giving her deeper insight into her own resentment than she could have ever produced by herself. She got right emotionally and she stayed sober, something she was never able to do on her own.

My point in throwing around examples of seemingly bizarre invention methods is twofold: First, I want to show that, odd as it may be, Bailey's experience is not singular. She is not alone in having valuable, insightful material appear through her hand from some other, unseen source. In fact, this sort of experience is common. It's not weird—it's boring and ordinary. We *always* accept ideas from invisible sources when we write, even if they don't always move our hands or speak to us from the center of the Earth.

Second, these seemingly weird but actually commonplace stories point to the fact that there is a dynamic but often unseen dimension of discovery that surfaces in moments when our writing surprises us. The playful, agency-distributing imagination contains all kinds of figures, from "God" to "The Social," and from imagined audiences to red-eyed, leather-winged sex brains from the next dimension. This generative, communicative, agentive, and *populated* imagination is always at play—to one degree or another, and in some way or another—as we write.

In 1960, Richard Shaver and his wife Dottie were going broke on their small farm in Lanark, Wisconsin. Shaver's early stories had run their course. The sci-fi fandom had decided against him and his work, and the magazine that had published his stories had gone bust. But just before the Shavers sold their farm, Dottie found a couple of weird rocks and showed them to Richard. One looked like the Virgin Mary; the other had the shape of a child's foot. Pondering the significance of his wife's find, Shaver was struck by a sudden insight, which is to say that he made a discovery: These were no ordinary rocks but the record left behind by extraterrestrial civilizations that knew how to imprint stone with 3D images. They were *singing rocks*, rocks that contained the choruses of prehuman history. The Shaver farm was littered with these rock-book-photographs, or "rogfogo," as Shaver now called them.

Over the following months, he discovered a process for scanning these rocks, transferring the images to film and using his paint brush to reveal the long-hidden history of an alien civilization on canvas. Now, neither you nor I would be able to reproduce Shaver's method for accessing the images supposedly stored in these rocks, and Shaver's career was littered with accusations of fraudulence and insanity. He, in fact, spent time in a state institution for the criminally insane. But Shaver's stories and paintings exist, which means they must have come from *somewhere*. And those closest to Shaver say that he was not lying, at least not intentionally, about where his ideas came from. He really did believe his discovery process involved sentient beings in the center of the Earth and ancient alien 3D photographers. He heard the voices, he had the visions, and he was convinced of their reality and value.[24]

He had to be. *They* needed him to be.

How else could a painting spring from a rock? Or a story from the hollow Earth?

Like me, Richard Shaver may have been "crazy," but I don't think he was pretending. And I believe his rogfogo are real, if not entirely actual. I mean, these rocks may or may not actually be 3D polaroids left by ancient Earth visitors, but they were exactly that to Shaver, and as such, they had real consequences for his creative output and for many other parts of his life: personal, social, and spiritual.

The imagination has a reality of its own, at the very least in the form of psychological and material consequences for those who *play* and those who *believe*, which is, to some degree, all of us when ideas appear in our minds as we write.

9

A BENEVOLENT, INVISIBLE AGENT OF DISCOVERY

If you strongly identify as someone with a rational-materialist perspective on life, you may find that all this talk of invisible agents and strange imaginings has given you a case of the "But Reallies." You'll know if, while reading this book, you find yourself saying things like, "Maybe Shaver thought there were books in his rocks, *but really*, he was nuts," or, "Sure, Bailey may have experienced her writing process as spiritual, *but really*, that's just more proof that social conditions write themselves through us as we inscribe," or even, "I can see how addicts might need to believe in something spiritual, *but really*, it's all a trick of the mind."

We come down with a case of the But Reallies anytime we feel an impulse to reinterpret someone else's experiences in terms that make us feel more comfortable. This is a problem that occurs all the time in ethnographic research, even when researchers try hard to avoid it. They interview people who are not like them, who tell them things that they don't understand, and then they reframe everything they've heard using theories and language appropriate to their academic discipline—in so doing painting over the transcripts with a big red brush to say, "I know, I said I was here to learn from you, *but really*, I'm just going to use your stories to say things people in my field already want to hear."

If you're an addict and my discussion thus far of invisible, imaginal agents gives you the But Reallies, you have my sympathy. You are not alone. Like you, and like me, plenty of addicts in recovery do not start out as big fans of the "God stuff" in the Twelve Steps. Many of us come to recovery with religious backgrounds that we do not care for and a distaste for anything that smells like religion. The advice I give my sponsees is the same advice Piers gave me: Bring all your doubts to the table, but give this thing a fair try. Do the work with an open mind and an open heart, and see where it takes you. If it changes your ideas about spiritual stuff, cool. If not, that's fine too. But don't preemptively shut yourself off from a life-saving experience just because you think it smells funny.

If you are a non-addict and have reasonable objections to talk of invisible beings, the stakes are much lower for you than they are for addicts, which is to say that your commitment to a rational worldview is probably not going to kill you anytime soon. But I would still ask you to adopt a similar attitude. Bring all your doubts and critical thinking to bear on what I have to say in this book, but please also give it a fair shake. Rather than rejecting these ideas out of hand, sit with them awhile and see how they *feel*. This stuff is weird, and it can be hard to understand. But the stories of the folks I interviewed have a lot to teach us about writing. Specifically, they can teach us about the way writerly agency is distributed among visible and invisible agents during moments of discovery. Within a writer's imagination, entities of all kinds can be summoned for their powers of insight and persuasion in order to accomplish the task of coming up with things to say. We can think of these entities as *real*, at least to the extent that writers experience them as such and they have material consequences for writers and their writing.

Addict or not, if you are a religious person, I realize that my loose talk of spirit boards and voices from the hollow Earth, of the similarities between talking rocks and messages from God, may be troubling to you. "Sure," you may say, "these are interesting phenomena, *but really*, they are dangerous, perhaps even demonic, and are certainly nothing like prayer." In a later chapter, I will discuss different safety measures and ethical standards for listening and responding to strange voices, but for the moment, I'd like to acknowledge that there are real differences between, for example, Merrill's poetry and Bailey's inventory writing. While Merrill ended up with strange ideas and bizarre poems, Bailey ended up with a new perspective on life and the ongoing ability to remain sober. And so, I believe we can distinguish between the various influences of invisible agents primarily by the effects they have on our lives and our writing. It is, in general, a good idea to be wary of those inner voices that would cause harm and chaos in our lives. It is also a good idea to be in close contact with those that heal and sustain us.

In Bailey's case, there are four important observations to be made about the reality of "the Spirit" and the consequences it has for her writing process. First, Bailey reported her hand moving and performing inscription without her conscious participation. Her experience shares much in common with other acts of automatic writing.[25] To a lesser degree, Bailey's report resembles that of writers who discover meaning and purpose during the writing process itself. Flannery O'Connor, for example, said: "I have to write to discover what I am doing. . . . I don't know so well what I think until I see what I say."[26] Like O'Connor, Bailey did not have access to her "own" insights until they had already been produced on the page.

Second, once Bailey read the new insights that had appeared, she immediately recognized them as of foreign origin. Unlike O'Connor, Bailey cannot bring herself to claim ownership of the writing. It does not seem to her that she discovered what *she* thought by writing; rather, the page contained something that she would "never, ever, ever" think. Nor does Bailey feel that the insight arose from her own unconscious, like a dream or an intuition might. Instead, for Bailey, the sensation of discovery is very distinctly *other*.

Third, when Bailey read her writing, she immediately recognized it as not only useful and true ("Wow, that's exactly the answer!") but also *truer* and *more useful* than the insights she had produced mentally on her own. Bailey did not gain clarity about her resentment when she mentally rehearsed it on her way home from work, but she did gain insight when she wrote and experienced another agent moving her hand. This "truer" truth led Bailey to conclude that the invisible agent moving her hand is a benevolent one, one interested in helping her come to know such truths about herself and, in knowing, to be free of resentment. Whatever "the Spirit" is, it appears to act within Bailey's writing process as a force of discovery, one that gives her better answers than she can arrive at on her own.

The appearance of this benevolent, invisible agent of discovery leads to a fourth and final point: Bailey attributes her writing to an entity she refers to as "the Spirit," and this attribution seems perfectly appropriate and natural to her—even logical, given what she experienced. If she could not make the desired discovery on her own, and if something outside her wrote *through* her to produce that discovery, then it follows that there must exist some kind of entity that is a) more powerful than she is, b) more insightful about her resentments and relationships, and c) caring enough to reveal what it knows. Through her writing, Bailey has acquired what is, to her, empirical evidence of the reality of a spiritual being. This is an intimate power, one that can move her hand to inscribe helpful truths, a power that knows her better than she knows herself. Through an act of writing, this power offered proof of its existence to Bailey in the realm of her lived experience.

Whatever else this thing might be, it is real, which is to say that Bailey experiences it as real, and it has material consequences for her writing, her self-representation, and her recovery. Some people would even argue that this "Spirit" is *more real* than you and me: it seems to intervene in our world from some higher-order plane of existence. And it comes up with better, more insightful things to say. It could even hijack Bailey's hand to inscribe those insights all by itself, indicating that it has more power than we do over the material world, even over our own bodies.

At this point, you may want to say:

"*But really*, it was just a cognitive process."

"*But really*, it was just the expression of social forces."

"*But really*, it was a moment of chaos, of writing itself showing its power."

"*But really*, this whole thing is nuts!"

Maybe so. It certainly *could be* any of those things, but I would ask you to set aside such perspectives for a while longer. Jumping to an already known, comfortable conclusion too early would cause us to miss out on the wisdom of experiences like Bailey's. And there is more weirdness to come.

"Pray, and Then You Write"

LAVERT COX'S STORY

Lavert's story describes several kinds of recovery writing practices. He begins by telling us that these practices work when addicts are willing to change and become receptive to the guidance from a power greater than themselves.

Prayer is a vitally important part of recovery for me. You gotta be willing to listen and then be obedient to what God is saying to do, 'cause many times God doesn't answer me with what I want to hear. Like, you ask God, "Should I date such and such?" and God will say, "No, stay away." But you crank the car up and then you go straight over to her house, and now you're both drunk 'cause you didn't listen. If you're fortunate enough to make it back to the rooms, you start over again. That's my story: I messed up so many times, so many times. I couldn't hold on to a sobriety date, and I was so down about it, I tried to kill myself. I came real close to getting out of here.

When I finally got to working Steps, my sponsor had me start with a little life story, identifying the powerlessness of my situation. My sponsor had a form he'd taken from an AA pamphlet with questions on it. I had to read these questions and answer them, so I did a little write-up on my life. I really wanted some relief, so I was anxious to get started, but it was kind of scary. He taught me that the first thing you do is pray before you pick up the pencil. *Pray*, and then you write. You pray for an open mind. I pray that God will help me to be as honest as I can with myself.

Because a newcomer is gonna come in, and they're not all that honest. You need help. You really need help being honest. I had a lot of lies that I had told for so long that it felt like they was truth. But after you peel through some layers, you get down to the real truth, and you find that there's a lot of add-ons, a lot of embellishing situations, minimizing wrongs that you had done—that kind of thing.

When I showed my writing to my sponsor, he would proofread it and give it back to me, kind of like how a schoolteacher would give you back your homework with all the errors marked so you could redo it. It wouldn't be grammar, but he would send me back to peel through the layers and get more honest with myself, because until you can see the truth about yourself, you're really just spitting in the wind. So you gotta be able to see the truth.

That's the approach I use for people I sponsor too. A lot of times, we minimize our part in our retelling of situations, so I ask them questions. I'll say: "You know, you played a bigger part than that. Was it her fault that you got in the car and ran off and didn't come home for a couple of days, out getting drunk? Or was it you just wanted to get drunk and needed an excuse, so you caused an argument?" You want them to see the truth about some stuff. And when they own up to it—you know, like, "Yeah, you right; you right, ok"—then they go ahead and rewrite or add some more truth to their writing. It's just helping them get in touch with some real basic stuff, just like a kind of soft soap to help them get clean.

But when my sponsor did that with me, it was humbling. First of all, it was embarrassing. But once I accepted it, it gave me a sense of relief. You got this person you really look up to and respect and admire—your sponsor. You're building this rapport with them through the writing and through sitting down and going through this information, and they help you to probe through it and dig and find the truth in situations so you're no longer blaming others. The real crux of the problem is me—my attitude, my outlook on life, and my interpretation of situations and events. So, it was a humbling experience, but you also get a sense of relief once you face the truth and accept it. It was like a weight was lifted up off of me, but then I got anxious. Once I had that sense of relief, I got anxious to get rid of all of it—the weight of all those secrets. I got a real sense that you're only as sick as the secrets that you keep. And the fear is that if you don't get completely honest, you're gonna get drunk again.

After the life story, my sponsor had me write about my ideas on higher power. I had religious training in my early life, although I got away from that later. I knew about God and religion, so tapping into a higher power was not a difficult process for me. I knew how to pray.

I do the same thing with my sponsees. I have them write down what they would like their higher power to be. I don't try to force on them my image of what I think God should be. I just let them format a god of their own understanding, a god they would like to have in their corner. I let them begin where they are and go from nothing to something, and then from something to a more effective, more powerful belief. You just put it down on paper, and we just start from there.

Once I had my image of God, my sponsor told me that old riddle: Three frogs were on a log, and one of them decided to jump—how many were left? All three, because one made a decision but none of them took action. So, you make a decision to change your life, but what are you going to *do*? So I have my sponsees list three to five things that they're willing to do differently in their activities or their lifestyle. Just whatever they're willing to do. That's a starting point. It's like coming out of the gate right there, and we set some goals to go to our next station.

For instance, someone is willing to be home at ten o'clock every night. If that's what they can start with, we'll start with that. And then we list some goals we're shooting for. Not only are they willing to be done and home by ten but they'll help the kids with homework or some other task. Let them start wherever they're at and have some short-term goals and some medium-range goals and that kind of thing.

After that was moral inventory. I had heard so much in the meeting rooms, with people making it seem like inventory was like a ferocious lion eating me up. I had a lot of anxiety about doing that. However, once I began to write—again, I prayed before I picked the pencil up—stuff started coming out. Stuff just started bubbling up, and it was very emotional. It was some days I wrote and just cried, but overall it was a sense of relief that I had never experienced before. I hadn't told anyone yet, but just me facing it, getting it on paper—it gave me relief. You hang on to these things and you stuff them down inside of you, and you pack it down and you put some more misery on top of that. But once you start writing and all that stuff starts coming up out of you, it's like somebody turns on a water faucet—it just starts spewing out. You're getting it down on paper. You're getting to write it down. And then you get to look at it in black and white. It's such an eye-opening event.

Then you go and share all that with your sponsor and get free of all that. When you go the wrong way in life, it's like walking with ankle weights on, but it's been so gradual that you don't realize that you're bogged down. Little by little, you get further and further and further away from your principles until you're up to your neck in a sea of dishonesty. You're getting more and more bogged down as you go, but you don't realize it until you unstrap them weights. Then you see how free you feel again, how easy it is to make a step forward. And it's a real powerful, powerful feeling. Because then you're spiritually centered once again. You get aligned with your true values. You get your moral compass back. And it's a real, good, satisfying feeling to get that weight off of you.

And basically, that's what the writing was about for me—just being able to put down on paper some of the events of my life, and then rewriting and rewriting 'til I got to the truth of the matter.

And then sharing it with my sponsor. That was priceless because, me being newly in recovery, it had been a long time since I did any looking at myself. But how can you recover if you don't know what the problem is? So, writing is putting pen to paper until you can see the truth, not theorying it up in your mind. That's where the illness is—it's in your mind. Your disease is in your thinking. It's like a neurosurgeon doing surgery on his own self. It ain't gonna work. You gotta get it down on paper in order to see the facts.

That's why I advise my sponsees to journal. Just to keep a log, a daily log of what happened that day and how they feel about what happened. If you have an emotional day or event, or if a situation comes up, sometimes you need to release the frustration. You can get it out by praying and writing rather than going to your local bar or getting a six-pack. You sit and pray for a while—maybe sit down with a cup of tea—and start writing, getting it all out. What that does is, after a period of time journaling, you're able to look back through the book and you're able to see where you've grown. Some things that used to have you bewildered and confused—now they're just like little mole hills where they once were big mountains. Things that had you twisted all up like a pretzel emotionally—today, they just don't even faze you.

I shiver sometimes when I think about where I was and where I am today, man. It's just amazing what God has done in my life. I am so opposite to the guy I was when I came into recovery. I am a minister of the gospel at my church. To come from where I come from and to be where I am today? There's no doubt in my mind that it was God. I could never on my own bring about what has happened in my life.

How to Write
Three Frogs on a Log

As Lavert's "three frogs" anecdote illustrates, a decision without action doesn't make any impact on our lives. If we decide we want to live in relationship with a higher power, then we have to ask ourselves: *What does that decision look like* in action*? What can I actually* do *to make this relationship concrete?*

To do this exercise, take some time to pray before writing. Ask whatever is out there in the universe to show you some things that you could do differently in your life. The goal of this reflection is to arrive at three "frogs on a log," by which I mean three places where you've been reluctant to live in relationship with your higher power. Once you have the frogs down, you'll figure out how to make them jump.

1. Find your frogs: Write down three sticking points, places in your life where you know you could be more honest, unselfish, or loving to others.
2. Jump 'em off the log: Write down three concrete actions you can take to change your behavior.
3. Get honest: Share your findings with a sponsor or an understanding, trustworthy friend who can hold you accountable.

4. Stay honest: Check in with that sponsor or friend regularly for a while to tell them what it's been like to change your behavior this way.

10

HOW I MADE MY SURRENDER

Piers told me that if I wanted to work the Twelve Steps, I had to make my peace with the God stuff. He didn't care what I believed, or if I believed in anything at all. But I was going to have to take the leap and surrender. That meant, at the very least, I would have to go through the motions of praying to The Great Whatever: "I am broken and can't run my own life, so could you do that for me, please?" Because I grew up in an evangelical church, I'd done this sort of thing before. We called it an "altar call." The preacher would say a bunch of awful stuff designed to make you feel bad about yourself, and then he'd say, "Come forward, if the Spirit calls you, and rededicate your life to Jesus Christ." If the sermon worked and you felt really bad about yourself, you'd plod your way to the front of the sanctuary and get on your knees to ask Jesus into your heart for the ten millionth time. These cycles of sin, shame, and rededication were, in my view, a toxic process to which I had no interest in returning. Ever.

But Piers said that making a surrender was the entry point to this new way of being, the only real hope I had of feeling at peace inside myself. I wanted that peace, desperately. Even so, there was no way I was going to put myself back through the evangelical ringer. This tension between my desire for change and my resistance to the all-too-familiar religious tones of the program created a real problem for me. My head was abuzz with conflicting feelings and ideas. Why not just try this surrender thing? Would I really rather be dead than a born-again Christian? Actually, yeah. Maybe I would.

Piers said I should take a week to think about it. If I wanted to make a surrender, we would do it then. That was a rough week. And I didn't make it all the way through. Each day, all day long, my brain shouted back and forth at itself:

MAKE A SURRENDER!

NO, THANKS!

BUT YOU WILL FEEL SO MUCH BETTER!

LOOKS LIKE A CULT TO ME!

YOU WILL LITERALLY DIE!

OR TURN INTO A MINDLESS ZOMBIE? WHAT A CHOICE!

On and on, my brain yelled at itself like that, from morning until deep in the night.

About four days into "thinking about it," I broke. The stress and strain were too much for me. As I headed to the library in search of distraction, everything suddenly went silent all around and within me. I remember this event happening at nighttime, and it starting to snow. Gentle flakes falling through the street lights. But when I run the calendar, I find that it actually happened in summer. So no snow. I think my memory is trying to interpret this weird, sudden inner and outer silence in material terms. It was like what happens when the snow falls and all the animals get quiet, and the noise of traffic is muted. It was soft. Soundless. A gift from above.

In the midst of this silence, a phrase came to my mind. Over and over again. It fell through my awareness in little flakes of light: "thy will, not mine, be done." *What a shitty thing to think,* I thought. It's a terrible phrase. In church, it was used to strip people of their free will and turn them into Jesus-robots. It meant: "Feel bad about yourself and do what we tell you." What garbage.

But it somehow sounded different this time.

I closed my eyes, and I was given a vision of my life up to that point. I saw my lifestream as if it were a flowchart that began with my birth and headed straight forward until it reached the first moment in which I had been able to make a decision for myself. In that moment, I had picked the thing that I most wanted, the thing that I thought would make me feel good, without any other consideration. And so the flow chart branched downward. I was just a bit less happy after that moment, a little less satisfied. But the line moved on, straight forward, until the next point of decision. And again, I had picked what I thought would make me feel good. The path branched downward once more. This pattern repeated itself over and over again throughout my life, with the universe presenting points of decision and me acting to please myself. Every time, the same result ensued: my life shifted to a trajectory where I was more restless, more unsatisfied. Over and over again. Before, during, and after active addiction, the pattern was always the same. I did whatever I wanted and the results were always crap.

That was my life, run on my own power. I was like a computer with only one program, a program called "How will this make me feel?" I had no other possible response to life's choices. No inner resources that would permit me to act another way. At my core, I could see things only through this very limiting lens.

My programming had led me to the point I was at now, wrestling with whether to die, get high, or make my peace with the "God" stuff and surrender. For the last few days, I had been trying to make this high-stakes, life-or-death choice the same way I had made all the previous ones. I was attempting to pick the option that would make me feel good. Then it dawned on me: if I actually did make *this* choice through *that* old program, I could expect the same old results. I looked forward on the timeline. There weren't too many branches left. Two, three more? Then my lifestream would drop into oblivion.

But what if there *were* another program? What if something out there in the universe—something beyond the tiny boundaries of my little ego and its desires—were willing to show me a different way to choose? I mean, that would be awesome. It would radically improve the whole trajectory of my life. What would you even say to something like that? Wouldn't you want to say something like, "thy will, not mine, be done"?

Something in me, some persistently and deeply held tension, released itself as if I had been tightening all my muscles my entire life and suddenly let go. Only, instead of muscle tension, it was *me* who got released. My ego deflated with the goofy whine and sputter of a rubber balloon. I started crying real ugly, like snot-coming-out-my-nose crying, just as I passed into the library. I rushed past the startled librarian, ducked into the bathroom, and locked the door behind me. I was on my knees over the floor drain, but I couldn't remember the words to the prayer Piers had taught me. So I just said something simple, like: "I don't know what to do. Please help me."

Immediately, my internal state shifted. I stopped crying. I felt dumb and embarrassed. But I also felt grounded. Like the fight was over. Even though this Twelve-Step thing was weird and smelled way too Christian for me, I was going to give it a try. And that felt good. Peaceful. Not ecstatic or transcendental or anything. Just . . . good. I knew that I was going to be okay. I wasn't going to jump off a bridge. I wasn't going to get high. I wasn't going to be depressed or crazy. I was on solid ground now. Something was with me, and it wasn't ever going to go away.

And that is what surrender means. It means you are going to be okay. You don't have to struggle to hold yourself together anymore. You don't have to try so hard to make your life successful or meaningful or moral or attractive or whatever it is that you've been striving for. Stop trying. Stop striving. Let yourself be. See what happens. There's another power at work in this world besides your ego. Step aside for a minute and let yourself see what it can do.

11

Do We Really Have to Give Up Everything?

Surrender is a difficult thing to explain to people who have not experienced it because from the outside, it looks completely nuts. I've heard addicts new to recovery protest the idea of surrender in all kinds of different ways. "What!?" they'd exclaim. "You're just supposed to stop doing everything and see what happens? Quit your job? Stop doing chores and paying the rent? You want me to just lie down in a field of flowers somewhere and hope that everything works out? What kind of plan is that?"

This kind of objection relies on the mistaken notion that surrender means making an absolute commitment to *passivity*. We make this kind of objection when we lack the imagination to envision our lives as directed by a power other than ourselves. If we let go of our will, we think, there will be nothing left to motivate us, nothing to run the show. We'll just go limp, fall to the ground, and we'll have to hope that someone comes along now and then to feed us.

But surrender is not passive. It is *active*. It's just that our activities are now motivated and directed by something new. People in recovery tend to call this new power "God," but you needn't think of it that way. You aren't required to give your ascent to any set beliefs about the nature of this power. What is required is that you completely cease your efforts to run your life on your own. And that can be a hard thing to wrap your mind around.

I worked at an in-patient drug and alcohol treatment center for a couple of years before returning to school. During those years, part of my job was to introduce new guests of the treatment center to the basics of Twelve-Step recovery. We read through the early chapters of the AA Big Book and discussed our experiences with things like compulsive using, obsessive thinking, out-of-control behavior, painful consequences, and the failure of self-control. All this discussion built up to an understanding of personal powerlessness, which is the basis for making a surrender. After two weeks of groups and discussion, guests would take a "Third Step," which meant getting on their knees in the chapel and saying a prayer to indicate that they were turning their will and their lives over to the care of a higher power.

Many guests went into that chapel and prayed, but not too many actually made a surrender there. Sure, they got on their knees and said the prayer like everybody else, but that was as far as it went. They were told that a "Third Step" was the next phase of their treatment, so they went through the motions. But making a surrender doesn't mean getting on your knees or saying a specific prayer. And it certainly doesn't mean jumping through hoops at a treatment center. Those guests who became actively involved in their own recovery and achieved long-term sobriety invariably had a moment of reckoning—sometime during their stay, or even well afterward—in which they were confronted by their desperate need for change and their inability to provide that change for themselves. They asked a higher power for help not because it was the next phase of treatment but because they suddenly knew, from the core of their being, that they needed it.

Unfortunately, these guests were the exception rather than the rule, and there was no predicting which ones would experience this sudden change of heart. Nothing that we staff members did caused guests to surrender. In fact, much of our efforts in this direction backfired, producing mere *compliance* with our wishes rather than a surrender at depth to something greater than ourselves.[27] Like desperation, surrender just sort of happens sometimes. You can provide an environment conducive to recognizing powerlessness; you can explain basic principles of recovery and tell your story over and over again; but you cannot make people surrender. You can't even make them understand what surrender means until they are ready to see it.

I once got to witness a true moment of surrender. Normally, these things happened privately, with guests locking themselves in their bathrooms or walking alone out into a field to pray. But this one time, it happened in the middle of my group. We were reading from a chapter of the Big Book called "How It Works." The chapter suggests that "most people" (not just addicts, mind you) normally try to "live by self-propulsion":

> Each person is like an actor who wants to run the whole show. . . . If only people would do as he wished, the show would be great. Everybody, including himself, would be pleased. . . . In trying to make these arrangements our actor may sometimes be quite virtuous. . . . On the other hand, he may be mean, egotistical, selfish and dishonest. . . . What usually happens? The show doesn't come off very well. . . . He decides to exert himself more. He becomes, on the next occasion, still more demanding or gracious, as the case may be. . . . Is he not really a self-seeker even when trying to be kind? Is he not a victim of the delusion that he can wrest satisfaction and happiness out of this world if he only manages well?[28]

I'd read this passage a million times to a million groups, but somehow, this time someone *got it*. I didn't say or do anything special in this group. I just read the book like always and gave my usual spiel about surrender. This guy's whole face lit up:

"You mean I don't have to try so hard anymore!?" he asked.

"Right," I said.

"I've got all this pressure to be a man and be a provider and be strong all the time, and I don't have to have that pressure anymore!?" he asked.

"Not anymore," I said.

"Something's just going to take care of me now!?" he asked, starting to choke up.

"That's right," I said. "You don't have to worry about *anything* anymore."

"Oh my god!" he shouted, and he began sobbing. Big, heavy, tearful sobs moved through this guy as he let go of his entire life's project of presenting himself as the perfect picture of a "man." It was okay to be weak. It was okay to accept help. It was okay to be powerless and to need something stronger than him to fix his life. It was all, suddenly, okay. And he understood that from the core of his being.

When this man's sobbing had subsided, I looked around at the rest of the guests in our group. Of the five of them, two were completely freaked out and dissociating. One was deeply affected by what he had just witnessed, but still presented fear and hesitation. The remaining guest was completely unimpressed. "I have a question about that," she said, dryly. "Like, do we *really* have to give up *everything*? Just to take a Third Step?"

She was staring salvation in the face and trying to get it at a discount. She wanted the freedom of having given up everything without actually giving up anything. She didn't understand what she was seeing because like most addicts—like most *humans*—she wasn't ready for it yet.

"Yeah," I answered. "We really do."

12

MAKING CONTACT

The sole purpose of desperation is to enable you to surrender, which is where its real value lies. If desperation is a gift, then surrender is the thing the gift does when you unwrap it, pull it out of the box, and stick the batteries in. When I say that desperation motivates us to do things we wouldn't otherwise do, surrender is my first case in point. Most normal, rational people don't turn their will and their lives over to the care of an invisible being that may or may not "exist." You have to be really desperate to do a thing like that.

My interview transcripts are full of stories of addicts who hit a wall in their lives and desperately sought help. When they came to the Twelve-Step fellowships, they, like me, were repulsed by the idea of surrender, but they held their noses and dove in anyway because they were desperate. They had no better options—no reasonable way out of their predicament—and so they agreed to this rather unreasonable way out instead.

Jerry E., for example, is an alcoholic and a retired banker from Middle America. When he was already thirteen years sober, Jerry had a spiritual crisis. For thirteen long years, he was hanging on to sobriety with all his might, essentially unchanged from the man he was when he was drinking, the only difference being that—for all those years—he never once enjoyed the relief that came from taking a drink. It was torturous. "Unrecovered" was the word Jerry used to describe it. Abstinent, but miserable. At the time, he was just about ready to die:

> To take as much of the drama out of it as I can, I could not stand the idea of going another day in the kind of psychic pain I was in. And that's the only label I can put on it: the psychic pain of being separated from the Spirit, being separated from the world, being separated from other people. It was so painful that I really did not want to live any longer. I was just barely able to function. I would wake up each morning and think, *I can't go through another day.* Somehow, I'd struggle through to the evening and try to go to sleep, but I couldn't—I just couldn't—because my mind wouldn't quiet down.

In this miserable state, Jerry was introduced to an AA meeting, where they described what was to him a novel approach to the Twelve Steps. This approach required treating the Steps as a set of actions rather than a bunch of ideas. You had to *do* the Steps, not just read and think about them. In this meeting, members told stories about how their lives changed radically for the better once they started taking action, Step by Step.

But Jerry found himself deeply conflicted when he learned that the process would require relying on "God." The idea of giving up control over his life to a non-material—probably imaginary—entity seemed unsound. How was he to deal with the program's insistence on higher power when he didn't believe and didn't even *want* to believe in such power? He describes the conflict and its resolution this way:

> I left the meeting one night, and I was walking up the street, trying to come to terms with this whole higher power thing and not having any luck. Man, I was struggling so hard! And as I was walking, it finally came to me that I have nothing to lose. I don't even need to know who or what I'm praying to. So I'll just pray to whatever is out there in the universe. And that was what I did. I just looked out into the universe and said, "Okay."

With that simple gesture—looking into the night sky and saying "okay"—Jerry began his relationship with "whatever is out there in the universe," a relationship that sustained him through the Twelve-Step process and that still nourishes his spiritual life decades later.

The addicts I spoke with generally agreed that this kind of gesture, this giving up on one's resistance and opening oneself to the possibility of higher power, was the foundation of their recovery. And as with Jerry and as with me, most of them said they could not or would not have made that gesture without first becoming desperate.

The logic here is fairly straightforward: if you realize you can't make your life work and your best plan is to die, then the idea of asking an invisible agent to run your life for you becomes— if not really more appealing—at least worth a try. This logic had to be explained to me with an elaborate flowchart visualization of my life. Some people, like Jerry, require a little less hand-holding. His statement of "I have nothing left to lose" is telling. In that moment, Jerry's desperation unlocked the possibility of surrender. In such moments, the "nihilist" position ("Life is meaningless, so I might as well die") shifts ever so slightly into an "absurdist" one ("Life is meaningless, so I might as well do this weird, ridiculous thing"). This shift from nihilistic despair to absurdist desperation, which justifies surrender, is all we need to begin recovery.

Post-surrender, Jerry began the process of writing a "Fourth Step moral inventory," a lengthy project of self-examination and moral reflection, and he found that "whatever is out there in the universe" joined him in the work. At the time, Jerry lived by himself in a small apartment. He set up a chair and a little bookshelf near a sliding glass door, where he could look out on a pond while he wrote. Jerry called this his "spiritual corner" and said that the space "was very conducive to my mind getting quiet."

"Getting quiet," Jerry said, is important to writing a moral inventory because we don't discover the truth by ourselves in recovery writing. We have to ask something else to show us. The discoveries Jerry needed to make were not ones he felt he could come up with on his own:

> If I'm going to write inventory, I've got to get a quiet mind, because I'm actually going to ask the Spirit to guide me in this process. See, I'm a guy who lied to himself. I need to allow my mind to get quiet, so I can finally see the truth. When I had trouble, I would sit there in that chair, and I would tell God: "Hey, I'm stuck. I don't think I'm ever going to see any truth here other than what I'm already thinking."

And in response to that prayer, "God" or "the Spirit" or "Whatever Is Out There" would provide insight. Where Jerry was lying to himself, the Spirit told him the truth. In Jerry's case, this divinely delivered insight did not come in the form of an automatic hand or a spirit board's inscription. It came in the form of an inner vision that shifted his orientation toward past events and allowed him to see his own moral failings in situations involving people he was still angry at. For example:

> I had a resentment where I kept believing she was more to blame than I was. Gradually, as I put a little prayer and meditation into it, she just . . . it was almost like a cartoon where the other person dissolves. The next thing I knew, I was left there alone. It was just me and what I had done. God will always reveal the truth if you wait long enough.

A lifelong resentment and preoccupation with the wrongs of another person suddenly evaporated before Jerry's eyes, allowing him to see, and therefore record, his own personal shortcomings. Because Jerry could not make this discovery on his own, and because he had specifically asked his higher power to show him the truth, he knew that his inner experience of shifting perspective and insight was enabled by something beyond his own rational mind. He had made what the Twelve Steps call "conscious contact with God."

These moments of insight, structured by prayer and inward listening, became the whole point of inventory writing for Jerry. He began to use his moral inventory specifically to make this kind of God-assisted discovery. His purpose in writing was not to complete an assignment or to express his feelings, or even to figure himself out. And it certainly wasn't to produce grammatically perfect, lovely-to-read prose. Instead, the point of writing, in his state of surrender, was *contact*.

From desperation to surrender, and from surrender to contact—I saw this pathway repeatedly in many addicts' stories, always with writing practices playing a central role. Writing transports addicts along the path from desperation to surrender and then to contact by affording the experience of discovery. When we discover the truth about ourselves, we also discover our relationship with a higher power.

How to Write
Your Own Surrender Prayer

The AA Big Book contains a prayer that many people refer to as the "Third Step prayer," meaning it is the prayer that they use to make a surrender. Here's the text of that prayer:

> God, I offer myself to Thee—to build with me and to do with me as Thou wilt. Relieve me of the bondage of self, that I may better do Thy will. Take away my difficulties, that victory over them may bear witness to those I would help of Thy Power, Thy Love, and Thy Way of life. May I do Thy will always![29]

Narcotics Anonymous also has a prayer commonly called the "Third Step prayer," and it is used for the same purpose. Much more to the point, it goes like this:

> Take my will and my life, guide me in my recovery, show me how to live.[30]

There's no one right way to say a prayer like this. The important thing is that your words express your desperation and your desire to receive help from a power greater than you. As a result, sponsors sometimes ask their sponsees to write their own versions of a surrender prayer. This was the case for Maureen D., who told me she was "struggling a lot with some of the Christian language" of the AA Third Step prayer, so her sponsor gave her the option to write it in her own way. Maureen's version stripped out the overly religious language and replaced it with words more appropriate to her own understanding of a higher power.

Other addicts told me that they rewrote their prayers of surrender at different times in their recovery in order to address new needs. For example, Dorothy wrote a new version of the Big Book's prayer when she realized that in addition to her alcoholism, she was a food addict:

> The changes I made to the prayer were specific about the ways I was acting and my obsession around food and body image. It was more direct than the original about where my selfishness was coming out and about asking for specific help.

To write a prayer of surrender:

1. Pick one of the prayers above or a similar prayer from another anonymous fellowship.
2. Identify the parts of the prayer that don't fit your understanding of a higher power.
3. Identify the parts of the prayer that could be more specific about the powerlessness you are personally facing.
4. Draft a version of the prayer that
    a. is addressed to your higher power,
    b. acknowledges that you are broken and powerless in specific ways,
    c. asks for help and guidance to recover.
4. When your prayer is ready, set aside some time to get centered and say your prayer aloud to your higher power.

"Something Heard You and Understood"

MATT D.'S STORY

Matt describes his experience with writing regular moral inventory every month for many years. He concludes that there is something special about writing that reveals to us truths about ourselves and places us in contact with a higher power.

I got sober on a recovery commune, and then I lived there for fifteen years after that. When I got there, they basically said: "Pray every morning, and when you are in real serious trouble throughout the day, use repetitive prayer. Have your inventory ready in five days." And that was it. They just said, "Write your inventory." At that time, it mostly came back to the seven deadly sins. Later, we had a guide for writing inventory with a list of character defects. We had a lot of different things that people did. Some people used St. Augustine's prayer book because there's a whole bunch of character defects in there—really helpful stuff. But for the most part, when we had new people, we just said, "Look, go write down all the stuff that you know is wrong and is bugging you." It was based on the premise that you were going to do this writing every thirty days, so you took your own inventory as best as you could. If there was something that you hadn't yet fully realized, you were going to have opportunities to see it as you went along. The idea was that this was going to be a regular thing now. That was how it worked.

Normally, I would start by putting down the thing that I didn't want to say, if I had one. I felt like it wasn't honest not to spill the beans on that. I also wanted to get it over with because, you know, you're afraid of what the person's going to say. You're ashamed, but you also want relief. You just want to get it out and done with, and you know that once you're done saying it, it's over. So I usually put that sort of thing first.

Then I would start off with pride. A lot of times, I would just write the word "pride." If I really felt like I needed it, I might give a definition or something. But pretty much I would just write the word "pride," and I would write out the character defects related to that. I would go through different forms of what pride would be, like, under "pride" would be "arrogance," "vanity," "self-will," and so on. Then I would go into those things: *Where have I been self-willed?* And I would start to write them out. *How about arrogance? Where have I been arrogant? Egotistical? Vain?* And then the next would be anger, so: *Did I get angry at anybody? Do I have resentments toward anybody? Did I act out on any of that?* And then next would be lust. It would be the same thing. *Did I indulge in lust? Were there any particular actions I might have committed that were lustful? Fantasies? Thoughts?* Then I'd just continue through the rest. There's an easy way to remember them all: PALE GAS—Pride, Anger, Lust, Envy, Gluttony, Avarice, Sloth.

I wrote inventory and confessed it to a sponsor or in a sacramental way to a priest every month for many years. It was undeniable that you would see some repetition. Month to month, they were mostly the same things. You could almost just read what you had read the month before. It became unbelievably obvious that your relationship to your character defects was such that, even though they bugged you, either you were kidding yourself about really wanting to do something about them or you really were powerless to do anything about them. But it was very hard to deny the fact that they were repetitive.

People tend to think of their character defects in a static way—I mean, yes, there are things that you never do again, but what you never do again is an *action*. You always have the character *defect*, which is behind any number of actions. At one point, I might be punching people in the nose, but at another point, I might be saying bad things about them to other people, and at yet another point, I'm just saying bad things about them in my head. It's the same defect whether I'm punching them or just thinking about it. Your actions change, but the character defects remain, and you're still acting out on them.

Most of the time, the experience of writing inventory and sharing it was really moving. I was overwhelmed with the feeling of being sorry for what I had done, and I just had the feeling of having an undefended heart. Writing inventory like that, you felt close to God because you needed Him. And you knew it. And you were sitting still long enough to face it.

Writing it all down was helpful because it's very hard to organize yourself. There's something about actually having the intention of revealing to another human being things that you did oftentimes in secret (or if not, things whose exact nature you often did not fully admit to yourself at the time). So, to premeditatively sit down and actually take the time to write things down in order to tell someone else—it's something that's been recommended forever and I think that's because there's no way to really organize all that in your mind and be able to tell it. You need the writing to organize it for you.

When you get a piece of paper and you start to write, it opens this doorway to this dimension of yourself, of your psyche. That door normally remains closed, but you start to write and that door opens and all of a sudden things start flowing out that you didn't expect. You're shocked: "Holy cow, I didn't realize I did this many things wrong," or, "I didn't realize I had this much stuff going on." Very few times have I had that experience without writing things down. Writing has a component to it that gives you a window to look into yourself in a way that I've never been able to do just mentally. It happens when you write. I know I'm not alone there. I've heard a lot of people say the same.

Through doing this kind of work, I went from talking about what I did that was wrong to actually identifying character defects and how I acted them out. Your perspective becomes different because you start to see the problem as not just separate actions in your life. All of a sudden, you start to break yourself into different compartments. I see that there's an arrogant side of myself, for example. You start to see these character defects and the myriad ways you act on them. It's not even fully by intention. It just happens with experience. It gives you a deeper look into yourself. Through the window of that character defect, I can review myself in a way that is more mentally efficient. It gives me a better hold on what my problems are.

By going through this process, you get an immense feeling that God is real, and I think that happens especially after you share your first inventory. I mean, it's almost universal. If it's really honest inventory, it's almost universal that people come out with, "Holy shit, God is real." That feeling is something that was there all along, but the things that you read were blocking you from it. You were fucking nuts for years, and all of a sudden, you feel like something heard you and understood you and is going to give you a way forward in life. You see these things about yourself in a way that's been tempered by God's desire to have you. He wants you cleaned of these things and freed from these things. You have a certain kind of freedom that comes from virtue, but you also have actual compassion for yourself.

It's a very strange thing, but the more that we get to see about ourselves, the more that we have compassion for other people too. The things in them that normally would bug the hell out of us, we come to see in ourselves. I didn't make up the process, but it works. God is the truth, and the closer you get to the truth, the closer you get to Him. It's not just a nice little thing to say, it's something you can realize and feel for yourself.

13

LET YOUR MIND BE LIKE A RIVER

In earlier chapters, I related some stories about strange moments of discovery: Bailey's story of writing moral inventory and finding that her hand automatically inscribed answers for her; biographies of famous writers who used spirit boards or who said their fiction was written in collaboration with dreamland faeries, ancient aliens, or voices from the center of the Earth; Jerry's story of praying for insight and having a sudden inner vision as a result; and just before this chapter, Matt D.'s story and conviction that recovery writing is accompanied by an intense feeling that "God is real." Each of these stories describes a discovery experience that may be strange but actually is not all that unusual. The dynamics present in automatic hands, spirit boards, and answered prayers are actually far more common than you might think. The process of discovery—of hoping certain ideas will show up until, somehow, they do—is a really weird phenomenon by nature, one that involves all kinds of unusual agents.

While we usually frame things like spirit board messages as anomalous, while centering and normalizing the experience of rational thought, the true situation is reversed: spirits are more normal than reason, which is to say that the regular flow of human thinking is irrational, spontaneous, and autonomous—independent of our control. Thoughts are always like specters from beyond: they appear unbidden, have their influence on us, and do not easily bend to our will. In fact, thinking is aberrant and more than a little deceptive when it makes us feel like we are rational actors in full control of our minds. Discovery, therefore, is *always* like having our hands move on their own or having a god whisper secrets into our ears. It signals the arrival of a message within ourselves from somewhere—or some*thing*—beyond ourselves. It's *wild*, in every sense of the word: undomesticated, undisciplined, and unreasonable.

Let's try an experiment so you can see what I mean.

Any form of silent meditation will suffice to give you a sense of where ideas come from. For the sake of this chapter, I'll present a meditation adapted from centering prayer as discussed by the Cistercian monk and writer Thomas Keating.[31] To do this experiment, find a place where you can be alone and undisturbed for up to thirty minutes. Turn off your cell phone. Turn off all screens of any kind and anything that makes noise. Do whatever is necessary to keep your pets and/or children distracted. In short, create an environment and a window of time with as few interruptions as possible.

Then, put your body in a position such that you will be comfortable without having to squirm around every five minutes, but not so comfortable that you will fall asleep. Bodies and comfort levels differ, so pick whatever position suits you best for this purpose. The standard recommendation is to sit in a chair with your feet flat on the ground, your back straight but relaxed, and your hands resting on your lap.

Set a timer for however long you want to sit. Ten minutes will be fine for the purpose of this experiment. If you want to go deeper, you could try fifteen or twenty.

When the timer is set, close your eyes.

Take a few slow, deep breaths and release any stress and tension from your body.

Once you are comfortable, relaxed, and undistracted, imagine yourself sitting on the bank of a wide river. Your job during this time is to rest and to watch your thoughts go by. Whenever you have a thought of any kind, let it float past you as if it were a boat on this river. You can see your thoughts in all their detail as they pass by, but they won't linger. They'll drift away down the river and out of your mind. Thought after thought will pass this way. Your job is just to observe each one and let it go.

At some point, perhaps very quickly, you will notice that you are completely wrapped up in one of these thoughts. You are *thinking* about it, imagining situations and consequences, hashing out points and counterpoints, anticipating the possibilities, getting emotionally involved in it, dwelling on the details. When you find that this has happened, imagine that you are now standing on one of the boats and going downstream with it by accident. You were supposed to sit and watch, but here you are, all tangled up in the rigging. No problem. This is a simple and common mistake. You needn't feel guilty. In fact, we all make this "mistake" all of the time in our daily lives, and most of us who meditate do it frequently during our meditations. The correction is just to gently take yourself back to shore, wave a fond farewell to the boat, and let it go down the river with all the rest.

Repeat this process of watching the boats go by, getting tangled up with one or another, and floating gently back to shore to watch again. Keep yourself in this imagined space until your timer goes off. Then, give yourself an additional minute or two of quiet before transitioning back to your day.

Long-term regular, even daily, meditation will be most revealing, but even if you are able to sit and observe your thoughts for only ten minutes, two things should become clear: First and foremost, you are in no way in full control of your own mind. Sometimes, thoughts pass peacefully; other times, they pull you from the shore and carry you away. Sometimes, your thoughts will evoke strong emotions: restless resentment, worried anticipation, anguished longing, or morbid reflection. Other times, they will inspire your creativity or get your intellect puzzling over and trying to solve some curious problem. Whatever the case, it is our thoughts that pull us from the shore into the day-to-day buzz of thinking, not we who direct their flow. In daily life, we normally assume that the thoughts we have are *our own*, meaning that we are in control of them and are purposefully producing them. We even experience ownership over our thoughts when we are all tangled up in them during meditation. But as soon as we sit quietly beside the river to watch the boats go by, we get a clear sense of how *sticky* thoughts can be. They have a power, a gravity, and an energy all of their own.

The second thing that should become clear upon observation is that the thoughts we experience appear *entirely without our conscious intervention*. We don't sit on the riverbank and place orders for the kinds of boats we'd like to see. Nor do we build the boats ourselves and then sit back to enjoy the fruits of our labor. No. We just sit on the bank passively and our minds pop off thought after thought without any intention or effort on our part. Thoughts show up, they pull us aboard, and tangle us in their perspectives and concerns until we realize what has happened and float ourselves back to the observer position.

You might say: "Sure, but aren't you purposefully directing your mind to sit on the shore? And can't I think of anything I want—say, for example, the perfect ham sandwich—anytime I want?" And the answer to these questions is: Yes. Of course. But personally, I don't last very long on the shore before some sticky thought carries me away. And thinking of sandwiches on purpose inevitably leads me to unintended thoughts about lunch and grocery shopping, and, "Oh crap, I was supposed to pick up ice cream for the kids, wasn't I?" The thoughts just tumble on by themselves. When I ask myself why I decided to think of a ham sandwich in the first place—that is, why I thought of ham instead of peanut butter, or why sandwiches at all instead of elephants or algebra—I have no good answer. The thought just appeared, and I claimed it as my own.

If our thoughts are always emerging from beyond ego-consciousness, without careful crafting on our part, then the ideas that occur to us when we write—the vague figments we reach for with pens hovering just off the page, the ones we cannot know until we see them in black and white—these ideas are not the products of a purely logical, intentional process either. They may well be the products of social processes or randomly firing neurons. Or they may be—as many addicts have told me they are—the products of invisible agents like "God" and "the Spirit." In any case, we can say that discovery, even when it is very weird, can be understood as the product of the normal ebb and flow of thinking, the base premise being that thinking itself is very weird. It does not belong to us the way we normally think it does, for just like the planchette on a spirit board, our thoughts are never really—at least not entirely—under our control.

14

BUOYANCY

If you're an addict like me, all this talk of the autonomy and power of thoughts should be hitting close to home. You likely remember times when uninvited ideas popped into your mind and pushed you back into active addiction. Thoughts have real power over us addicts. If the wrong boat shows up on our river and pulls us aboard, we'll be sailing into yet another relapse, and eventually into death. Our thoughts, as you may have heard in meetings, are trying to kill us. And that's a real problem, especially considering we can't control if and when a killer thought will appear, or how much power it will have over us when it does. We just have to sit around waiting, watching, and praying for our mental river to remain relapse-free.

In Big Book circles, we tend to talk about relapse as something that is caused by a "mental obsession," a powerful, behavior-altering thought about using that drives us back into active addiction. The example the Big Book gives is of some drunk eating a sandwich with a glass of milk. Suddenly, he thinks: *Hey, why don't I put a shot of whiskey in my milk? It can't hurt me on a full stomach!* He jumps aboard that thought without a second's hesitation and runs aground in the hospital after an ugly bout of blackout drinking.[32] Because of experiences like this, we addicts are used to the idea that we are not really in control of our thoughts. We know all too well how our minds can pull us onto the relapse boat, even with an obviously dumb discovery like "whiskey-milk." Once we're on a boat like that, we charge ahead, foolishly thinking we are in full control.

A rational person, faced with dangerous thoughts of this kind, would want to exercise some kind of control over them, with a strong effort of will aided perhaps by cognitive-behavioral therapy, and a pill or two to slow the boats down. But that is not the answer presented by the Twelve-Step fellowships. Instead of forming better mental defenses or exercising greater control over our faculties, we *surrender*. We just let the river flow wherever it will, even though it could easily, at any moment, kill us. Surrender is scary. By surrendering, we make ourselves vulnerable to our own minds—the very things out to get us. When we write, we make ourselves more vulnerable still. Sitting with pen in hand, we wait—open, receptive, allowing anything and everything to float past our shore. We just let all the boats come, hoping to God that none of them will be our last.

In this light, surrender doesn't make a lot of sense.

But it does work:

> I came into this program believing that I was never going to get better and be free from my addiction. I had arrived at this place in life where I was like, "There is no fucking way I will ever wake up in the morning and not want to do heroin." And then they tell you the answer is to write some things down?

This is Cythia, a therapist and artist on the East Coast. She's also a drug addict and alcoholic with a history of disordered eating. Cynthia told me that in spite of her initial dubiousness, writing was largely responsible for her recovery:

> I was in a place where I was willing to do the work, but the amount of trust you have to have in order to think that writing this shit down is going to make a difference? It's just like, *This is crazy*. But then you start writing. And it's weird, you know? You write these things down, and you turn it around, and the spiritual void that was inside you that you were filling with all these maladaptive coping skills like drugs or sex or

purging or anorexia or whatever—it alleviates all that. It just blows my mind. It's not sorcery, but it's definitely interesting.

When I asked Cynthia to explain *how* writing alleviates all the suffering and maladaptive behaviors of a drug addict, she spoke about the clarifying effect of written discovery, which came as a result of spiritual connection:

We live in a world of stories that we tell ourselves about why we are the way we are. I'm visual, so I'm picturing it like a big clusterfuck, like a nest, up there in the ether. It's above you and around you all the time. I had never been able to parse it all out, but writing made me separate things and let me see it all on paper. When I wrote, something greater happened to me. It's like the way artists used to speak about the Genius—when something would come through them, and it wasn't even *them* creating the art, like, they weren't necessarily even taking credit for it, but something was happening to them. I was really trying to allow that to happen for me. I wasn't attached to the things that were happening in my writing. I was just letting them happen, like I was trusting that if somebody's name showed up in my inventory, then it was supposed to be there. I already believed that there was some type of energy or force greater than myself, but I didn't know how to access it. The writing was a really cut-and-dry way of gaining access. It was like, *Here's a way in.* So I'm tapping in, and I'm gonna let whatever happens take over. It's like submission to the process, or like a surrender and a letting go. We hold on to that clusterfuck nest of shit with a death grip, but in writing we let some of it unravel, let it unfurl a little bit. We sort of dial in and let the parts come out in the order they need to come out. Then you're writing down a resentment or whatever it may be, and you're seeing your place in it, and then, like, all of a sudden, it gives you perspective and intention.

In her writing process, Cynthia shifts into a receptive state and lets something else express its point of view through her. The experience, she said, is very much like the time she almost drowned:

I was working at the treatment center where I had written my inventory. Some of us went out to the river to swim. As we were walking along the river, one of the guys was like, "Follow me!" And he jumped into the water, but he didn't tell me that there was this rock that you had to grasp onto almost immediately or you were gonna get taken downstream. I was just like, "Yes!" And I dove right in. I came up for air quickly, but I was getting sucked under and the rapids were moving really, really quickly, and I was getting thrown around, and I was fighting it. I was fighting, fighting, fighting to get to the surface, and I realized that I was going to drown if I kept wasting energy fighting like this. And so I just let my body go completely slack. And I was just like, "Surrender."

Slowly, I floated up to the surface, and I was fine and it was okay. To me, it was such a physical, metaphorical representation of recovery. I was like, "Woah, that is exactly what I have been doing on paper."

In the river, Cynthia fought the current and sank. She realized that fighting was a waste of energy, so she relaxed her muscles and was delivered from harm by the natural buoyancy of her body. Ironically, it was the struggle to survive that kept her submerged. In Cynthia's recovery writing, the same principle applied. She had been fighting the natural flow of life, building such a heavy and thick nest around herself that she was drowning in it. If she kept on fighting life, she would die. So she surrendered. Just as her body's buoyancy had saved her from drowning in water, some natural or supernatural power now saved her from drowning in active addiction. Ceasing her struggle, making contact, and allowing another power to guide her thoughts were what Cynthia had been doing "on paper."

When you have a mind that's trying to kill you, the answer is not to try to control the mind. The answer is to relax, float to the surface, and see where the river takes you. If you can do that much, then "some type of energy or force" that's greater than yourself will show up. A buoyancy. And it will order your thinking for you, including the discoveries you make when you write.

15

DISCOVERING RECOVERY

Writing aids recovery by enabling the experience of discovery, the process by which writers come up with ideas for what they are going to write. This process can seem strange and mysterious at times, but only because human thought itself is strange and mysterious. Our thoughts, including the thoughts we call "ideas," arise from somewhere beyond our ego-consciousness, somewhere "upstream" relative to our normal flow of thinking. Discovery—especially when it is difficult—turns our awareness toward the unknown source of our thinking and asks us to be both focused and open. We are focused on a specific question, but we must open ourselves and wait for the right answer to show up.

Discovery may be centrally important to recovery writing, but from the perspective of academic writing experts, discovery is only one aspect of a writing process, which also includes things like drafting and revision. Writers do discover ideas and write them down, but then they usually think about what they've written, consider the impact of their words on their intended audience, and repeatedly revisit and improve their work until they believe it will achieve a desired effect. So why is discovery singled out as especially valuable to addicts in recovery? Why is this aspect of writing prized, when other aspects—like revision, for example—are almost completely neglected?

One answer is that addicts in recovery value the experience of writing much more highly than the quality of prose produced. In most cases, a polished piece of recovery writing would be a contradiction, almost an oxymoron. Unless it is a public-facing work, recovery writing rarely aims to be "well written" or even grammatically correct. Its goal is to produce transformative experiences for the addict, nothing more. And discovery is the aspect of writing that produces experiences of sudden insight.

A second reason why addicts in recovery value discovery is that discovery and recovery have a lot in common. Discovery, like a miniature version of recovery, involves a small degree of desperation, surrender, and contact, and—to a degree—it always leads to a transformation of relationships.

Desperation may be too strong a word to describe writing outside of a recovery context, but discovery does always begin with an acknowledgment of lack—we need an idea but do not yet have one. We sit before the blank page, hoping for the right thought to come. We might employ various methods to help us generate an idea. We might mentally construct a detailed communication problem to solve, for example, or study the norms of a chosen genre, but at some point—even if only for a moment—we will have to turn our attention to the absence of a good answer, and wait for one to arrive from beyond ourselves.

This waiting, in a very small way, is an act of *surrender*. The ego must let go of its pretense and allow something to arise in the mind from beyond its control. When an idea does arrive, we have a moment of *contact* with a source of knowledge beyond our ego-consciousness. This moment may be quickly lost as the ego hurries to appropriate the idea, but it occurs nonetheless. And once the idea arrives and is accepted by the ego, our relationship to the task at hand is transformed: we now have an idea and can move forward, until we are stuck and must make a small surrender once again.

Note that this process holds true even for something as mundane as making a grocery list. We know we need to go shopping, but we don't yet know what we need to buy. We sit quietly and pose a question to our minds, "What do I need from the store?" Somehow, ideas begin to surface, and we write them down. We might make a tour of the fridge and pantry to see if that sparks any further thoughts. List made, our relationship to the task of buying groceries is transformed—we are now ready to shop. We have adjusted ourselves to an emergent need in life through an act of discovery, which involved—in a very small way—*desperation* ("What should I buy?"), *surrender* ("I'm open to ideas for this list"), and *contact* ("Oh! I should get toothpaste").

The difference between grocery lists and recovery writing is simply that in recovery writing, the stakes are significantly higher. While grocery lists aim to transform our relationship to shopping for food, recovery writing aims at the transformation of *all* our relationships—even our very way of relating to life—and so its impact is much more profound and therefore more obvious. In recovery writing, the fundamental dynamics of discovery, which are present in most acts of writing, are made visible because they are asked to perform high-stakes work with remarkable outcomes: spiritual experiences, transformations of personality, renewal of relationships, and lasting abstinence. Even though these results are clearly more impactful than the ability to purchase needed groceries, the underlying principles are the same. We lack needed insight, and so we must open ourselves to insight from beyond the ego. Then, from sources unknown, the ideas come.

One way to think about recovery is as an always ongoing process of discovery. In fact, addicts often talk this way about recovery in meetings, saying things like, "More will be revealed," or, "Recovery is like peeling the layers of an onion." These statements speak to recovering addicts' continual need for new experiences of discovery. By making contact with the source of ideas and maintaining a relationship with it long-term over the course of their recovery, addicts discover a new way of life.

For example, Leah O., a Midwestern graphic designer and compulsive overeater, began her recovery writing process when her sponsor asked her to write "a want ad for a higher power." This want ad was just what it sounds like: a written job description for the position of God. Leah's ad advertised for a higher power that would make her feel "really safe and good":

> Something like a cross between the best qualities of my mom and Galadriel from *Lord of the Rings*—not the movie version, the book version. You know, just completely strong but also loving and simple and beautiful and maternal. I have never associated myself with somebody who needed to believe in some happy Wicca goddess, but that just felt good to me. The idea of this loving, beneficent, sort of warm, maternal power that could love you and hold you and be there for you and tell you everything is going to be ok, but also be totally badass and take care of stuff. That's what I wanted my higher power to be.

Leah felt weak in her addiction, so she needed someone strong. She was wounded and hurting in life, so she needed someone nurturing to care for her. In writing her want ad, she discovered a workable idea of higher power—someone to whom she could willingly surrender.

But Leah's discovery of her higher power did not end there. Her concept continued to evolve over the course of her recovery as she made further discoveries. The want ad, she said, was "like a working title for a song" that was meant to get replaced as the lyrics took shape. But Leah's "working title" was replaced not with a more exact definition, instead with something hard to even put into words. Her higher power, she said, became an "internal feeling of opening up and feeling a power greater than [her] day-to-day, normal, blocked-thinking self." This "God

Feeling," as she called it, didn't "look like Galadriel or George Burns, or anything else." While the loving, maternal, powerful qualities she originally wrote about "might certainly be elements" of this feeling, the feeling itself was "all-encompassing": "It's more just like, *Wow*. I can't quantify that. It transcends anything that I could verbalize."

In order to maintain regular contact with this "God Feeling," Leah does a lot of writing, which means a lot of discovery. She writes "morning pages" using instructions from Julia Cameron's *The Artist's Way*. She writes "Dear God letters" and "little intention writings" based on Esther Hick's *Law of Attraction* and Helen Schucman's *A Course in Miracles* (two books, incidentally, that claim to be the products of dictation from spirits). She also writes reflective journal entries based on daily inspirational reading of short excerpts from works of recovery literature paired with reflective questions. Leah described this practice as a means of discovering and rediscovering how to live life:

> What will happen is that I'll be busy, busy, busy, frustrated, uptight, and anxious. I'll stop. I'll write out the question, and then I'll write my answer to the question after reading a little blurb from the Big Book or whatever. And writing it helps me to bring whatever the problem is that I'm having into the other kind of perception—the program-based perception. It'll reacquaint me with this other way of thinking. It diverts whatever negative, train-wreck thinking I was having. And then I get to get out of my own head, be of service to someone else, and distract my diseased mind from doing whatever it was trying to do.

In this way, Leah uses writing as a regular and reliable way to move from what she calls the "chatter and noise and general discontent" of her everyday thinking to the well-attuned perception of the "God Feeling" within. Anytime she falls out of sync with her higher power and into a "busy, busy, busy, frustrated, uptight, and anxious" frame of mind, she can return to a state of "program-based perception" through one of her writing practices. In short, like most of the addicts I spoke with, Leah uses discovery to maintain her recovery.

HOW TO WRITE
A Profile of Your Higher Power

Leah's "want ad" was a useful practice for her in early recovery, even though her actual concept of higher power evolved considerably with further experience. When she was hesitant to make a surrender, listing the desired qualities for a power she was willing to "hire" did double work for Leah: First, it enabled her to identify a higher power she could trust. Second, each of the qualities Leah listed was something she needed from an outside source. For example, strength and maternal love, listed in her want ad, were qualities Leah felt she could not provide for herself. She was powerless over her addiction and deep in shame, so she needed someone strong and loving to help her turn her life around. In short, writing a want ad for a higher power enabled Leah to give voice to her desperation. She named the places where she was broken and crafted the image of a being that offered her real hope.

Leah wrote her want ad early in her recovery, but it seems to me that this exercise could be useful anytime we feel some hesitance around surrender, no matter how long we've been sober or how well we think we know what our higher power is.

To write a profile of your desired higher power:

1. List the places in your life where you feel broken, vulnerable, and powerless. Where are you hurting the most? What is lacking in your life? Where are you falling short of your ideals?

2. List the things that you need and don't seem to be able to provide for yourself. What is missing from your life? What inner resources do you lack? What kind of power do you wish you had?

3. Name or describe some people or fictional characters who have the things you are missing. Who has the kind of power and resources that you need? Remember that Leah used only the best qualities of her mother, excluding her personal failings. So feel free to describe specific aspects of people or characters rather than their whole personality.

4. Ask yourself: What would a higher power be like if it could provide all the power I am lacking? If it had all the things I need? What if it were a combination of all the qualities of all the people and characters I named? What would a higher power like that be like? And what if it were willing to help me?

5. Write a description of that higher power.

6. Ask it to help you and to guide you to a better way of life.

7. Remember that this is a "working title" version of a higher power. Be open to revising your understanding as the Spirit reveals itself to you through experience. In time, it may be valuable to repeat this practice.

"The God Box"

CATHY C.'S STORY

Cathy discusses several writing practices, all of which are focused on making discoveries and putting her in contact with a power greater than herself. Cathy finds value in writing as a means to physically, literally let go of the problems she's facing by placing them in her higher power's hands.

For me, writing is a spiritual experience just as much as a physical thing. For instance, I did a program that Julia Cameron is famous for, called "The Artist's Way," for twelve weeks. We formed a little Artist's Way group online and all went through it together. The practice of writing three pages every morning no matter what comes out—even if it's just, "I hate to write these pages! I can't believe I agreed to do this program, blah, blah, blah"—all of a sudden, you realize you are writing about your resentment against your mother. You didn't even realize you had this resentment. It just comes tumbling out. I didn't realize how much junk I was keeping in my mind. Writing is physically doing something with my hand that allows that stuff to roll out onto paper so I can let it go.

I've had a lot of different sponsors over time, and the action of writing something down—getting it out of my head—was something all these sponsorships had in common. One sponsor told me to make amends to myself. I didn't write myself down on my amends list, and she looked at the list and said, "There's someone missing." I was like, "What do you mean?" She said, "You're not on there." She had me make amends to myself by writing letters to the little girl in me. She said to write with my non-dominant hand so as to mimic a child's writing. Another sponsor told me to write down all my dreams in a different color in my journal and told me that sometimes, what comes out in your dreams is very pertinent to what you are not willing to, or not able to, connect to in your waking life. Yet another sponsor was responsible for me writing down my heart's desire, basically answering the question: *What do I want to have my life look like?* And she had me list everything: the ideal partner, all the way down to specifics, like sandals versus shoes. Really detailed stuff. And then she had me put it away, then, a few years later, pull it out and see how it's going, see whether or not that stuff materialized. It's been a very powerful practice.

I also had a sponsor who asked me to write down all my fears and all my resentments daily and put them physically in my God Box, then close the lid. I went to a recovery conference one time, and they had these little boxes that were made with popsicle stick-sized pieces of wood that were glued together, and that's where it started. I found a plain wooden box in a Hobby Lobby or something. Over the years, I'd write stuff and I'd put it in there. I'd push it down—it's crowded—and every once in a while, I'd pull stuff out, read it, and then burn it, basically returning it to the Earth. Anytime I burn something, it's like a gratitude to my higher power that the thing is gone. It's out. It doesn't need to stay in the box. He's taken care of it.

The box itself is very plain. The only thing it has written on it is Gᴏᴅ Bᴏx in blue marker. It's small, not huge. The top is not a hinged top—it just comes straight off—and it has little rope handles. When I put stuff in my God Box and close the lid, it gives me a little bit of distance from the problem. Also, AA is my main recovery, but I also go to Al-Anon. And in Al-Anon, I learned that I don't like to let things go. I hang on to things. I try to fix things. And I try to do it by myself. The God Box represents for me a practice in which I can not only get it out of my mind and my body, but also put it somewhere in an act of physically letting something go, physically letting it leave my fingertips, putting it in the box, and then putting the lid on top. That physical action helps me remember that, okay, I've put it in there. There's my problem over there. It's no longer mine to solve. It's literally in my higher power's hands.

I can say, "Let it go, let it go," and mentally, it does absolutely nothing for me. But if you tell me . . . I heard a Beatles song one day when I was having a lot of trouble. I heard "Let It Be." I was like, "Oh, I may not be able to let it go, but I can leave it alone." I think for me, especially in early recovery, if I didn't feel like my higher power was working fast enough, I would think, "Okay, maybe I can fix this myself." I'd take back all my prayers. It's like the story of a kid who takes his broken toy to God and asks him to fix it, and God says, "Of course." But then the kid comes back and asks, "Have you fixed it yet?" He's like, "Patience, my child." The child gets all like: "I'll take it back. I'll fix it myself." And then tries to and ruins it more. That's been me. If I could just remember to physically let it go—that helps me leave it alone.

There was another time when I was not doing too well, and I wrote down a lot of stuff that was bothering me. I was at the beach at the time, and I had done a lot of meditation and prayer. I looked at the ocean, and at that moment, I thought: *This is definitely God. This ocean—this gulf—is bigger than me. Look at all this water. It can absorb so much. It can absorb all my problems. There's so much water that it can take all my worries and cleanse them.* So I ended up going and taking these pages I had written in the journal, and I tore them up into little pieces and threw them in the water. I watched them drift away. It was truly a good release practice. It was the same thing as the God Box. It was like: *These are my worries. I'm physically going to give them to you. And I'm going to watch them as they drift—physically—farther and farther from me.* I will never forget that moment. It was a really powerful experience.

I haven't looked at some of the stuff in my God Box for years, but I think I would be surprised. Like: "What? That was a problem?" But at the time, I was probably in tears over it. I kind of think about it as a time zone difference between me and my higher power. I write something down, and I feel like this situation needs to be alleviated immediately, but it's going to happen on God's time. It's helped me realize that: One, I have to have patience; and two, I hate patience. But, three, to be patient is really just to go busy yourself—do something else. I'm not supposed to sit and watch water boil. It's a time for me to go out and go to a meeting, reach out to someone new, invite someone to lunch who I know is lonely or just having a hard time—it's to get out of myself. I'm able to do that because I trust that a higher power is out there conspiring for my best. It's an act of faith every time I put something in my box, close the lid, and walk away.

I've written several inventories too, and each one was different. I would say the most memorable one was the one I wrote without a sponsor, and this is a good reason for sponsorship. I was going to ACoA meetings (Adult Children of Alcoholics), and I decided that I needed to write an inventory and I didn't need a sponsor. So I sat down at my kitchen table one night, and I started writing: "I'm lazy. I'm a perfectionist. I'm gay." That was the big secret on my list: "I'm gay, and that is wrong." I had no guidance, no spiritual foundation. I had nothing. It was just a self-abuse fest. Someone very, very kindly said: "You know, I don't think that should be on your inventory. Why don't you check that out with somebody else?"

Once I finally got with a sponsor, she was very, very kind and gentle. I've had sponsors who were the kick-my-ass type, but the first one I had was kind and gentle. I would go over to her house, and she would make me lesbian coffee, which was really Folgers with a touch of cinnamon. I would go out into her backyard and sit on her swing, and she would have me write. I've always been the person who is hardest on me. Always. She was warm, welcoming, accepting, and she was just listening. Absolutely, positively no look on her face of surprise, no look on her face of judgment. It was simply . . . it was an exercise. I'm reading this, and she's listening.

I've been very lucky. I don't think it's a mistake that I've had very spiritual-minded sponsors who encouraged me to write things down—letters to God, for example. That's who I write to now in my journals. It always starts with, "Dear God." And I can tell God anything. Before, I was just writing to . . . I don't even know. I was just writing in a journal. Now, I have an intention, somewhere to pin my hopes, my fears, my resentments, my pain. I'm writing to someone and asking for help. It has changed a lot. So I'm a martial artist, and there is very much a difference between a martial artist who just punches in the air and one who punches and visualizes punching something. In other words, putting intention behind it makes a difference. And the same thing is true when I write letters to my higher power. I'm having a communication. It's a moment in which there is absolutely no doubt that my higher power exists. For me, it is just as beneficial as punching a bag whenever I'm really frustrated or really angry. It's the same result. I get it out of my body. I get it out of my mind. I let someone else in on the crazy thinking that's going on. And I let someone else help me to alleviate the pain, to be able to clear my head enough to see the solution, and to be able to have enough courage to take action.

I really believe that anyone can do this work. You don't have to be a writer. You don't have to have a good grasp of the English language—grammar, punctuation, spelling. You just have to look at yourself. Get it out of your head. Get it on paper. Get it out of you. See what it is. Accept it. And then let it go.

16

WRITING THAT HEALS

Sometime in the mid 1980s, psychologist James Pennebaker and graduate student Sandra Beall designed an experiment to test the psychosomatic healing properties of emotionally expressive writing.[33] They already knew that there was a link between undisclosed trauma and poor physical health outcomes, and they had seen the first evidence that participation in psychotherapy resulted in lower rates of hospitalization and lower medical costs in general. What was missing was a study that demonstrated a direct relationship between disclosure of trauma and improved physical health.

Pennebaker and Beall had undergraduate students write in isolation cells in their laboratory and then tracked their visits to the student health center for the next six months. In the lab, some students were given writing prompts on "superficial or irrelevant topics," asking them to describe, say, the details of their dorm room or the shoes they were wearing. Others were given these instructions: "Write continuously about the most upsetting or traumatic experience of your entire life. . . . Discuss your deepest thoughts and feelings about the experience. . . . Write about what happened and how you felt about it, and how you feel about it now."[34]

Needless to say, the two groups had very different experiences with the writing itself. The first group simply wrote about their dorm rooms or their sneakers, set down their pens, and went on with their lives. But students in the second group were deeply affected by the writing prompt. All participants in this group wrote about deeply painful events in their lives. Several cried in the laboratory. Many were haunted by recurring dreams about the experiences they described. When the results were in, it was clear that this second group—in spite of the psychological discomfort they experienced—benefited both emotionally and physically from their participation in the experiment. They reported deeply valuing their experience with this kind of writing, with several seeking out Pennebaker on campus months later to thank him for allowing them to participate. They also had half as many visits to the student health center over the next six months compared to the control group. Somehow, writing about traumatic or upsetting events supported their physical wellbeing.

Many subsequent studies have found a positive correlation between expressive writing and various physical health outcomes, including enhanced quality of life for breast cancer survivors,[35] more rapid surgical wound healing,[36] and improved treatment outcomes for patients with moderate asthma.[37] In addition, in their survey of research in this area, Karen Baikie and Kay Wilhelm found that expressive writing was associated with significant health benefits like reduced severity of rheumatoid arthritis, reduced pain and greater physical health for cancer patients, better immune response to HIV infection, reduced hospitalizations for cystic fibrosis patients, lower pain intensity for women with chronic pelvic pain, shorter sleep-onset latency for poor sleepers, and speedier post-operative recovery.[38] While not every study showed a beneficial or significant result, the general consensus of this research is that emotionally expressive writing really does lead to improved physical health outcomes.

So, what about the healing that Cynthia experienced as she wrote moral inventory, by surrendering the same way she had surrendered in the river? She clearly felt that writing inventory was a healing practice. It helped her sort through the nest of trauma and entrenched emotions she was stuck in, and as a result, it saved her from the necessity and inevitability of drugging herself to death. Cynthia is not alone in this understanding. All of the addicts I interviewed understood their recovery writing as a healing practice, with both psychological and physical benefits. As Joe C., a treatment professional, put it: "This writing helps me to stop injecting heroin. I would say that's a physical benefit right there." Notably, heroin abstinence is the kind of physical benefit that would register very clearly in the results of a long-term controlled study: drug addicts who stop using drugs don't overdose and don't destroy their bodies in other ways that would land them in the ER or the morgue. Measurable results like that support Pennebaker's work.

Further, the healing that Cynthia and others experience in recovery writing is related to the disclosure of troubling emotions. Cynthia's "nest" metaphor articulates the value of emotional expression, and the inventory she wrote required the disclosure of a lifetime's worth of resentments, fears, and troubling sexual experiences.

To some extent, then, the healing experienced by the students who participated in Pennebaker and Beall's study is the same kind of healing experienced by addicts who do recovery writing. Yes, the stakes are higher for addicts—*not dying* is clearly a better health outcome than paying fewer visits to the school nurse—but in both cases, writing is used to share private pains with another human, and this improves psychological and physical wellbeing as a result.

It would be reasonable to assume that if there are strong similarities between the subjects of Pennebaker and Beall's study and addicts in recovery, then Pennebaker's explanation of psychosomatic healing holds for recovery writing too. He argues that keeping emotionally charged secrets is physically taxing and thus negatively influences long-term health. Therefore, disclosing those secrets, whether orally or in writing, lessens their negative influence.[39] This explanation is perfectly logical for Pennebaker's study, but I would argue that it falls short of accounting for the benefits of recovery writing for four reasons:

First, Pennebaker's explanation does not encompass the experience of many addicts who have had to cycle through many detoxes and treatment centers before finally finding their recovery in a Twelve-Step fellowship. Many of us have been through all kinds of counseling and therapy, making a host of disclosures to different professionals in a variety of treatment modalities. If mere disclosure were enough to heal us, we would have recovered a long time ago. Discovery, rather than emotional expression, is the element of writing that can best explain the kind of changes addicts experience through recovery writing.

Second, Pennebaker, like any other scientist, aimed to produce a rational and material explanation, which makes no mention of spirituality and has no use for "God" or "the Spirit." Applying Pennebaker's theory to recovery writing would therefore be reductive: it would suggest that the spirituality of addicts is marginal or irrelevant to the "real" cause of recovery—emotional expression. I would argue that reductive explanations like this are problematic because they disregard important aspects of human experience.

Third, Pennebaker had nothing to say about the unique qualities of *writing*. In his view, disclosure and emotional expression are valuable be it in the form of oral or written statements. What matters is the truth telling, not the medium it happens in. While I think this claim would receive broad support in recovery communities—where oral and written disclosures are equally valued—we have already seen addicts express the special value of writing to their experiences. Nathan said he never could have made the oral disclosures of his Formal First Step without writing first, and disclosures of the type made by Bailey's automatic hand are a highly writing-specific phenomenon. There are unique qualities to written disclosure that are worth attending to.

Fourth and finally—and also most importantly—Pennebaker's theory treats healing as a property of individual writers and their bodies. In other words, according to Pennebaker, when I write about my emotions, my body somehow gets healthier even if nothing else changes in my life. The healing is contained within the individual, independent of relationships or environmental factors. But in recovery writing, healing is wholly *relational*. Recovery requires addicts to transform their relationships not only with an addictive substance or behavior but also with literally everything and everyone they know. In my interviews, respondents told me stories of radical changes in the way they related to friends, family, co-workers, their jobs, the very idea of work, institutions, religion and religious ideas, food, sex, romantic partnership both in practice and as a concept, and so on. The list of changed relationships was long, for what had changed was these addicts' way of being in relationship—their *relationality*. Where they had once been overwhelmingly obsessed with the personal needs of their addiction, they were now radically grounded in their care for others.

The healing that results from recovery writing is based on *discovery*, not expression. It is inclusively *spiritual*, not reductive of human experience. It is also *social*, not personal; *shared*, not private; and *relational*, not individual.

17

NEW LIFE, NEW RELATIONSHIPS

Jerry told me his whole life prior to writing inventory had consisted "really of one singular thought, and that thought was, 'What's in it for me?'" After writing a moral inventory, he "got clear about the fact that recovery isn't going to be about [him] getting anything ever again."

Jeff H., a heroin addict and recovery professional, said something similar: "Before I wrote inventory, the relationships I had were based on the external value they presented in my life. Now, my relationships are based around common interests, real sharing, and a genuine desire to be around that human being."

For Julie B., an alcoholic who works for an insurance company, the changes in her way of relating to others were coupled with a sense of ease in being herself: "I became much more comfortable with who I was, like, even the physicality of how I felt in my body as a woman. But also, I started to have real interest in how other people were doing, and not always in the way that it related to me. I'd just stop and listen to people."

For Britni C., an addict and freelance writer, the most obvious post-inventory change was the way they related to men: "I used to walk into a room and—even if I had a boyfriend and I wasn't actively looking—want to see if men were looking at *me*. I wanted to talk to a random guy to see if he liked me." But after the inventory process, they said, "I don't seek attention from men at all anymore."

For Jen, whose story is at the start of this book, the most obvious change took place in her relationship with her children. She said: "[Without inventory] there would be a little poisonous hole in the universe where the mother they needed was supposed to be. I can't necessarily draw the causal link for you, but I can tell you right now my inventory notebook is why my teenager gave me a hug today in my kitchen."

These are significant changes. Here, we see lifetime patterns of self-absorption, self-loathing, attention seeking, neglect, and self-harm all suddenly reversed after a confessional writing practice. Interestingly, none of these statements is specifically about sobriety from drugs or alcohol. When I asked addicts to describe the healing benefits of recovery writing, they spoke about changes in the way they related to other people, to their bodies, and to their worlds. Then, when I butted in with a tongue-in-cheek question like, "Well, that sounds nice, but what does it have to do with staying sober?" they would laugh knowingly. The dramatic relational changes recovery writing produces don't relate to addiction in an obvious or direct way. And yet, for someone who has recovered this way, the connection is obvious. When we heal our way of relating to others, we also heal our way of relating to addictive substances and behaviors, almost as a side effect. Importantly, this does *not* work the other way around: our relationship to life doesn't get better when we focus on just trying to fix our addictions. It is only by healing relationally that we can attain reliable abstinence.

Bob P., an alcoholic who works in advertising, told me a story about how it felt to be freed from compulsive drinking after writing inventory:

> Shortly after I finished, I got on a plane to go on a business trip. Business trips up until that point had been really bad for me because I would wind up raiding the penny bar. I got onto

that plane and I sat down. I really felt safe and protected. It was calm, and it was very practical. It wasn't magical. It was this very calm knowledge that I was going to go on this trip and I was going to be fine. There was going to be no drinking. I had somehow crossed a threshold.

These results are almost incidental, automatic. Once we straighten out relationally, we just feel like we are in "right relationship" with the world, and that includes being in right relationship with drugs and alcohol.

This means, too, that recovery writing brings about broad changes in an addict's life well beyond the hoped-for change of lasting sobriety. In fact, several addicts I interviewed drew a hard distinction between "recovery" and "sobriety." For them, sobriety just means holding on to basic abstinence without making any other changes. An unrecovered life of mere sobriety is a painful one marked by depression, anxiety, even suicidal tendencies. Recovery, on the other hand, means entering a whole new way of being in the world. In this way of being, sobriety comes naturally and easily, as if on its own.

The new person who emerges from recovery writing can be surprising to the writer. The changes we experience don't seem like the results of our efforts, and they add up to something more than the product of the insights we were given while writing. We are just *really different* all of a sudden, in ways we can't fully explain.

Take Maureen D., an early-thirties drug addict from New England. When we spoke, she was almost four years sober and a college student working as a resident advisor at a transitional living facility. Her story—from struggling with addiction and abuse to finding herself in a new way of relating to the world, including her own history—represents one of the clearest expressions of relational transformation that I've encountered.

After her surrender, Maureen wrote an extensive moral inventory, which she told me profoundly changed her. When I asked her to give me an example of how this writing had changed her, she told me this story, which includes references to domestic violence and Maureen's discovery of compassion for abusive strangers:

> My window was open. It was late at night, and these two very drunk men were walking home from a bar. They were talking in a disgusting and crude way about one of the men's partner. One man was yelling at the other about how he needed to beat the shit out of her to put her in her place, which was very overwhelming, considering that I had just come from an abusive relationship.
>
> But my reaction surprised me. I remember lying there and feeling so much love and compassion for these two men. It just wasn't like me. I had felt compassion and empathy for another woman in my situation, but to also feel compassion for an abuser was really huge.
>
> There's so much tremendous pain and evil in the world. I've spent my life separating myself from that, telling myself, "Those are bad people, and I'm a good person, and these are the reasons why." But the process of doing all of that writing blurred those boundaries. I don't feel like "us versus them" anymore. I feel like I'm in the world with a bunch of other people who are all being yanked and pulled around by this awful mess. Compassion has led me to be open and receptive to the world in all of its different complexities and shades and confusion. To be able to stand and look that type of evil in the eye and not fall into it and not accept it and not say that it's all right, but to just stand there and have my sense of self—it's beautiful.

Maureen recognized the violence and cruelty of the passing men, yet, to her own surprise, she found herself identifying with them in a spirit of compassion. Gaining compassion for abusers is not a requirement for recovery—and may not even be desirable for many addicts—but for Maureen, this surprising identification represented a turning point. Because she had written and shared the depth of her own moral failings, she was now able to understand what it must be like to be these men—drunk, suffering, eager to pass on that suffering to others, and living alienated, abusive, hard-hearted lives. Maureen saw the depth of their depravity without either approval or condemnation—and without reacting in self-destructive ways. Instead, she simply bore witness. By discovering this new way of relating to the "awful mess" of this world, Maureen also discovered a new power and freedom. She discovered a self who is not retraumatized by a reminder of past violence, who does not immediately spiral downward into shame or despair, and who does not need to bury her consciousness under a drink or a drug. In a word, in her new relationship to the awful mess, Maureen *recovered*.

18

ALWAYS ONGOING RE-ATTUNEMENT

In order to understand how simple acts of confessional writing could lead to the kind of relational healing that Maureen D. experienced, we can borrow a concept from theorist Thomas Rickert, who describes an ambient persuasiveness that is a feature of our environment and is all around us all the time. For example, as we walk down a city street, advertisements, street signs, traffic patterns, social norms, and brief encounters with strangers all work together to shape our thoughts and behavior. Likewise, as we hike through the woods, the paths, signage, sounds and smells, encounters with wildlife, and the sunbeams breaking through gaps in the canopy collectively and persuasively shape our experience. And the process through which we adapt ourselves in relationship to the rest of the world—to the pressures of this ambient persuasiveness—is what Rickert calls "attunement."

In explaining this concept, Rickert points to Heidegger's example of a Black Forest farmhouse, which Heidegger tells us was built by "earth and heaven, divinities and mortals" who "placed the [house] on the wind-sheltered mountain slope looking south" and "gave it the wide overhanging shingle roof whose proper slope bears up under the burden of snow, and which, reaching deep down, shields the chambers against the storms of the long winter nights."[40] Rickert observes that this farmhouse is "richly interwoven into its sustaining environs," that "the house is built from material given by the land and placed just so as regards the land's features; it takes part in what the landscape occasions [and] . . . declines to force itself over the land or to master it."[41] The farmhouse is shaped by snow and wind, soil and stone, and farmers and sunlight. Each of these entities has its own effect on the dwelling, influencing its placement and structure. The farmhouse is attuned to all this ambient persuasion: its roof is suited to the wind and snow, its windows to the winter sun, and its rooms to the farmer's needs.

Maureen's story speaks to a radical act of attunement, or even of *re*-attunement. She grew up in a "world with a bunch of other people [. . .] all being yanked and pulled around by this awful mess." In various ways, those people yanked and pulled her around too. And so, Maureen adapted herself to the ongoing trauma of living in this world by what was for her the best available means of attunement: heroin. But heroin brought with it other problems—further traumas—and Maureen was left to either die or adjust herself once more. As she was exposed to other addicts in recovery, Maureen discovered a more productive means of attunement. Rather than adapting to life by way of heroin, she would adapt by way of "higher power"—in her case, the power of empathy, love, compassion, and truth. This new attunement proved remarkably resilient in the face of potentially retraumatizing events. The world was still a challenging, painful place, but Maureen had become a person of great empathy who could look that world in the eye and retain her sense of self.

Most of the addicts I spoke with entered a similar state of attunement. In fact, this is what they meant when they said that they had "recovered" from addiction. They meant they had a new way of life, a new way of being, and a new relationship with the world.

But, like any ideal state, this one is not easily maintained. As time passes in recovery, addicts re-enter life and take on new responsibilities like work, school, romantic relationships, paying off old debts, and being helpful to our families. As our lives change and grow, we must learn to attune ourselves to the new pressures that these responsibilities introduce. Rickert's theory anticipates this development. He suggests that our world and our responsiveness to it are always changing: "Attunement is nothing static. It is always ongoing, and achievement of some sense of harmony or synchronicity would, on this account, be fleeting. It is not given that we are simply at home, in ourselves, in our lives, in our world."[42]

We addicts know all too well that we are not simply at home in ourselves, our lives, or this world. We feel this not-at-home-ness in the marrow of our bones. It's why we became addicted in the first place. In recovery, if we cannot or will not stay well attuned to the realities of this world—if we instead try to make ourselves comfortable in life by some other material means— we soon find ourselves in the throes of addiction all over again. Accordingly, many of the addicts I spoke with write regularly to attune and re-attune themselves to life's emerging traumas and complications.

Jerry, for example, told me that well into sobriety, he developed a long-standing resentment against his boss that finally came to a head:

> My boss was an old crank. He would walk in on Monday morning, and he'd walk right by my desk and not say anything. Just walk on by. I'd think: *That sorry rascal. He could at least say hello.* I mean, Christ, this went on for two years. Anyway, one day, he didn't speak to me that morning, and that evening the thought crossed my mind, *You know, I've never said hello to him either.* So I did an inventory on him.

Remember that Jerry's experience of inventory writing involves prayer, followed by an experience of revelation. In Chapter 14, he described being stuck on a resentment against a woman until he prayed and her image evaporated out of his mind, leaving him to see only himself and his own conduct. Something like that happened again for Jerry when he wrote about his boss. As a result, he realized that he had behaved poorly in a whole bunch of ways. The next morning, he had a changed attitude:

> I went in and I said, "Yesterday, when we were talking about that one particular customer and I gave you my idea and you gave me your idea, well, the longer I look at that, the more I realize that I was wrong and you were right." And he said: "You know something? I never thought that I would hear you say you were wrong." [Laughter] He and I became really, really good friends after that, and it all stemmed from the fact that I was finally willing to say I was wrong.

Anne, a director of special education and an alcoholic, told me a story like this too. It began when Anne's husband, also an alcoholic, was diagnosed with terminal cancer. In physical pain, and in a state of resentment against his diagnosis, Anne's husband often lashed out at her verbally. "He was sick for a long time and drifted away from his Twelve-Step practice before he died," she told me. "An un-practicing alcoholic with cancer and pain isn't always a lovely creature."

Not surprisingly, Anne was not immediately the perfect angel of compassion in this situation. The two argued frequently, and their relationship grew increasingly tense. Unsettled, and slipping from her own spiritual center, Anne turned to her inventory-writing practice for guidance:

> In the end, I used my writing in my resentments around not having the husband I thought I should have or thought I deserved. I knew that his life was coming to a close, probably in a year or two, and I decided that I wasn't looking for a perfect husband anymore. I was a woman who was going to make sure that when he left the planet, he knew he was loved. It took a long time to get there, but I was able to do that with some measure of joy. Exhausting, but yes, joy.

In a recovery context, healing is relational. It changes the way we relate to other people and to the world we live in. Through the guided discoveries of recovery writing, we reform ourselves into people who are better attuned to the pains and pressures of ordinary human life—drunken strangers, grumpy bosses, dying husbands, and whatever else life throws our way. By being made new in our relationships, we don't need to turn to a substance or behavior to cope with the pain of living. Instead, we continually re-attune ourselves to life.

"Untangled and Unencumbered"

CARLOS ISAIS'S STORY

Carlos describes a variety of writing practices he has used throughout his recovery, including a practice of emotionally expressive writing. Each practice has allowed him to adapt himself to a different aspect of sobriety.

I started practicing as a Buddhist in the late 1980s when I got sober the first time. I didn't do the Steps back then, but I did talk about them a lot. [Laughs] When I relapsed, I ended up in the psychiatric ward, and then I wandered the streets of downtown LA. But I maintained my Buddhist practice throughout my drinking. I was not a perfect adherent, obviously, but if I had totally lost that connection, I don't know that I would have survived.

When I got sober again, I had to come to terms with AA spirituality because the Big Book was written from a Judeo-Christian point of view. I was like, "Oh man, this can't work for me!" But the Big Book was written by middle-aged white men in the Midwest in the 1930s, so of course they got their spiritual and cultural references from the Bible. And they were some pretty whacky guys, going out into the forests and having seances and shit, you know? Not your stereotypical, goody-two-shoes type of Christians. When I really stripped away all the things that appeared dogmatic and actually looked at what they were saying, it was just basic spiritual principles.

So I started looking for a sponsor to take me through the Steps. There was a guy who kind of helped me out while I was looking.

He asked me to write out a definition of my powerlessness. When I showed it to him, he said, "Well, that's not really what I was talking about." In the meantime, I had found a sponsor, so I never got to ask him what I was supposed to do instead! [Laughs] But writing it helped me anyway. At the time, my main beef with Twelve-Step recovery was the concept of powerlessness. I didn't see how it could be healthy to say that you had no power, but then I wrote out my definition and it clarified things. I just wrote that obviously, I wouldn't be in the situation I was in if I had any power over my life or my addiction.

The most crucial writing I did was the moral inventory, which meant taking an honest appraisal of my life and of how my compulsions warped my character. I've written many inventories, but the first one was just the columns from the AA Big Book. In the columns, I listed my resentments, the causes of my resentments, and then how each resentment affected my life, like if it hurt my pride or how I felt about my relationships. After that, there was a specific inventory about my sexual conduct.

I know for a lot of people, writing inventory throws them into a depression. Bill Wilson calls it "morbid reflection." I think that's because people write like five-hundred-page inventories. I would call that morbid reflection not getting honest. But, because I had been practicing as a Buddhist for so many years, I was able to detach from the inventory a little bit and look at it. Some of it was surprising, like that I was capable of stealing from people I cared about, or that I lied so much I lost track of the truth. I'm not a sociopath, so I would have to convince myself that what I was doing was okay, and I was surprised at the kinds of things that I could rationalize in order to keep going in my addiction.

It took me three weeks to write my first inventory. When I had finished, I read it to my sponsor, and then he asked me to tell him my life story—everything that I could remember. It took a long time. And then he said, "Okay, so you're basically telling me that you're a liar, a cheat, and you're not trustworthy." Then we went back over everything I had said and broke it all down by each of the Seven Deadly Sins. It was a relief. At the time, I couldn't have told you why it was a relief, but on reflection, I think it was because it finally simplified everything. It made my problems into something I could understand. It was nice to have it all untangled.

I did my second inventory in a Big Book workshop that involved more extensive writing and more extensive prayer. At some point in that process, I realized that different things were showing up. Things that I thought were okay in my first inventory were not okay in this new one. Things that I didn't or wouldn't include in my first inventory came up, and I included them. For example, in my first inventory, I didn't feel that I owed any explanations to some family members who were hard on me, because they didn't understand what I was going through as an addict. [Laughs] In my second inventory, I realized that they didn't need to understand me. It only mattered what I had done to them, and what I needed to do to set it right. The second inventory helped me to be more dispassionate, to separate myself from the emotion and just look at the facts of my behavior. After that, I could approach my spiritual practice relatively unencumbered, meaning I could seek to improve my conscious contact without all that baggage weighing me down.

When I teach people to write inventory, the instructions I give depend on the person. Some people are not really good at expressing themselves in writing, or they find that writing is frustrating, and they'll never go through the process if you ask them to write too much stuff. In that case, you show them the basic writing but don't ask for as much detail. You get the details when you talk about it together. But some people are better at expressing themselves in writing; you can tell they are intellectual types and it's more freeing for them to use written words. In that case, I will ask them for more detail.

For six or seven years, I wrote daily inventory. My sponsor had me make lists of what I could have done better that day, and what I had done right. He said, "When a store does an inventory, they don't just count the broken shit, so write down the good stuff too." It wasn't like a huge thing every day. It was usually just four or five things, and that would be it. Just a little bit of reflection on my day before I went to bed at night. It helped me to stop beating up on myself and to see where I was making progress. It also honed my ability to see problems and set them right more quickly. The funny thing was that sometimes, stuff that was in the good column one day would end up in the bad column on a later day, and even then, it wasn't always where it should be. Like, maybe one day I'd have in my *good* column that the guy at 7-Eleven gave me the wrong change, so I got an extra dollar! Then, the next month, when it happened again, my *bad* column would say, "I got the wrong change, but I gave it back even though I'm broke." [Laughs] So I could see where I was making improvements over time.

These days, I think any expression or any kind of reflection that I do is part of my recovery. If I'm having difficulties, I'll just write. If I'm really, really uncomfortable about something and I can't put my finger on it, I start writing down everything that I'm feeling and everything that I'm thinking. Not in a structured way. It's just a series of words, or a lot of exclamation points, or, you know—whatever. And it usually doesn't make sense to anyone but me—and half the time not even me—but I'll just write words, phrases, and whatever I'm feeling. It doesn't have to make sense. It's actually a big freedom to not make sense. But that also can make it hard to reflect. I guess, maybe it's like looking at a Pollock painting: it doesn't make any sense, but you know you're feeling something when you look at it. I work through stuff that way. It isn't something I learned in AA. I learned it in therapy, but it's a fact-finding mission the same way all the other Step writing is. It's clarifying. And it lets off steam.

I've used this practice for clients in the detox where I work too. I've had people who were flipping out and wanted to leave, and I said, "Well, just do me a favor and write for a second." They ended up staying in detox because they felt better about whatever it was. It doesn't always work, but sometimes it does. I think—especially if somebody is sick and in withdrawal—the writing takes them off of whatever they're physically feeling at the moment. It gets them engaged in something besides, "I feel sick!" you know? When people feel that way, they work themselves up into a tizzy so they can rationalize leaving the detox, and the writing can defuse that a little bit. And sometimes, a little bit is all it takes.

HOW TO WRITE
Two-Column Nightly Review

Carlos described a daily inventory practice that he used for many years. If you want to give this practice a try, keep a notebook where you're likely to find it at the end of every day—like at your bedside. Each day, divide the page into two columns, and label them like so:

What I could have done better	What I did right

If you want to make this a prayerful exercise, you might start by asking a higher power to show you whatever it is that you need to see about your day. If you want to be more meditative in your approach, you could take some deep breaths to center yourself, and then think back through each moment of your day, starting with this moment, now. Follow the stream of events—moment by moment—back to the beginning of the day.

Of course, you also don't have to think too hard about this exercise. To fill in the first column, you can just think about the question, *What could I have done better today?* and write down whatever answers come.

Likewise, for the second column, you can pray or meditate on your day, or just ask yourself, *What went well, what did I do well?* and write down whatever comes to mind. As Carlos mentioned, this does not have to be super involved or take a long time. He just wrote down a handful of answers each day. The real value, as he described it, lies in looking back over the facts after you've been doing this practice for a period of time. Try to commit to doing this for a month or two, and then read back over your days. Do you notice any patterns or any changes? What is different between your most recent entries and your earliest ones? This can be a great way to identify any recurring challenges and to track your spiritual growth.

19

SPIRITS OF DISCOVERY

So far, I've been talking about discovery as the act of receiving ideas from an abstract *source*—an "upstream," an unknowable mystery. However, in writing, it often happens that ideas come not from a depersonified "cloud of unknowing" but from a familiar face. The Source appears to us wrapped in the skin of friends and family, of peers and rivals, of people whose attention we fear or desire. These *inventive spirits* populate our imagination and guide our thinking as we write. By calling them "spirits," I mean that they are human or fantastical persons who inhabit our imaginations. By calling them "inventive," I mean that these spirits exert persuasive influence over our discovery processes, and occasionally, they even act as the source of desired insight. In any given act of writing, the writer may notice, dialogue with, and attribute some part of their discovery to these spirits.

To the extent that writing experts have explored the significance of inventive spirits, they have done so under the label "audience." In broad strokes, writing scholars recognize that audience can be real people who read and interpret an author's text, but the "audience" many scholars are interested in consists of those living inside the author's head. It is the audience *as imagined and represented by the writer* that has the most influence over their writing process, including the ideas that come to them in moments of discovery.

For example, Walter Ong treats an author's audience as "a fiction." For Ong, this means that writers mentally construct a general readership and cast them "in some sort of role" like "entertainment seekers" or "reflective sharers of experience."[43] Writing for this useful abstraction allows writers to generate ideas that are appropriately entertaining or reflective, as the case may be.

Likewise, cognitive researchers Linda Flower and John Hayes found that imagined audiences help writers make discoveries. They found that thinking about an audience is a regular, recurring feature of "expert" writers' processes. They concluded: "Good writers create a particularly rich network of goals for affecting their reader. Furthermore, these goals, based on affecting a reader, also helped the writer generate new ideas. . . . Setting up goals to affect a reader is not only a reasonable act, but a powerful strategy for generating new ideas."[44] The desire to affect readers leads writers into a relationship with an imagined audience. Testing their emerging thoughts against the reactions of this audience helps writers decide whether to accept or reject ideas as they appear.

Theories like Ong's or Flower and Hayes's are useful insofar as they point to the value of imaginal figures who influence the writing process, but they are limited in their scope. For one thing, these theories focus strictly on *audiences* when, in fact, there are many types of spirits that haunt writers' minds as they write. Parents, siblings, friends, past writing teachers, former lovers, people we want to impress, podcast hosts we would love to be interviewed by, fictional characters, long-dead authors, gods, Ouija board monsters, ancient alien photographers—there is no end to the variety of figures that might show up in our minds with something to say about our writing. These figures can significantly influence our writing process even though, in many cases, we have no reasonable expectation that they will ever read our work, meaning that they don't really fit into the category of "audience."

Another limitation of audience theories is that they do not represent the full power and potential of inventive spirits, which can act autonomously, speaking directly to—or even *through*—writers as they write:

> So, this happened when we first started doing the prayer, and this is really creepy. Corey can attest to this too, and it is bizarre.

This is Joe C., a recovery professional and heroin addict. He told me about "two way prayer," a writing practice that involves written conversations with "God." One sits quietly with a notebook, asks God a question, and then writes down whatever God says in response. As Joe began writing two way prayer with his friend Corey, they received uncanny confirmations that God really was participating in their writing:

> We would go away for the week, and we would come back to read to each other. I remember there was this time when I read first. As I was reading, Corey started laughing. He didn't say anything. He just started laughing. Then, when it was his turn to read, he had written exactly the same thing—verbatim. A couple of times, actually.

The odds of two writers independently coming up with identical language in response to a similar prompt are, of course, extremely low, especially when the prompt is something as open-ended as "ask any question you want and see what God says." And the odds of this happening more than once would be vanishingly rare. Joe told me this experience felt like good evidence that the voice he and Corey were recording really did originate from a third party. And his conviction only grew as he taught two way prayer to others:

> I've done this probably with somewhere in the ballpark of thirty to fifty people, and the voice that people hear generally seems the same. It uses the same sort of language. Talks about the same things. Always in this loving sort of manner.

Always wants the person to reach their full potential. Says things like: "My child, I love you. Why don't you try being more compassionate today?" Now, whether or not you want to call it "God," I don't care, but at the very least, everybody seems to have that voice. So it's as if there were one being throughout all these people.

This voice, clearly, is not an "audience" in any traditional sense of the word. Whatever this thing is, we can say, at the very least, that it is something more than a generalized category like "entertainment seekers" or a cognitive network of goals for affecting readers. This spirit seems to be actively and autonomously participating in the writing process of these addicts.

20

THREE LETTERS

Whether or not you want to believe that Joe was recording the actual voice of God in his notebook, you have to respect his caution and skepticism, even of his own experience. He did not tell me that he was without doubt. Instead, he said that he encountered commonalities, similar language, and sometimes even identical responses among people's writing when they sat quietly, asked God a question, and wrote down whatever came to mind. There are other ways to explain these commonalities, of course, and Joe wasn't even fully committed to calling this voice "God" at the time of our interview. He only said it was *as if* the voice were one being. What was remarkable to him was the fact that something good and loving consistently appeared in the notebooks of recovering addicts every time they asked for help and listened for answers.

In talking about "God" this way, we have strayed well outside the bounds of "audience." Whatever spirit was haunting these two way prayer sessions, it acted less like an audience member and more like a co-author. Just like the strange bat-creatures in Merrill's poems, an invisible agent of some kind was understood to be the source of language that appeared in these texts. Even so, I think these kinds of co-authors share some important qualities with "audience," traditionally understood, which is why I want to discuss them under a shared label: *inventive spirits*.

To understand the relationship between "ordinary" spirits, like imagined audiences, and "extraordinary" spirits, like "God" and "the Spirit," I find it helpful to imagine the writing process of a woman at different times in her life as she composes a series of three letters:

1. A letter to her mother, still living;
2. A letter to her mother, deceased;
3. A letter *from* her deceased mother.

I want us, in imagining each of these distinct writing processes, to focus on the role that the woman's mother plays in each case. As the woman writes these letters, she senses and responds to her mother in different ways, and her "mother," in various states of being, shapes her daughter's writing processes variously.

When composing her first letter—the one to her living mother—the woman expresses her thoughts and feelings to her mother as an actual audience. She knows her mother well, and she knows that her mother will receive and respond to whatever she writes. And so, as the woman considers what to say in this first letter, her mother influences her writing process in two ways: first, as a real, responsive reader, with whose values and judgment she must *contend*; and second, as an imagined respondent, whose needs and interests the woman must, to some degree, *invent*.[45] Let's say, for example, that the woman is writing to tell her mother that she has decided against coming home for Thanksgiving. She knows her mother will be disappointed and will respond poorly to the news. This anticipated disappointment puts pressure on the woman to craft her letter in a way that minimizes her mother's negative response. However, because she does not know exactly how to word her letter to achieve the best result, she has to *imagine* her mother's response to each turn of phrase. Through trial and error, she starts her letter in different ways, crumpling up pages and throwing them away when she imagines a negative reaction from her mother. In this way, "Mom" is both a real person whose responses she can anticipate and an invented figure whose responses she must discover in an imagined internal dialogue. As the woman writes, her inner representation of her real mother and the imagined version of her mother as an audience blur into one figure, who responds—in this case with disappointment—to everything she writes.

At this point, we can already make some interesting observations about authorship. When we ask the question, *Who is writing this letter?* we must answer that the letter is a collaborative effort. Clearly, the woman is writing. She is doing a lot of thinking and putting words on paper, but she is also clearly not writing alone. The imaginal mother is also writing the letter by causing the woman a great deal of frustration and provoking her to revise repeatedly until she can get the language just right, or at least good enough to send. Even so, this collaboration is still fairly one-sided, with the woman doing most of the work. She's the one drafting, representing her mother's reactions, and revising her work.

However, when the woman composes her second letter—the one to her *deceased* mother—the dynamics between the author and her mother shift. The woman knows her audience can no longer respond to her writing: her mother cannot read or respond to this second letter, at least not in any ordinary way. And so, this woman has lost (or has been freed from) her mother as an actual audience and now writes to her purely as an imaginal presence. Writing letters to the deceased (or letters to the living that one does not intend to send) is a practice most common in therapeutic contexts, where the goal is to help the writer express things about a relationship that they would not be able to express normally.[46] In this kind of therapeutic writing, the audience is imagined as an attentive, non-responsive participant to whom the writer can say absolutely anything. Whereas the woman was conflicted about how to raise the subject of Thanksgiving in her last letter, she can now tell her mother, bluntly and directly, all the things she thinks and feels about their relationship, including her frustration at Mom's lack of understanding about previous holiday plans.

However, even though the woman is unconstrained by the living presence of her mother, she may still find herself hesitating to put some of her feelings on paper, afraid to offend her mother's memory (or her ghost). Her imagined audience, because it is built from her psychological history with her mother, still offers resistance. In this resistance lies the letter's therapeutic value. By overcoming that resistance and expressing herself honestly and thoroughly to her mother, the woman can experience some closure to this troubled relationship, and perhaps even feel closer to her mother's spirit as a result.

In this second letter, Mom-as-audience still plays a vital role in shaping the woman's text. Though her mother has died, this woman still is not writing alone. She is writing *with* and *for* an imagined presence, who cannot and will not respond negatively to her feelings anymore. This mother is silent and receptive, a source of resistance at times but still welcoming once the resistance is overcome. In short, this inventive spirit enables the woman to write down what she thinks and feels about her relationship with her mother. Without that support, it would not be possible to write this second letter.

But what happens when the woman writes her third letter, the one *from* her dead mother? She sits before a blank sheet of paper and speaks to her mother's ghost, asking that it guide her hand. Then, the woman writes as quickly as possible, making every effort not to reflect on or even notice what she is writing. She inscribes with haste, trusting that somewhere in the resulting text, a message from her mother will appear. When she reads the result, she discovers a message in her mother's voice, telling her things that her mother would want her to know, things that the writer feels she would not, could not, and *did not* think of on her own.

In this case, the mother takes on a very different role in the writing process. Previously, the woman wrote *to* her mother and allowed Mom-as-audience to influence her writing more or less passively. Now, Mom is doing the writing. The woman holds the pen, but her mother moves her hand. As a result, she genuinely feels—and gains tangible evidence—that her mother is communicating with her from beyond the grave.

This new writing relationship, while striking and odd, is not really different *in kind* from the last two examples of working with inventive spirits. The difference is one of *degree*. In the case of all three letters, the woman did not write alone. She wrote each letter with the active participation of an imaginal figure. In the first letter, this spirit provided disappointment, provoking many revisions. In the second letter, it provided a measure of resistance, balanced by a therapeutically productive silence and receptivity. In the third letter, Mom's spirit provided *actual language*. As we move from letter two to letter three, we aren't really entering a fundamentally new situation; we are just turning up the knob to the max on "audience participation," so to speak. In the third letter, the woman's mother is simply participating more fully and more actively than before.

When Joe and the others practice two way prayer, they are doing what this woman is doing in her third letter. They are asking an inventive spirit to say whatever it wants through them. They switch seats with their "audience" for a moment, so to speak, so that they can sit and listen while the Spirit puts words on their page.

HOW TO WRITE
Two Way Prayer

If you'd like to try your hand at writing *from* one or more spirits, two way prayer is a good place to start. This form of written prayer was a central practice for the Oxford Group, a non-denominational Christian evangelical movement that began in the 1920s and still exists today under the name Initiatives of Change. All of the founding members of Alcoholics Anonymous, the first Twelve-Step fellowship, were members of the Oxford Group, and all of AA's practices—including those encoded in the Twelve Steps—were drawn from early AA members' experiences with the Group. Two way prayer, however, was one practice that the alcoholics left behind when they formed their own fellowship. While the essence of this practice is recorded in the Big Book's instructions for prayer and meditation,[47] two way prayer is never named in these pages, and the practice itself is not strongly emphasized either in the text or in current Twelve-Step culture.

The essential elements of two way prayer are fairly simple: you sit quietly with a notebook and write down everything that you think, without exception or self-censorship of any kind. But these simple elements—you, a pencil, a notebook, and literally everything that goes through your head—conceal a more nuanced spiritual practice. You may notice that these same elements are also common in many other practices that don't necessarily result in the voice of God appearing on the pages of your journal. Automatic writing, as practiced by late-nineteenth-century spiritualists and later taken up by Surrealist writers in the early twentieth century, also involves writing without self-censorship, with the goal of contacting ghosts (in the case of the spiritualists) or the writer's own unconscious mind (in the case of the Surrealists). "Freewriting," or "personal writing," as practiced in many English composition classrooms, also involves the unrestrained, uncritical expression of thoughts and feelings, this time with the goal of helping students discover their own voices, or their own ideas, or in any case, a workable answer to the problem of what to write for their term paper.

Though freewriting, automatic writing, and two way prayer all share common elements, the practices are clearly different in their emphasis and in the degree to which they recognize their material as originating from an outside source. For English teachers and Surrealists, the ideas that burble forth during unrestrained writing are *yours*, even though you may struggle to explain exactly how you arrived at them. But for spiritualists and the Oxford Group, ideas come during unrestrained writing clothed in the personage of an invisible other, a spirit who generates and voices these ideas, and offers them to you.

What distinguishes between spiritualist automatic writing and two way prayer is not only the nature of the spirits imagined—ghosts and God, respectively—but also the degree of skepticism each applies to the product of writing. For the spiritualists, a message from a ghost is just that. For the Oxford Group, any thought that hits the page, even one that strikes the writer as especially powerful and spiritual, could easily be just a product of the writer's own mind. And so, messages from God must be sifted carefully from the noise and chatter of the writer's ego-based thinking. This sifting takes place in a two-stage process called "checking." The writer tests each thought against a set of moral standards, and then meets with another two way prayer practitioner to get their input.

There are many instructions for two way prayer. The ones I offer here are excerpted from an early Oxford Group pamphlet by John Batterson:

RELAX

Sit in a comfortable position. Consciously relax all your muscles. Be loose. There is no hurry. There needs to be no strain during these minutes. God cannot get through to us if we are tense and anxious about later responsibilities.

TUNE IN

Open your heart to God. Either silently or aloud, just say to God in a natural way that you would like to find His plan for your life—you want His answer to the problem or situation that you are facing just now. Be definite and specific in your request.

LISTEN

Just be still, quiet, relaxed, and open. Let your mind go "loose." Let God do the talking. Thoughts, ideas, and impressions will begin to come into your mind and heart. Be alert and aware and open to everyone.

WRITE!

Here is the important key to the whole process. Write down everything that comes into your mind. Everything. Writing is simply a means of recording so that you can remember later. Don't sort out or edit your thoughts at this point.

Don't say to yourself:

This thought isn't important;

This is just an ordinary thought;

This can't be guidance;

This isn't nice;

This can't be from God;

This is just me thinking, etc.

Be honest! Write down everything! A thought comes quickly, and it escapes even more quickly unless it is captured and put down.

TEST

When the flow of thoughts slows down, stop. Take a good look at what you have written. Not every thought we have comes from God. So we need to test our thoughts. Here is where the written record helps us to be able to look at them.

a) Are these thoughts completely honest, pure, unselfish, and loving?

b) Are these thoughts in line with our duties—to our family—to our country?

c) Are these thoughts in line with our understanding of the teachings found in our spiritual literature?

CHECK

When in doubt and when it is important, what does another person who is living two way prayer think about this thought or action? More light comes in through two windows than one. Someone else who also wants God's plan for our lives may help us to see more clearly . . .

OBEY

Carry out the thoughts that have come. You will only be sure of guidance as you go through it. A rudder will not guide a boat until the boat is moving. As you obey, very often the results will convince you that you are on the right track.[48]

21

PRAYER, INNER CHILDREN, AND AN ACTIVE IMAGINATION

Father Bill W. is a retired priest and an alcoholic who has been practicing two way prayer for the last couple of decades. He told me he stumbled on to this method—rarely practiced today—when an AA archivist introduced him to the Oxford Group:

> I was twenty years sober at the time. I was missing something inside and I knew it, and I knew that upping my number of meetings or taking one more trip through the Steps just wasn't gonna do it. He [the archivist] gave me a number of books on the Oxford Group, and I really went into it. I found very quickly that two way prayer was at the heart and soul of their practice, so I started doing it. It sounded strange at first, listening for God's voice and writing down the thoughts that come, but I stuck with it.

The initial strangeness of the practice soon wore off, and Father Bill became invested in making it his own. He told me that Oxford Group literature did not have great instructions on the practical details of two way prayer (Batterson's pamphlet notwithstanding). Different authors described the practice differently and gave conflicting advice. So, Father Bill let his writing process guide him to a version of the prayer suited to his own needs:

After a while, I gave up on writing down all the thoughts that came. It got to be pretty obvious when my thoughts were distracted from prayer, so I stopped writing those down. But even so, it was all disjointed thoughts in the beginning— free-floating thoughts that just came in. At some point, I added a question. I started taking a quick inventory of myself. *What's going on internally? What's going on externally? Am I peaceful, or am I not?* And I'd focus on where I was not peaceful—not okay inside or outside—and then ask for help: "Lord, I'm scared about this. I'm anxious about that. Please help me." Then I would switch into listening mode and begin the guided writing. After a while, I said, "I think God can speak in paragraphs," so I tried to keep that flow going. It was a train of thought, and I tried to get it down. When I did receive specific guidance to do something, I started putting a little box next to each item, and then the next day I would go back and check it off if I had done it.

Father Bill's two way prayer practice evolved further when he began introducing therapeutic ideas into his writing, beginning with dialogue between himself and his "inner child." John Bradshaw's inner child theory suggests that a more authentic, spontaneous, playful, creative, soulful version of ourselves— our inner child—gets left behind during development when we experience shame and feel a need to hide this part of ourselves.[49] As Father Bill put it: "I grew up learning to hide my wounds, keep them buried, and put on the façade or persona that everybody creates to be acceptable in our culture. But I did that at the price of the child. And therefore, I lost the spontaneity, the creativity, and the playfulness. I became really serious." The purpose of dialoguing with the inner child is to heal from the shame that led to this separation in the first place. To begin that healing, Father Bill told me, you first have to "go in and find the kid":

A friend of mine found his inner child in the closet in a fetal position. That's where he left him. And so he goes to him. He talks to him. He's gentle and patient with him. He gives him all the love and attention that a little kid deserves instead of all the abuse and shit that *he* got as a kid. And so a very beautiful dialogue ensues where the kid is afraid and the parent figure is coaxing him: "Trust I will come back. I will come back. I'll be here tomorrow. You'll see. You'll see." And then—son of a bitch—you *better* be back tomorrow or the kid is gonna be pissed.

At first, Father Bill practiced inner child writing and two way prayer separately, but before long, they began to bleed into one another. Once the inner child figure was a regular part of Father Bill's imagination, "Jesus" began referencing "the kid" during two way prayer: "Sometimes, I'd go to Jesus, and I'd ask a question, and Jesus would say, 'Talk to the kid.'" As an example, Father Bill read me the following excerpt from his two way prayer journal:

Jesus: Feel me in the wind. Drop your unnecessary defenses and allow me access to your heart. Know I am always here and you fail to see me, fail to welcome me. I take no offense from this. Only it saddens me. So feel the kid's feet now as you carry him on your shoulders. He opens the door to me. He gets it; you don't. Look to him for your salvation.

Self: (to the kid) I have you and I'm holding you tight.

Kid: Hey, big guy. You didn't notice me in your meetings of late. I recognize the kids in others. I'm not threatening to them but you are. Hell, you threatened me for years. But what a team we make! You do your part, and I'll do mine. When this happens, everything changes. So let's go and have a fun day!

Jesus: How pleasant, my brothers! I love you both, and I provide the spirit that bonds us all together. Let this be your trinity today.

Three-way dialogues like this became commonplace in Father Bill's two way prayer practice. In time, he came to understand them as a variation on the Jungian practice called "active imagination," in which the patient identifies inner complexes and figures, gives names and images to them, and then enters into dialogue with them:

> Jungians tend to talk about "shadow" and getting in touch with "shadow characters" and dialoguing with them, but it's really the same process. You are bringing into consciousness that which is in you and is unconscious. I tell people: "Imagine if God were to speak to you, what would he say? Use your imagination, and start to write."

Through further practice with active imagination, Father Bill began to identify other inner figures and include them in his two way prayer sessions:

> I try to identify energies in me—energies that take over, particularly. I'm a control freak, which I got growing up in an alcoholic family. I take on huge responsibilities, but behind those responsibilities is *drivenness. If I could be responsible enough, maybe I could keep control in the house. Maybe there won't be an explosion if I can just make everybody happy.* So that's the energy that's going on inside of me. My image for this energy—this character—is Atlas. He carries the world on his shoulders. Well, I've carried the world on my shoulders since I was five or six years old. When that energy shows up, I start talking to him in my two way prayer. I do a little Jesus, and then I go into an in-depth meeting with Atlas: "I felt your energy yesterday. I felt you stirring inside of me." And he'll speak: "Yeah, because if you're not doing what you're supposed to do, then I gotta do it." I apologize to him. I thank him for his energy. To take their energy is to take their insight, take whatever gift they have. So it's a dance. You're drawing their energy, but it's channeled, and Jesus is present in the process.

As you can see, Father Bill's two way prayer practice has evolved significantly since he started researching the Oxford

Group. Over time, he adapted it to meet his own needs and blended in elements of inner child work and active imagination. The result is a rich, deep, and healing daily engagement with inventive spirits.[50]

22

INNER WORK

The method of active imagination was developed by the Swiss psychiatrist Carl Jung after his public break from Sigmund Freud in 1913. The following years were a difficult time for Jung psychologically. To navigate through a period that his various biographers have described as something between a fit of creative introspection and a full psychotic break, Jung kept a journal, recording his hallucinations (or visions, or imaginations, depending on your point of view). Many spirits appeared to Jung during these waking dreams, and his dialogues with them formed the basis of all his later psychological theories. One important feature of these dialogues was Jung's insistence that each figure that appeared to him should explain itself: *Who are you? Why have you appeared to me? What is the meaning of this encounter?* By asking these questions and recording the answers he received, Jung was able to "integrate" unconscious material into his consciousness. In other words, he was able to understand the nature and purpose of his visions, thereby transforming these unnerving experiences into psychological insight.

Accordingly, Jungian psychology begins with the premise of an active, populated unconscious mind, one full of "complexes" and "archetypes." These figures embody varying degrees of personal and impersonal psychological material and have personalities and motives of their own. Because they exist below the threshold of consciousness, they know things about us that we do not. They hold secrets and wisdom, so entering into dialogue with them offers us a path to deeper self-understanding. Some of these figures, built primarily from repressed material, offer insight into our personal histories. Others, connected to primal human instincts, speak to us from a perspective that transcends our limited life experiences. Gaining the wisdom of these inner figures is what active imagination is all about.

Robert Johnson's *Inner Work* provides an excellent, practical primer on active imagination. Johnson describes this practice as "similar to dreaming, except that you are fully awake and conscious during the experience. . . . You allow the images to rise up out of the unconscious. . . . In your imagination, you begin to talk to your images and interact with them."[51] In its "purest form," active imagination involves simply sitting and waiting for the images to appear on their own, but Johnson suggests that one could start with a figure from a dream or with a strong feeling instead:

> We often have something vague and invisible in the unconscious that bothers us. . . . Moods, worries, depression, inflations, and obsessions all come within this category.
>
> When this happens, you can go to the unconscious in your imagination and ask the unseen content to personify itself. . . . If you do this, an image eventually comes into your mind . . .
>
> Any quality within you can be personified in this way and persuaded to clothe itself in an image so that you can interact with it.[52]

Once we have invited the unconscious to personify itself, our job is to interact with the image that appears. Our goal is to arrive at an understanding of this imaginal figure and to discover what it wants from us. Making this discovery requires a certain openness to the image and a willingness to listen to what it has to say:

You may know how you feel about something; you may know what you have to say to the inner person; you may know who you are looking for when you go into your imagination. But you don't know what the other person is going to say until he or she says it. You don't know what the inner people are going to do until they do it. . . . We make no plan or script. We simply begin, and then let come what will. Whatever flows spontaneously out of the unconscious, without manipulation, without guidance or control, is the stuff of Active Imagination. . . . Active Imagination begins with the principle that you must respect the unconscious and realize that it has something valuable to contribute; therefore, the dialogue must be between two intelligent equals who respect each other.[53]

Johnson recommends addressing these self-personifying, unconscious figures directly and inviting them to speak freely, like this: "Who are you? What do you have to say? I will listen to you. You may have the floor for this entire hour if you want; you may use any language you want. I am here to listen."[54] Once an invitation like that is made, and we are present and receptive to the image, the results will likely surprise us:

They answer back. You are startled to find out that they express radically different viewpoints from those of your conscious mind. They tell you things you never consciously knew and express thoughts that you never consciously thought. . . . Because these interior beings have "minds of their own," they say and do things that are new to us—startling, often enlightening, sometimes offensive to our egos.[55]

These exchanges should be conducted in writing, says Johnson, because the act of writing keeps us focused and the written record enables study and reflection. By actively engaging our imaginations and recording the results, we capture what otherwise would have been a passing mood or a semi-conscious fantasy and convert it into a conscious relationship between ourselves and the population of our unconscious minds. With regular practice, this relationship develops into a rich exchange between our egos and the rest of our psyches:

> The ego actually goes into the inner world, walks and talks, confronts and argues, makes friends with or fights with the persons it finds there. You consciously take part in the drama of your imagination. You engage the other actors in conversation, exchange viewpoints, go through adventures together, and eventually learn something from each other.[56]

The life of active imagination is a life of regular written exchanges between us and a host of inventive spirits.

23

A Chorus of Inner Parts

When I asked Father Bill who else I should interview about two way prayer, he directed me to a friend of his in Germany. Martin H. learned two way prayer from Bill. He began by asking "Jesus" for guidance, then advanced to conversations with several "inner children," and then discovered many more figures—or "inner parts," as he calls them—through active imagination.

Martin is a sex addict and alcoholic who retired early due to an acquired disability. He read several examples from his prayer journal to me—some brief, with only a few characters, others longer and involving multiple voices. The most extensive example Martin shared with me was prompted by an inner struggle he experienced over whether or not to return a friend's phone call.

Martin told me that Hellen, the friend in question, was a recovering alcoholic and a great support to others but had halted her own personal growth: "She's marvelous at being helpful but she's stuck, and this is painful for me." But why, Martin wondered, was it so hard for him to even consider returning her call? To find out, he started to write.

In the space of a few pages—and about a half-hour of writing—Martin conversed with thirteen of his twenty-one inner parts. More precisely, more often than not, they conversed with each other while Martin watched, listened, and wrote. For example,

"Fear," the personified figure of all Martin's fears, asked all the inner parts which one of them was scared, and Martin's inner child responded. In another exchange, "Maria" and "Jesus" spoke several lines to each other. Later, all of the parts joined together to make a prayer of surrender. Each voice had a unique personality and perspective, and each offered a confession or a piece of wisdom to the group.

What follow are excerpts from Martin's journal, which he read to me, with occasional interruptions to introduce the *dramatis personae* or explain references made by his inner parts. In the following passage, "Me" refers to Martin:

Martin's Inner Dialogue

Me: Lord, I see Hellen in my inner eye. She is carrying a huge stone without realizing that the name of her stone is always changing. It is her way of life to obsess about herself and her problems, carrying this stone. You know that I have avoided calling her back for weeks now. Help me to show compassion, love, and patience. Teach me your will in this regard.

Jesus: Martin, come into my arms. You feel threatened by her. She is drowning, and you fear you will drown with her. You rely only on your own strength, and you can't imagine that I will guide you close to her without letting you fall into the abyss of her depression.

Fear: Who feels threatened about Hellen?

(Little Martin, my younger self, raises his hand.)

Little Martin: I can't stand any other problems. I need help, but no further burden.

Fear: Now you, Martin, understand why you have become avoided by others despite your efforts and goodwill. They fear that your problems are contagious and you will infect them with your disability.

(Ragey appears. He is the defiant, indignant, true lover of truth in me.)

Ragey: That's complete bullshit! But it's also the way they think, so it is the truth as well. OK?

(Error appears. He is half-mature, half-youthful energy. He has good intentions but is easily deceived.)

Error: That's why you have to come under my shield of protection. Let everything be between God and your inner parts. We will act but only after our union with God. Not before and not without it.

(Leader Dag appears. He is named after former UN leader Dag Hammarskjold, and he represents human energy at its peak.)

Leader Dag: Clarify your issues at the table with two way prayer, but outwardly practice AA spirit. Do not condemn, judge, argue, or criticize. You might spoil a later opportunity to help.

(Abraham appears, the father of faith inside me.)

Abraham: Understand we have given away our earthly lives to serve Yahweh.

(All the inner parts kneel down to welcome the arrival of Maria, who has dedication, who is suffering, who is humble. Maria and Abraham bless all the inner parts. Then all stand up and hold hands.)

Little Martin: I confess I don't feel fear anymore of Hellen.

(The ten-year-old me smiles.)

(The fourteen-year-old me nods.)

(The Broken One, me when I was thirty-one and became disabled, is resistant.)

(CC appears, who is the well of creativity and chaos inside me.)

CC: I feel I should speak out, but I feel so mute.

(The monk and nun appear, holding hands and crying; they are simplicity and focus and truth and love.)

The monk and nun: Yes, we feel it too! What a plucking of energy!

Maria: Do we feel Hellen's trauma, or is it ours, Jesus?

Jesus: Both. You will only be helpful if you have solved this issue yourself. Judging is no answer at all.

Maria: I feel powerless.

(Jesus smiles.)

Jesus: You are. You all are. Surrender what you cannot solve to me alone.

(All join hands.)

All: We surrender Hellen and all the ways her behaviors disturb us to you, our Lord.

(And then comes something which is amazing—Whirly. Whirly is a whirlwind inside me, and he takes all the issues off the inner parts and carries them to something greater.)

Jesus: Martin, guard your limit. Stop here. You cannot do this. It must happen to you. Rest. Then receive guidance for the rest of the day. Go now.

Through these exchanges, Martin learns that his youngest inner child is scared of Hellen, scared that her burden will become Martin's. He gains the insight that this fear is identical to that felt by people who avoid him because of his disability. After many figures share their wisdom, insight, and blessing, Little Martin is no longer afraid, and several inner versions of Martin at different ages approve, until the spotlight moves to the Broken One—Martin at the age of the traumatic injury that left him disabled. This figure represents a second internal struggle in relation to the expected phone call: Martin's memory of personal trauma is triggered by Hellen's depression, and this stifles him. His inner parts help him distinguish between Hellen's trauma and his own, and they all collectively turn to Jesus for help in overcoming their trauma while supporting Hellen in her own growth. In the end, the guidance is for Martin to rest and allow the process to continue within him.

Martin described this session as a "very long and intense" one, but pointed out that he gained clarity and insight that are often hard-won. "Years ago, I would have struggled with this energy for weeks," he told me. The result of this writing was a "body shift," a physical sense of relaxation and dissipation of stress. "Even though you see your problems more clearly," Martin said, "you feel relieved; you feel free."

24

FROM CONTACT TO ACTION

Recovery writing begins in *desperation*, drives us to *surrender*, and opens into *contact* with a source of wisdom beyond our egos. In two way prayer and active imagination, we can see how contact, in turn, leads us into *action*. Both two way prayer and active imagination suggest acting on wisdom received from inventive spirits. Robert Johnson suggests that a session of active imagination should culminate in you "[taking] the *essence* you have distilled from it . . . and [incarnating] it by doing physical ritual or by integrating it into your practical life."[57] The end goal of active imagination is for you to respond symbolically or practically—but in any case, *physically*—to the wisdom of the figures you've met in your unconscious. Johnson gives the example of a young man who dreamed about junk food and discovered a link between the dream and his habit of wasting time on superficial and unfulfilling relationships. So, this man bought himself a cheeseburger and buried it in his backyard: a symbolic funeral for his old way of life.[58]

For the Oxford Group, the whole point of two way prayer was to discover "guidance" or messages from God related to God's specific plan for your life. This guidance could be as general as a suggested attitude one should take toward life, or as specific as a place to be and time to be there on Saturday afternoon. Oxford Groupers reasoned that, for example, if the creator of the universe tells you to send fifty bucks to your cousin in Detroit on Thursday, then you'd probably better send that money, even if it seems like a weird thing to do. Importantly, failure to follow through on guidance would result in the tap getting turned off—no obedience, no more guidance. John Batterson's pamphlet puts it like this:

> What if I don't seem to get any definite thoughts? Guidance is as freely available as the air we breathe. If I am not receiving thoughts when I listen, the fault is not God's.
> - Usually, it is because there is something I will not do:
> - something wrong in my life that I will not face and make right;
> - a habit or indulgence I will not give up;
> - a person I will not forgive;
> - a wrong relationship in my life I will not give up;
> - a restitution I will not make;
> - something God has already told me to do that I will not obey.
>
> Check these points and be honest. Then try listening again.[59]

A regular objection to advice like this is that it runs the risk of making us look and act like crazy people. If we believe that we have been specially guided by God or by some powerful inner archetype to do specific things in the world, we may end up acting in ways that are embarrassing, harmful, or self-destructive. One doesn't have to look too deeply into history, or even current events, to find examples of bad behavior justified by religious conviction. So how could it possibly be a good idea to act on imaginal dialogues with gods and spirits? Maybe not, at least not always. Jungian psychologists and Oxford Group members are well aware that not every impulse or idea is a good one to act on, and not everything that feels like God-given guidance will produce good results. And so each group has its own series of safety protocols meant to prevent harmful behavior.

For Jungians, the first safety protocol is, of course, the therapist, with whom the client will discuss an appropriate ritual for honoring the insights provided by inner figures. The therapist's help is supported by what Robert Johnson calls the "ethical element" of active imagination:

> First, you add the ethical element by holding out for the attitudes and conduct that are consistent with your character and your deepest values.
>
> Second, ethical balance requires that we not let one archetype or one part of ourselves take over at the expense of the others. We can't sacrifice essential values in order to pursue one narrow urge or goal.
>
> Third, we must nurture and preserve the specifically human values that serve human life, that keep practical daily life going, and that keep our human relationships alive.[60]

In essence, the work of active imagination must be grounded in principles that would prevent us from doing harm or acting in ways inconsistent with our core sense of self.

For the Oxford Group, safely acting on guidance requires a process of "checking." Any guidance two way prayer writers receive is checked twice: first against a set of moral principles—honesty, purity, unselfishness, and love—and then again in consultation with another two way prayer practitioner. The process of checking guidance is meant to prevent writers from assuming too quickly that everything that flows from their pen is divinely inspired. When we write *all* our ideas down, we are likely to record some things best left unacted on, things that should be easily flagged as dishonest, impure, selfish, or unloving. Failing that, such ideas will hopefully be caught and corrected by a fellow practitioner with more experience and discernment.

In short, there is a real danger of acting poorly if, for example, we assume that our writing is always divinely inspired. At the same time, an insight is not of much value unless it is acted on, and so if we want our writing to change our lives, we will have to move from the page into action. Jungian psychologists and Oxford Group writers both suggest that if we remain grounded in moral principles and if we consult with trusted advisors, we have a better chance of staying sane and healthy as we take the discoveries gained from our conversations with inventive spirits and find ways to integrate them into our lives.

25

A TALE OF TWO TREES

The checkboxes Father Bill W. puts in his notebook are meant to remind him to act on the guidance he receives: empty checkboxes mean unfollowed guidance; full boxes mean a message from God seen all the way through. When I asked him about what following guidance looked like, Father Bill told me a couple of stories about trees:

> Fifteen years ago, my wife and kids were away visiting someone. I was alone, and I was doing my two way prayer. I was writing something nice and holy, I'm sure. [Laughs] And then this thought came—a crazy thought—and I wrote it down. The thought was, *Plant a tree.* So I kind of ignored it and went on with more holy shit after that, you know? [Laughs] When I'm done writing, I almost always will read what I have written. So, at the end of the process, I read that thought again, and this was what Oxford Group people would call an illuminative thought. It jumps out at you. It had a light around it almost. It *shone.* So I looked at that sucker, and I said, "Well, if I did that, I would feel stupid." Immediately, another thought came, *That would be a good thing for you, because you don't like to feel stupid.* It was like, "Oh shit, this little image has me!" It was my guidance. It was not dishonest or selfish. It didn't go against those principles in any way. So, for the purpose of being obedient to a part of me that my ego is not comfortable with, I did it. I went

to the nursery and bought a tree and I felt stupid. I came back to the house, and I planted it in the middle of the yard, feeling stupid the whole time. But feeling *obedient*. Stupid and obedient. And then, for fifteen years, every time I looked at that tree, it was my obedience tree. It reminded me.

Telling this story sparked another memory of tree-related guidance. Father Bill laughed at himself, and told me he was going to really embarrass himself by telling this one, but he went ahead and read a recent journal entry into the permanent record:

Dream fragment: I was at a meeting with a group of friends. Somehow, my little dog was there with me. It seemed inappropriate for her to be there. When we needed to leave, I said, "The dog will find her own way home." The meeting was several blocks from my house, and this seemed a dangerous thing for me to do, but when I got home, the dog was there.

Jesus: Trust your soul to lead you home. Let go of control. Let go of fear. Trust your lower nature to know what it is doing. Join with the Earth. You hide in your head and miss so much life happening all around you. Go hug a tree today. I mean this literally. Feel as foolish as when I asked you to plant one. In your "foolishness," you'll find my "fool" and he will set you free. Go do it now. Go do it now. Go hug the tree you peed on yesterday in the dark.

At this point, Father Bill was laughing too hard to continue: "He even pointed out the tree I was supposed to [extended laughing] . . ."

I hope you can appreciate the humor here. If you were going to put money on the kind of thing God would tell a retired priest to do, I'm guessing you wouldn't place your bet on "go hug the tree you peed on last night." And Father Bill wouldn't either. The God he dialogues with seems to have a knack not only for dream interpretation—His reading of the dog dream as a call for Bill to trust his instincts was brilliant—but also for guiding him to do exactly the thing that will give him a good laugh at himself:

Here's the thing—I did it! I hugged that tree. I'm a head guy, but where I find God is in my undeveloped sides. I'll never find God in my head. He will never come to me through a book. He'll come through a tree. He will come through the Earth. Sometimes, I just go dig in the ground, and when I get that dirt on my hands, there's a connection I feel that is undeveloped in me. If I were a farmer, it might be the opposite. It might be: "Go read a book." But I hugged the tree, being obedient and feeling foolish. I mean, two way prayer is not always those weird things. But it came up this week!

You may think that hugging a tree is a silly thing for a grown man to do, but you have to admit that it is not harmful or psychotic. It's just a gentle act of ego deflation for a guy who—like many of us—has a tendency to take himself too seriously. It's a reminder to get *grounded* and to *play*.

To be clear, none of this discussion is meant to minimize or erase the real difficulties that many people have with feeling "guided" by inner voices. Many people do hear harmful, violent, intrusive voices that upset their lives and can provoke them to behave poorly at times. But the voices addicts described to me in conjunction with their recovery writing were never cruel, nor did they ever encourage cruelty. These voices were loving and wise, and dialoguing with them gave these addicts a reliable source of surprising, humorous, ego-deflating insight.

"An Awakened Heart"

MARGARET'S STORY

Margaret's journal keeping, creative work, and activist writing each offer her different ways to discover herself in dialogue with her higher power. In contrast to active imagination and two way prayer, Margaret's practices do not produce direct transcripts from a divine (inner) voice or the voices of figures in her unconscious, but they nevertheless help her to make contact and take action.

Before I got into recovery, I felt as if I didn't really have a self of my own. I think I kept a journal as a way of holding myself together. There was so much confusion and anger and loneliness and sorrow. I kept many, many journals before I got into recovery, so I don't see writing in itself as sufficient. You can't write yourself into recovery.

But, after I got into recovery, writing was one of the ways I kept myself company. Journal writing in recovery helped me to articulate and understand the strong feelings that were moving through me. Early recovery was like taking the lid off all the feelings I'd been stuffing away, so there was a lot of emotional turbulence, and I needed to write my way toward clarity. Writing was a way of staying abstinent, too. I could write down my feelings on the page rather than acting them out, so if I was really angry, I could just write about the anger rather than eating over it.

I also found that I'd always been looking for God, although I'd hidden that from myself for a long time. When I was caught in the grip of addiction, I didn't know what to do with my spiritual longing. Part of my healing had to do with understanding and accepting that I have a deep longing for a relationship with God. That became very clear and I needed to write about it. So I turn to my journal when I'm reflecting on, "What is my life's purpose?" and, "Am I surrendered to God?" Or sometimes I'm deep in prayer, and then afterwards I need to jot down some notes about what I experienced. I often ask in prayer: "How can I serve you? How can I express your love in the world?" I feel that I'm given provisional answers. It makes me think of "manna for the day." I get enough for the day, that's for sure.

Chunks of my memoir came right out of my journals too. In *Holy Hunger*, there's an opening scene of a binge in the supermarket, which was taken almost verbatim from a journal account. But I didn't start out to write a memoir. I had been in recovery for fifteen years when I felt a deep desire to write about desire. At first, I thought I was going to write a very intellectual, systematic theology of desire. I mapped out the chapters. The first chapter was going to be about addiction, and then it was going to go on from there to other ways of thinking about desire. Then Henri Nouwen—thank goodness—suggested, "In your introduction, why don't you tell us some personal stories about why desire is so interesting to you?" So I started writing down stories, and eventually that became *Holy Hunger*.

Writing the book took me to a different, deeper level of healing in terms of understanding my own journey and also of making peace with my past, especially with each of my parents. Much was drawn from my journals, but much of it was new writing too. My intent in writing the book was to speak the truth in love—you know, that line from Ephesians. I needed to tell my story without blame. I wanted to be very honest about what had happened and how I'd felt hurt by things that happened when I was young, but I didn't want to settle into the framework of "I'm the innocent victim and you're the horrible perpetrator."

As I was writing, I realized that everything that my father and mother had done, I was completely capable of doing. When I was eight, my dad was drinking and my mother was depressed and no one was tending to the family dog when he slipped off the penthouse balcony, fell eight floors, and died. I remember being horrified. It was traumatizing. As I was writing that story, I was telling it as, you know, "Poor me—I'm eight years old and my father's out of control and my mother's not paying any attention." The same night that I was drafting that chapter, I happened to change the filter in the home aquarium where we kept some fish, and I did something wrong. By the next day, all the fish but one had died. My son was eight years old and he was horrified. I realized that it was a situation of "there, but for the grace of God, go I": everything my father had done, everything my mother had done, I myself was completely capable of doing and, to some extent, had actually done. That was a wake-up call. I knew I had to tell this story in a way that was more compassionate and mature, without finger-pointing.

All these years later, I don't maintain a steady writing practice in a journal, but whenever I go back to journal writing, I always feel refreshed and reconnected with myself. And I'm always writing in one form or another. I'm someone who needs to write and very much values good writing. There's something powerful about writing—it takes what's inside me and then puts it outside me on the page, so that I can look at it. It externalizes and makes visible something that until then was hidden. After that, in a sense, what I wrote about becomes more real—now, I can see it with my own eyes. Writing makes my relationship with God feel more tangible and real, and it keeps me real to myself as well.

There's also a great pleasure in creating beauty, in creating a sentence that really has meaning to me and that also has some beauty. I feel happy when I think, *I like those words*, or, *I like the rhythm of that sentence*, or, *I like how things fit together.* There's joy in creation, in creativity, in writing. I do think of that as Spirit moving through me. It's one way that God is expressed through me.

The most intense experience I've had of this was after the Oklahoma City bombing took place. I was shocked and I did not want to pray. I refused to pray. But several days later, I was practically pulled to my prayer cushion and I had a very intense experience in prayer. Afterwards, I scribbled down what I'd experienced. Later, it was published. I called it, simply, "A prayer after the Oklahoma City bombing." That felt like the most straight-from-the-source writing I've ever done in my life. It was completely unselfconscious and very open, as if my self had been blown open. It felt different from my usual writing process, which usually involves more labor and care. In fact, I love good writing so much that I will go back and rewrite journal entries even though no one but me will ever see them. This was something different.

Over the years, I've gotten more and more interested in and alarmed by what we're doing to the Earth. I feel as if the same God who gave me the power to reconnect my mind, body, and spirit in a healthy way is now sending me out into the world to try to help human beings to heal our relationship with the body of Earth.

Early in recovery, I had an experience in Minnesota in the back of a pickup truck. We were going through a field on a beautiful summer day—oh, the smell of the grasses—and we were headed off to go swimming in the river. Being newly in recovery was like being a baby who is in bliss simply because of the sensory experience of being alive. So, I was breathing in the scent of grasses and feeling the sun on my face, and just . . . the joy was an ecstatic experience of being alive: *I belong to the world. I belong to the web of life.*

That experience is an example of what it means to have an awakened heart, when we awaken to how beloved we are and also how beloved the whole of God's creation is—all of it, not just human beings, but the whole. Now, when I lead retreats, I often present a framework for the heart that helps us to be spiritually resilient in a time of climate crisis. The first step is an awakened heart. The second is the broken heart, where we allow ourselves to grieve; that's the experience of crucifixion. The third I call the radiant heart, which is about how we take action. It's how Spirit manifests in the world. You might call that resurrection, and that's where advocacy comes in. It starts with a very personal experience in our bodies and then moves into public advocacy.

I very much want to encourage myself and other people to keep spiritual experience as the foundation of advocacy work. We must stay rooted in our spiritual experience because it's so easy to fly off into advocacy and to end up being full of anger and resentment and anxiety, to get cynical and burned out. Of course, activists get anxious, for good reasons, but any of us can get violent when afraid. So I try to keep circling us back to the heart. Come back to the love, and then, out of that place of love, take your next action. When you get lost in sorrow or fear or anger, how do you come back to the experience of love? How do you reground yourself in the sacred? Those are questions that I want to help people to answer.

So, when I write sermons or when I write blog posts about healing the relationship between ourselves and Earth, in the background is my personal story of recovery. I do a lot of writing in that capacity. I write articles, blog posts, sermons, and I speak and lead retreats. It's an extension of—or an expression of—my own recovery. What I often say in my talks is, "If God can heal one crazy addict and can help this crazy addict to put her mind in right relationship with her body and her soul, is it not possible that God can help human beings as a species to come into right relationship with the body of Earth?" That's the big question I've been working with.

How to Write

A Resilient Heart

Margaret shared with me this set of reflective writing prompts, which guides us through her three-part framework for keeping our hearts grounded in spiritual experience while we take action to improve our world. Reflecting deeply on these questions helps us rediscover our relationship with the body of Earth, as well as our role in caring for it. Even if you are not involved in environmental work, this exercise is a great way to move through the process of discovery and recovery—from desperation to surrender, from surrender to contact, and from contact to action.

Margaret normally shares these questions with participants on her retreats. You can find out more about this exercise and Margaret's activism at www.revivingcreation.org.

Awakened Heart:
- What helps you to become aware of how loved you are and how loved all beings are?
- What habits, thoughts, or behaviors tend to block that awareness?
- How important to your spiritual life is staying connected with the natural world?

Broken Heart:
- Write or draw a prayer of lament or protest, confession or intercession.
- Where do you feel the pain of the Earth? Where do you hear the groaning of God's Creation?
- What are the losses you need to mourn? What are the tears you need to shed?

Radiant Heart:
- Who are the people who inspire you to do more than you thought possible? With whom do you hold hands, literally or figuratively, when you step out to make a difference in the world?
- If you knew you could not fail—if you were set free from all fear—what would you do for the healing of our world?

26

PLAIN OLD ORDINARY TRUTH

In this book, I have presented some rather unusual examples of writers and their writing. I've told stories of prayers that result in extraordinary insight, automatic hands that inscribe messages from beyond, spirit-board sex-bats from another dimension, a God-like voice that repeats itself verbatim to multiple writers, straight-from-the-source poems that flow from a higher power, and a host of inner voices that communicate with each other and with their writer autonomously.

Along the way, I've argued that these seemingly strange examples are not really strange at all—that, in fact, they are only extreme cases of the everyday dynamics of the writing process. Our minds naturally produce thoughts without the help of our egos. Ideas burble up to our consciousness on their own. Autonomous figures arise within us and tell us things that we did not know about ourselves, things we could not discover without their help. Every time we write, even when it's something as boring and ordinary as a grocery list, we engage with these imaginal figures— these inventive spirits—which shape our ideas about writing and can even write independently of our egos if we allow them.

Writing, even at its most ordinary, requires an inner conversation with these figures, even if we are speaking only to whatever inner figure guards our memories about what brand of canned beans to buy. Every act of writing, no matter how small, reproduces the recovery process in the necessary step of discovery. We must acknowledge our lack of an idea, surrender our ego to the flow of incoming thoughts, and make contact with the source of that flow. The result always changes our relationships and allows us to take new action, even if the change we experience is only that we are now able to purchase the groceries we need.

On the other hand, when we write for recovery, the resulting changes can be deep and significant, altering every relationship we have, including our relationships with ourselves, our addictions, and our higher powers.

To be clear, not every addict I interviewed reported weird experiences like automatic hands and choruses of internal voices. For some addicts, much of their recovery writing experience was rather uneventful. Piers, for example, told me that for him, writing moral inventory was a mundane and uncomfortable process:

> I got off to a pretty good start, and then I bogged down. It took the better part of three months to finish the thing. I got lazy and resistant to it. It felt just like ordinary procrastination. I told myself, "I'll do it tonight, I'll do it tomorrow, I'll do it this weekend," and then I wouldn't do it. My ex-girlfriend suggested that I make an appointment to read inventory to my sponsor to force my hand in getting it done, which it did, but I still wound up doing most of the writing the night before. I felt kind of frenetic and mad at myself, but I was going to do it anyway. It had that kind of messy, all-too-familiar feeling.

During Piers's inventory process, the unconscious forces lurking behind his resistance did not personify themselves and speak to him. Nor did he find himself making seemingly miraculous contact with a divine source of ideas and insight. He just sat at his parents' kitchen table the night before his inventory was due and worked at it as if he were rushing through a last-minute draft of a college essay.

Even so, we can see familiar discovery dynamics at work in Piers's story. He faced an emotionally difficult writing task but pressed on anyway because he was *desperate*. Piers's persistence in the face of his own resistance was in itself a form of *surrender*— he acted against the interests of his own ego (which would prefer to procrastinate and resist), trusting in the process to help him recover. And, even though his experience was fairly ordinary (no obvious gods or ghosts made an appearance), he did make *contact* with a source of ideas from beyond his own ego, which generated new insight as a result:

> I saw patterns in my history. I saw how I punished people who weren't necessarily the perpetrators. I saw how I used my own victimization to justify any number of behaviors. I saw a lot of hypocrisy—almost mind-numbingly so—in that I resented people for doing the things that I often do. It felt a little bit like seeing your backside, seeing a side of yourself you've never seen before. I was disturbed, but it was insightful. I could tell something was happening. I wasn't super excited about it, but I wasn't uninterested in it either. I was suddenly open to some things about myself that I'd spent a lot of energy avoiding.

By writing moral inventory, Piers gained moral insight. He saw his life history and his addiction in a new light, which prepared him to relate to others in a new way. And it is this experience of moral insight—more than moving hands, mystic visions, or dialogues with inner voices—that lies at the heart of recovery writing. In many ways, all the various weird experiences I've reported so far are merely different means of arriving at the central, moral fact of the Twelve-Step program: that we addicts begin to recover when we admit to ourselves, to our higher power, and to at least one other person "the exact nature of our wrongs."

Gods, ghosts, and inner children are welcome and powerful elements of recovery writing, but they are not strictly necessary. What is required is that we see and say the Truth.

27

How I First Wrote Inventory

The first thing Piers had me write was a moral inventory. He told me to start by making a list of my resentments—everyone and everything that pissed me off, irritated me, or toward whom or which I felt any amount of ill will. If there was ever a question about whether or not I had a resentment toward someone, I was supposed to imagine sitting across the table from the person. If that image made me uncomfortable, then I should add their name to my list. But Piers also told me not to waste too much time thinking about it. He said to just pray and put down whoever came to mind without second-guessing. The Spirit knew better than I did who belonged on my list. Piers gave me a week to get it done.

I spent most of that week convinced that I wasn't a resentful person. I named a few obvious resentments—with "myself" topping the list, "God" being second, followed by "church," and a few family members—and told myself I was done. Then I tried praying like Piers suggested. I asked God to show me whom to write about, and I waited for inspiration to come. Over the course of the next half-hour, names poured out of me onto the page—a hundred and twenty-nine of them. My last "name" was a summative generalization: "Anyone I've ever met or been around long enough to notice, even if I didn't know their name." Somewhere between the start of that week and entry 129, I'd gotten the message that in fact, I was a very petty person who held grudges against people sometimes just for existing in the same space as me.

There were, of course, many other, less abstract resentments on my list. I resented everyone in my family, immediate and extended. All my friends. All former bosses and most former co-workers. Ex-girlfriends. Classmates. Therapists and doctors. Celebrities. Presidents. People in the news. It was only toward the end of the list—once I'd reached a hundred names or so—that I found myself listing things like "people who cut me off in traffic," "people who are bossy," "people who are cheerful in the morning," and so on. I would later call these my "people who" resentments.

I resented a lot of people-whos.

When I showed my list to Piers, he nodded approvingly. His only correction was to have me take my own name off the list. "The purpose of inventory is to see our own selfishness," he said, "so we have to resist the impulse to put ourselves first, even on our list of resentments." Then he told me to format my work into four columns. The names I'd written would make up the first column. In the second, I was to write down the causes of each resentment. By "causes," Piers meant the reasons each person belonged on my list. He told me to be as specific as possible in the second column. He said that writing "he's an asshole" might be honest, but it was not as effective as something like, "He used to show up at my Little League games drunk and embarrass me." There was power in the details, Piers said.

In my third column, he said I should write down how the people I resented had affected my life. Specifically, I was supposed to sort the harm they caused me by the seven categories given in the Big Book: security, pocketbook, ambition, pride, self-esteem, personal relationships, and sexual relationships.[61] In this case, I was not supposed to go into detail, just write down the names of whichever categories applied. I wondered why we didn't elaborate. I had plenty to say about how former girlfriends had affected my self-esteem, for example, but the inventory process, as Piers described it, didn't allow for that kind of thing. Columns two and three were easy to write. I already knew that people were jerks who did mean things to me. All I had to do was write it all down.

After three columns were done, Piers gave me instructions for the fourth. This fourth column wasn't going to be about other people, he said. This one was about me and my moral shortcomings. For each resentment, I was to write down all the ways in which I had been *selfish, dishonest, self-seeking,* and *afraid.* For example, I'd written down a bunch of crap about my parents and how they had affected me. Now, I was supposed to write down all the ways I'd been selfish toward them, plus all the lies I'd told, plus all the things I did to keep up false appearances, plus all the fears that drove me to behave poorly toward them. Yeesh.

This fourth column was *not easy to write.* I thought of myself as a kind person who was treated poorly by the people in his life. Selfish, dishonest, self-seeking, and afraid? I couldn't see how those words applied to me.

Piers told me to pray each time I sat down to write and to listen for answers. The Spirit knew more about my relationships than I did, he reminded me, and it would reveal the truth if I asked.

I took my notebook to a windowless study nook in the library and locked the door behind me. I turned to a random resentment and reread its first three columns. I resented my cousin because once, when he was visiting, I spent a bunch of my paper route money on candy for us, and out of nowhere he asked me, with clear skepticism, "Are you even really a Christian?" At the time, being "really a Christian" mattered to me, like, *a lot.* I was an evangelical kid who had nightmare-inducing anxiety about being left behind after the rapture. I prayed repeatedly to ask Jesus into my heart out of fear that I had screwed it up all the previous times. I ground my teeth worrying that I wasn't good enough to earn God's grace. My cousin's question cut right to the heart of my religious fears. His parents were Bible-translating missionaries, so I assumed he looked down on me for being a comfortable suburban kid with money to buy snacks.

Where had I been selfish, dishonest, self-seeking, and afraid toward my cousin?

I thought about it for a while. Nothing came to mind.

Piers had given me a prayer, so I wrote it across the top of the page: "God, please show me the things that block me from you and others."

Then I waited, and I listened.

After a time, I heard a quiet voice inside me. "You didn't want to share," it said.

And it was right. I didn't want to share.

My cousin was one of four kids. I had promised to share my candy with him and *only him.* I told him not to tell his siblings—or my own brother—about our stash. My paper route money bought us a big bag of treats, way more than enough to go around, but if we let our siblings know about it, then it would be gone in a flash. And that's what I cared most about—having a secret supply of sugar under my bed, not making sure everyone got to share in our good time.

So, yeah, that was *selfish.*

I wrote it down, and as I did, it immediately occurred to me that I had been *dishonest* too. I planned to hide the candy, and I tried to make my cousin swear to secrecy. Keeping that information from everyone else was a lie of omission: it meant withholding information I knew would matter to someone else. Further, I was trying to keep secrets because I was *afraid* of losing my stash. And I was *self-seeking* too. I wanted to appear like a good cousin, a good brother, and a good Christian, even though I was keeping selfish secrets.

Something started to shift in me. Now that I could see a part of my selfishness, a new perspective came into view. A more sympathetic portrait of my cousin emerged. He'd grown up in a family of six without a lot of resources. When he had something good, he wanted to share it with his younger siblings. To him, that was what Christianity meant—caring for people, giving what you have to others so that their lives will be better. He didn't understand how you could be a Christian but also hide candy from your own family. Of course, a lot of Christians do shit like that, but not my cousin, at least not at that time.

And so, I had been *dishonest* on a deeper level: I lied to myself about my cousin's motives and perspective. I framed him as a judgmental guy who attacked my faith out of nowhere when he was actually a confused and caring person who just wanted his siblings to share in our haul. On a deeper level, my resentment was also *self-seeking*: it allowed me to cast myself as a wrongfully judged victim instead of a selfish candy hoarder. And what more was I *afraid* of? God, the rapture, my own moral failings, not being good enough for salvation, being exposed as selfish, losing my candy, being embarrassed—this resentment wasn't about my cousin at all. It was just a fantasy I'd invented so I could project onto him all the things I worried were wrong with me. And that was even more deeply *selfish* than I first thought. I damaged my relationship with my cousin instead of facing an uncomfortable truth.

I shut my notebook. I felt like someone had just punched me in the stomach, but I was also lighter somehow, like I'd been carrying a heavy weight and getting gut-punched had forced me to drop it. I'd held that resentment against my cousin for fifteen years. Now, it was gone. In its place was a mix of embarrassment, regret, respect, and compassion. I was sorry for resenting my cousin for so long over something so silly, and I was suddenly open to a better relationship with him. For just an instant, I caught a whiff of what it would be like to have this same experience—this same gut-punching release—with all one hundred and twenty-nine of my resentments. The thought of going through that process again was not entirely appealing, but the release and freedom that came afterward? I desperately wanted that.

HOW TO WRITE

Four-Column Resentment Inventory

The Big Book's instructions for moral inventory divide the process into three parts: resentment, fear, and sex. The book refers to the first of these—resentment—as the "number one offender," for "from it stem all forms of spiritual disease."[62] The basic principle here is that while other people really may have wronged us, our resentments only prolong our suffering. As many say in meetings: "Resentment is like drinking poison and expecting someone else to die." The goal of this inventory is to purge that poison from our systems so that we can live sane and sober lives.

As described in the last chapter, Big Book resentment inventory is normally broken up into four columns. The first three name each resentment, state its cause, and then describe how it affects us. Here's the example the book offers on page 65:

I'm resentful at:	The Cause	Affects my:
Mr. Brown	His attention to my wife.	Sex relations. Self-esteem (fear)
	Told my wife of my mistress.	Sex relations. Self-esteem (fear)
	Brown may get my job at the office.	Security Self-esteem (fear)
Mrs. Jones	She's a nut—she snubbed me. She committed her husband for drinking. He's my friend. She's a gossip.	Personal relationship. Self-esteem (fear)

After a few pages that describe the dangers of harboring resentment, the Big Book suggests we take a new attitude toward the people on our list: we should think of them as spiritually sick, just like us, and therefore should pray for them. "We asked God to help us show them the same tolerance, pity, and patience that we would cheerfully grant a sick friend. When a person offended, we said to ourselves: 'This is a sick man. How can I be helpful to him? God save me from being angry. Thy will be done.'" Following this suggested prayer, the Big Book offers these instructions:

> We resolutely looked for our own mistakes. Where had we been selfish, dishonest, self-seeking, and frightened? Though a situation had not been entirely our fault, we tried to disregard the other person involved entirely. Where were we to blame? The inventory was ours, not the other man's. When we saw our faults, we listed them. We placed them before us in black and white. We admitted our wrongs honestly and were willing to set these matters straight.

The book does not offer an example to show what a fourth column might look like, so here's an example that fills in the blanks for the imaginary person who resents "Mr. Brown":

Selfish: I'm jealous of my wife and I'm cheating on her.

Dishonest: I had an affair and kept it secret.

Self-seeking: I want everyone at the office to respect me more than him.

Afraid: I'll lose my job and my wife.

Here's another for the resentment against "Mrs. Jones":

Selfish: I care more about having my drinking buddy around than I care about his wife's wellbeing, or his.

Dishonest: He really does need the help. So do I.

Self-seeking: I call her names like "nut" and "gossip" to make myself feel better.

Afraid: I'm a hopeless drunk and my wife will probably have me committed next.

To write a resentment inventory:

1. Start by listing all your resentments—all the people, places, and things that cause you anger, irritation, or distress. These names will make up your first column.
2. Then, fill in the second column by stating why you resent each name on your list.
3. For the third column, make brief notes about how each one's behavior has affected you. You can use the list of categories offered by the Big Book: security, pocketbook, ambition, pride, self-esteem, personal relationships, and sexual relationships.[63]
4. Finally, for your fourth column, describe the ways in which you have been selfish, dishonest, self-seeking, and afraid in each relationship.
5. Remember that prayer is a useful ally in writing this inventory at every stage. Many addicts have found the discoveries made in this inventory to be their best proof yet that something out there really does hear us and care.
6. I should note that opinions differ about how many questions belong in column four. In addition to describing selfish, dishonest, self-seeking, and fearful behavior, some addicts also describe things like their "faults,"

"wrongs," "blame," and even "mistaken thinking," though the last phrase does not appear in the Big Book. Feel free to expand your fourth-column reflection if you like.

"You Need to Keep Writing"

BOB P.'S STORY

The Big Book Step Study groups are known for their rigorous adherence to the Twelve-Step program as described in AA's text. Bob shares his experience of and reflections on writing and extensive inventory with one of these groups.

I went through something called the Big Book Step Study program. I had been sober for eleven years and relapsed for a couple of years. When I came back, I followed the instructions in the Big Book for the first time in my life. I had a sponsor who basically said, "We don't do any writing until the Fourth Step because that's what the instructions say." We did Steps One through Three in one sitting, meaning we talked about the nature of powerlessness and then did a Third-Step prayer on our knees. Then he said, "You're not leaving here until you begin to write your inventory, because the book says, 'Next, we launched out on a course of vigorous action.'" He was going to follow the Big Book to the letter, and given the state I was in at that time—my wife was threatening to leave me—I was not going to question any direction I received, so we started the list right there and then. Over the course of the next week, I finished the first-column list.

I transposed what I had written to a laptop because I liked to type, but when I went to him with the list on the laptop, he shut it and said: "We write. We don't type." And I was like: "Really? You're going to be that way to me?" He was like: "Yeah, use a

notebook. If you want what I have, we're going to do what I did."
So I went back and I wrote it out longhand.

Once I believed I had a pretty thorough accounting of the people, institutions, and principles with whom or which I was angry, he had me go back and we actually divided my life into five-year segments. I populated each segment with everyone I resented from those years. If mom showed up when I was eight and she showed up again when I was twenty-eight, I was to treat those separately because probably, the natures of the resentments were different. So I had multiple people show up multiple times as I went through my life. Even so, I was told I had the shortest list of anyone, but I think my sponsor told everybody that. There were about a hundred and fifteen names.

My sponsor had me write my list in a notebook that had three columns. Then, for each name on my list, from top to bottom, I was told to fill in the nature of the resentment and what in my life was affected by it. After that came something called "the turnarounds"—the real difference between the Big Book Step Study approach and what I would call traditional "check mark" inventory writing. After I had finished column three, I got to that part in the directions that said, "We need to be prepared to look at things from an entirely different angle." My sponsor gave me the directions five minutes before a meeting started, and he brought me to one corner of the room and said, "Look at the room." Then he brought me to another corner of the room and said, "Now look at it." He was into this sort of symbolic stuff; a turnaround meant trying to look at a situation in terms of our role in it. So, what I did then was start a new page for each of my resentments, and I would write the resentment across the top, along with the words "selfish," "dishonest," "self-seeking," and "fearful." Then I would write about how I was guilty of those behaviors in the case of that particular resentment.

It was really difficult. We all know how resentments feel self-righteous, so to try to look at my role in them was really hard, and that's where I was when I last drank. I was so frustrated with the writing and just hit a wall and went off on a two- or three-day drinkfest. When I came back, my sponsor said: "You need to keep writing. I don't need you to go to meetings and tell everybody that you relapsed. I need you to keep writing." And that's what I did, and that was the last time I drank.

One of my favorite expressions is "AA ruins your drinking." What that means is when you go out and drink again, you get the exact same results as before, and the despair gets deeper. I was in a dark place, but to hear somebody say to me, "You just gotta push through the writing; we're not going back to square one; you understand what you're up against here," it just . . . you know, I think it was desperation. Maybe despair turns into the humility required for insight. It wasn't like all of a sudden, the writing was easy. That wasn't the case. But I was clear on what needed to be done. If I was struggling with something, I needed to ask for help and not try to do it on my own. I would talk to my sponsor or someone else and say, "I'm struggling with this one," and he'd say, "Well, did you look at it this way?" Sometimes, you just need a nudge and it cascades from there. For whatever reason, I was able to push through.

The turnarounds are where a lot of the work is done. That's where most of my writing was and where a lot of the writing is painful, but I find it to be an important part of writing. For example, I got beat up in New York City by a bunch of kids when I was about fifteen. I was up there at Columbia University on a class trip. I was a white guy in a partially African American neighborhood and it was 1986 or whatever, so I got beaten up and I was in the hospital. So I had this resentment about it, and when I was writing my turnarounds, I said, "Wait a minute, I didn't do anything wrong!" It was very hard for me to look at it from their point of view and at what I represented to them as a rich white kid from northern New Jersey, walking around Harlem as if I owned the place. That sort of resistance happened a number of different times: I would just look at the paper and think, "Uh, I can't find my role in this." My brain didn't really want to work that way. So prayer at that point, for me, was really just an act of humility, an act of submission to the process.

After resentments, I wrote a fear inventory, which came out of my turnarounds, and then a sex inventory followed that, then a sex ideal. After I took a look at all my behavior with all those women and saw where I had been selfish and where my behavior had been abusive, the sex ideal meant trying to write the opposite of all that.

All in all, the writing took me about four months. You hear legendary stories of people doing their Steps in an afternoon at the beginning of AA. You wonder how anyone ever wrote a full inventory in an afternoon. The Big Book Step Study program involves a tremendous amount of writing, whether that's good or bad—my experience is constantly evolving, but I think if guys get bogged down in it, then that isn't productive. Perfection can be the enemy of progress, and so I think there's gotta be a point at which you say, "You've got enough here to get going and if you think of some things that you've missed, you can put them in, but we need to get on with the process." So that's kind of where my head is if I have somebody who's really bogged down in the writing. I've also had guys who've gotten too methodical, to the point where they were really just filling notebooks, and I thought: "You know, we're getting a little repetitive here. How do we find progress without conceding thoroughness?" That can be tricky.

When I read my inventory, something happens, I think, in the verbalizing that is different from the writing. I think when we are saying that stuff aloud to another human being and we're reading our words, it changes the impact. It brings our words to life, but it also transforms us a little bit. I'm not a mystical sort of guy, but something happened that day for me. Something changed in me that is very hard to put words around. I immediately felt relief. I wanted to go forward and not go back. I wanted to see what this life had to offer; up until that point I had not felt that way.

I look back at my Fourth Step now and I chuckle at some of the stuff that I have in there. I think when you're reading and sharing, it excavates a part of you. I think that the difference between writing it down and saying it out loud is like that between digging something up and actually showing it to somebody. I believe that is transformative. I really do.

"The Person I Really Am"

JULIE B.'S STORY

Julie describes her experience working through the Steps, writing inventory, and achieving lasting change as a result. She also compares writing inventory to writing stand-up comedy.

Julie's story contains references to suicidal ideation and childhood sexual abuse.

I was suicidal coming into treatment. I was out of money, and I really didn't have any options left. I was willing to do anything if it meant that I would not be a miserable person who wanted to die. In my first weeks at the treatment center, I wrote a daily journal. I took a lot of notes and wrote some pretty crazy stuff. [Laughs] I would write about the person who was conducting . . . you know, for instance, there was a woman who worked there who was very bubbly and pretty but younger than me, and I didn't like her at all, so I sat in the group and wrote, "God, she's so annoying! I can't stand this woman!" [Laughs]

But then, at the end of the day, I would go and I would write, and all these uncomfortable things were coming up. Not having the ability to self-medicate like I had been for years, I just had to feel that stuff. I found it really helpful to just write it out. I wrote it out, and it was like I left it there on the paper and I didn't have to keep feeling that way. As a child, I kept journals, and I found that it was the same as back then. If I was feeling negatively, a lot of times, if I could write it down, some of that discomfort eased and I was able to just leave it there on paper. But when I go back and read my treatment journal, I'm like, "Wow, I was feeling very uncomfortable." I wrote a lot about the people who worked there and about fellow people in treatment, and all about how crazy *they* were. [Laughs]

The difference between journaling and inventory is that I take a much harder look at myself in inventory, and I try to bring my higher power into it. I push myself more to look at the ways I'm conducting myself that don't align with the person I'd like to be, or that could harm other people, or that could ultimately come back around and bite me in the ass because I'm being dishonest. In the treatment center, they provided me with a prayer to put at the top of every page of inventory, and that was, "God, help me to see those things in myself that block me from you and others." And then I started with making a list of all the people, places, and things I was resentful toward, whether I was angry or it brought up some sort of feeling of discontentment. I had no trouble making that list. Like, I'm kind of a student by nature and I like to please people, so I wanted to write the best moral inventory ever. I started to write my list, and it was my parents at the top, down to the people who were most influential in my life, and even down to like a couple of people in elementary school and stuff like that. Then along came the list of the things each person on my list had done to me. Again, I had no problem whipping that out. Then it was on to the turnarounds.

With the turnarounds, I did start to have an experience pretty quickly as I was writing out where I was selfish, fearful, dishonest, and self-seeking. I think that having the prayer written down on the top of the page started to involve my higher power. I could read that prayer at times when I struggled. I had some trauma, some sexual abuse in my past when I was a young child, and so it was really difficult for me to write through. How was I selfish in being abused as a child? I had to sit down with someone, and they explained to me that it wasn't about where I was at at the time of the abuse but where I was at today. That really helped me not to relive the abuse but to look at the ways that I acted out on the abuse as an adult. But it was a very uncomfortable process. I did anything that I could to avoid writing, but at the same time, I wanted people to like me and to think I was doing a really good job. I would make sure I was seen writing all day, but then the first opportunity I got, when no one was looking, I was flirting with this guy or doing anything to get outside of myself. In hindsight, there was a real, direct correlation between my reaching out for attention from men and my need to avoid looking at some of this stuff.

Through writing and prayer, the process started to become really personal to me, and I was writing such personal stuff that it started to feel like I was forming a connection with a power outside of myself. I was asking for help, and I felt like I was starting to get that help. I found myself alone on this bathroom floor in treatment, saying a prayer with earnestness. I was like, "I need some help here." After that, the writing felt more fluid. Inventory just kind of flowed out of me. In the past, I had always been stifled when writing things about myself, but now I found that things just poured out of me when I put pen to paper. I also found that I no longer had that very familiar, lonely feeling. I didn't say, "Oh, this must be God." I just kind of let it be. There were times when I stopped to wonder if I was just tapping into something inside myself, but I concluded that if I was praying outside of myself, then I wasn't praying *to* myself.

I ended up writing five or six notebooks' worth just for my fourth column. It was really overwhelming. I felt very raw and incredibly exposed. I was having these constant revelations, and it was really heavy stuff. I didn't talk much about it. I kind of closed myself off, but it turned me back to prayer. Throughout my teenage and adult life—and, of course, when I was drinking— people always told me that I was crazy, but through inventory, I started to really see my insanity in black and white, on paper. It became less and less easy to lie to myself about where I was in my life. I couldn't run from it. It was just right there in front of me, and I started to acknowledge that, for one, I couldn't drink anymore, and two, my problems went a lot deeper than the fact that I drank too much.

In the process, I really did start to notice a big shift in my ability to be honest. I'm a liar. I was always an exaggerator. I found myself, for the first time in my life, stopping myself and asking, like, "Is this true?" I started to be aware that I was lying as opposed to not thinking twice about it. That was a big shift for me. Then, after I read my inventory, the buzzing in my head stopped. I always . . . and this probably had to do with the physicality of alcoholism, but I always had an audible noise in my head, like a buzzing, and I had some auditory hallucinations in the last several months of my drinking. There was just a lot of noise in my head. After I read my inventory, it was legitimately gone. The offshoot of that was being able to sit in morning meditation much more easily. And I was very open to the fact that I could really be a different person, more genuine to myself, which was a little overwhelming but also really exciting. And so, at thirty-two, I started to explore who I was in a way I never thought would happen. I had a pretty strong sense of myself, and inventory really shattered that and let me start over.

I became much more comfortable with who I was, even the physicality of how I felt in my body as a woman, or just in general. I started standing up taller. I changed the way that I talked to people. I started to have a real interest in other people and I genuinely wanted to learn about them. I would just stop and listen to other people. I found that I was able to actually shut up and listen. [Laughs] So, yeah.

Lately, I've been taking a comedy class. I've found writing comedy to be cathartic. Then, getting up there and reading my jokes is interesting. I get to see people's reactions to my life, and my teacher said: "Oh, you're an alcoholic? I can't wait to hear your stories." And I immediately thought, *I don't know if you want to hear those things.* I'm exploring how some of my stand-up can bleed into my inventory, but I haven't really gone there with it yet. I don't really know how to approach it. I don't know that crippling alcoholism is that funny to people. We laugh about it in meetings, but I don't know if a regular audience is going to find that stuff that amusing. It's pretty dark. [Laughs]

So far, my comedy's been about my dating life and finding myself at thirty-eight, living alone with two cats, and what it means for me to be this crazy cat lady. I work in an office, and I think a lot of times, people see me as a very conservative-appearing person. So, when I went to do my open mic, I wore my work outfit and kept my hair up to play that up a bit. When I got up there and started to talk about masturbation and being single for ten years and some of the crazy stuff I've done, I think it added to the comedy that I didn't look the part.

Actually, I think stand-up is similar to reading my first inventory. I wanted the person I read to to know me better, and maybe through having them know me better, I started to see myself differently. Taking this class and getting up in front of everyone to talk about myself . . . it's been all these revelations that I can walk through the world and be a certain way, but when I stand up in front of people and read something that is one-hundred-percent me, I'm telling them who I am. It's been interesting to see people react to my humor and to realize: "Oh, yeah. This is the person I really am."

28

WHY GOOD INVENTORY FEELS BAD, AND HOW BAD SPONSORS DO HARM

Even though moral inventory can be liberating, the process of writing one is not always an easy or pleasant experience. For some addicts, even thinking of the ways in which they have been "selfish, dishonest, self-seeking, and frightened" can be challenging. As Bob P. told me, he felt "a resistance" when writing the fourth column of his resentment inventory: "I would just look at the paper and think, 'Uh, I can't find my role in this.'" Another addict I spoke with told me, "It was hard to put a name to the things that I was most ashamed of in the resentment."

Some of the addicts I interviewed offered theories about why the discovery of moral shortcomings is so difficult. One explained to me his struggle with this process: "I just didn't have any practice looking for my own mistakes. What I had was a lifetime's habit of blaming other people for my troubles. So the idea that I was gonna set those people aside entirely and just look at myself? That was hard for me to do."

Another addict told me: "I had been so consumed and preoccupied with thinking about myself all the time that looking at my resentments from a different angle was really hard. When I finally did get the clarity to do that, I felt really disgusted."

In order to overcome the inertia of lifelong mental habits, many of the addicts I interviewed turned to their higher powers and asked for help in seeing their moral shortcomings. Most reported some kind of direct experience with "God" or "the Spirit" or something similar during their writing process, and most of these reports centered around the fourth column of Big Book resentment inventory. They told me this column "required power that [they] really didn't have," and so it made them reliant on prayer. As a result, prayer was often cited as a means of discovery. It allowed respondents to receive the ability to "actually see some sort of truth" about themselves that was otherwise inaccessible.

Many strongly associated truthful writing with a feeling of connection to spiritual power. "I was becoming stronger, but it didn't feel like I was building myself into something," one addict told me. "It felt more like I was stripping something away. And every layer that I stripped away, I was more connected to this universal power." Another described inventory writing as "a process of trying to minimize what is [their] voice in the situation and leaving it open to God to fill that space." When prayer or some other meaningful gesture of surrender was followed by sudden insight into a moral failing, these addicts felt that their higher powers were helping them complete their inventories.

These moments of contact with higher power were seen as spiritual, even though they were not particularly pleasant. In fact, the insights discovered in column four of resentment inventory generally produced uncomfortable emotions. The addicts I talked to described this column with phrases like "horrifying," "so painful," "didn't feel good," "made me sick of myself," "uncomfortable," "disgusted," and "gross." One suggested the experience was not as bad for her as it is for most addicts because, "I'm one of those people who feel like a shitbag anyway."

Somewhat counterintuitively, these negative feelings were often associated with positive experiences of change and growth. What felt "gross" and "uncomfortable" for the addicts

I interviewed was recognizing the extent of their character defects and the harm they had caused others, recognitions which, though painful, were also seen as a corrective to self-deceit and a motivation for change: "I think having to write it out and see it meant I couldn't lie to myself about it anymore. It made me want to not be that person," said one addict. "I got to see myself in a different way, as if I were somebody else, and I thought, 'Oh, I don't like this guy,'" said another. A third told me: "It wasn't this magical feeling of letting go but of, 'I am so sick of thinking like that.' I couldn't do it anymore." While these discoveries were unpleasant, they also produced a desire for a new way of being.

The discovery process of Big Book resentment inventory was difficult for most of the addicts I spoke with, but it was always the most difficult for those who had a history of trauma, especially when the object of their resentment was also the perpetrator of their abuse. Several addicts told me they wrote inventory about people who had abused them physically, sexually, and/or emotionally at different stages in their lives. For these resentments in particular, respondents found the Big Book's suggestion to look for their own "defects" problematic or even potentially harmful. Such a suggestion ran dangerously close to asking victims of abuse to blame themselves for the actions of their abusers.

Addicts with histories of trauma told me that they turned to their sponsors with these concerns and were told that the goal of resentment inventory was not to take responsibility for the wrongs of others but to see the whole truth of each resentment, including their character defects that stemmed from their history of abuse. These addicts found value in writing down their own harmful responses to abuse, not because it revised their history but because it allowed them to revise their *relationship* to that history. As one addict put it: "I'm not a victim anymore. I mean, I can't say people haven't hurt me or that I haven't been the victim of situations. It's important not to diminish what happened. But it is a really incredible feeling to wake up and know that no matter what events happened, I do have control over how I respond." After processing their resentments through moral inventory, these addicts no longer felt trapped in trauma-reactive coping mechanisms. Instead, they found a way to be open to their own vulnerability to abusive behavior without becoming defensive and causing harm to themselves or others. This new way of being in relation to histories of abuse did not alleviate all symptoms of trauma, but it empowered respondents to let go of their most problematic reactions.

The result of resentment inventory sometimes looks like forgiveness, sometimes like the empowerment of an abuse survivor, sometimes like a deep understanding of humans who hurt other humans, and sometimes like all of the above. While inventory always produces a degree of vulnerability, this never means willingly making oneself vulnerable to a particular abuser or to further abuse. However, I also heard stories from addicts with friends who failed to complete the inventory process due to the harm caused by abusive sponsors. Such sponsors used inventory like a club to emotionally beat their sponsees. This violence was never more harmful than when the abusive sponsor applied it to a sponsee already suffering from a traumatic past. As one addict told me:

> I know somebody who went back out because her sponsor kept telling her that she wasn't doing her Step work right if she couldn't take full responsibility for the abuse she'd experienced. And she went out, and it was bad. She was shooting meth when she'd never done hard drugs before. It was really, really bad. I talked to her before she went out, and she was struggling so much with what she was told. She was shocked when I said to her: "That's not your fault. That's not what that means." So I think when we're getting writing instruction—in the wrong hands, it can actually be damaging for people.

"A Blip in My Notebook"

BRITNI C.'S STORY

Britni describes the emergence of a new voice from their recovery writing: first during an intense and uncomfortable moment in the middle of their inventory process; then through a shift in the tone of their public writing; and finally, as they wrote a memoir and discovered compassion for their former self.

Britni's story contains references to sexual abuse.

When I went to treatment, I felt excited to write resentment inventory because I thought I would be able to prove that all my resentments were logical. I also didn't think I was angry at all. I thought I was just a really passionate person. But my inventory was really long. I ended up with ten notebooks. I wrote for six weeks and my resentment inventory was most of it. Actually, my conduct inventory was also pretty substantial.

In my resentment inventory, I had a really, really hard time with some of the resentments, like around "people who are anti-choice." I was having a hard time with the selfishness piece. The person I remember talking to about it the most was a man on the treatment staff. He got me to see that whether or not I thought they were right, I wasn't willing to even entertain their way of thinking. If they tried to talk to me about it, I would have shut them down without hearing them out, in the same way that I was accusing them of doing.

Then there was this weird . . . almost like a blip in the middle of my notebook somewhere. I stopped doing the turnarounds in the fourth column the way I was supposed to. I was in the dining hall, and most of my fourth column came down, like, "I'm full of shit and I'm a fraud," over and over again. That was the biggest pattern I saw, and I was trying to find every way I could possibly think of to write it: "I am filled with shit. I am full of shit. There is so much shit inside me." [Laughs] All that just to avoid writing the same thing over and over again, right? And—I don't even know how—I just started asking all these weird rhetorical questions, "Who the fuck do you think you are?" and, "Is this who you want to be?" It's like I was suddenly compelled to stop following the format and to write these things instead. Something just needed to come out on the page.

I had written similar kinds of questions inside my Big Book, throughout the "We Agnostics" chapter. I was an atheist coming in, and so a lot of my questions were about, "Who the fuck do you think you are?" and, "What are you so afraid of?"—they were those sorts of questions. When I wrote those in my Big Book, I actually felt myself crack. Like, I felt I was cracking open, and something in me was starting to shift. I was letting something in, and it tended to come out in the form of those questions to myself.

It was those same kinds of questions that came out at that point in my fourth column. It was really quick. It was only like two pieces of inventory that looked that way, and I don't even remember who they were about. It wasn't like I was writing inventory about being abused. It was just somewhere in the middle. It made no sense, but I couldn't stop writing questions like that, and I actually felt like I was being stabbed while it was happening. It was horrible and really painful. It was like a literal heartache. My chest hurt. I felt like something was being ripped open. I physically felt that pain while it was happening.

In the moment, it wasn't a good feeling, but for me, I needed to hurt so that I could be willing to change. I think I had to write all of my inventory . . . everything I had written before that was just so I could get to whatever happened in that blip. Whatever it was that I was compelled to write . . . I just needed to write it. This is where I start to sound weird because I think I was being compelled to write by God. [Laughs] A lot of people think that's fucking crazy! [Laughs] But my version of a higher power is not subtle. My higher power has to make it clear so that even I, this skeptical person, have to say, "Alright, there's something here, and I don't have to know what it is, but it's much bigger than me."

I will say I'm often referred to sponsor people who have trauma histories because I do trauma-informed Step work, and some of the ways that we talk about finding your part in the turnarounds can be really, really destructive in the hands of someone who doesn't understand how to interpret that for people who are childhood sexual abuse survivors, for example. Before I went to treatment, I had done a shit ton of work around not blaming myself for both the abusive relationship I had been in and my assault. So, as soon as I realized what was going to happen in the fourth column, I went to a staff member, and I was like, "I'm not doing this, absolutely not," and she was like, "Don't worry about it until you get there." She walked me through the process of saying, "It is not my fault what happened to me, it is not my fault that someone else chose to violate me or take advantage of me, but I can also acknowledge that I am responsible for the way I used my trauma to manipulate or hurt other people in the aftermath." It showed me that the coping mechanisms around my trauma were not helping me. They were hurting me, and they were hurting other people. So now, I do that work with other people. I will say: "That is a valid coping mechanism, and a super common one. And it has still caused harm." We are responsible for acknowledging the harm we cause, even if it came from a trauma-reactive response. We were hurt, and we hurt other people.

Writing and gaining that insight were valuable for me because putting it down in black and white was the only way to shatter the lies I told myself and the delusional beliefs I held about myself as a victim—and not just as a trauma victim, but as a victim in the sense of, "Why is everyone so mean to me? Why is my life so hard?" For example, I might think, "I can't believe that this girl was so horrible to me!" and then I'd write my fourth column and say, "I'm dishonest; I slept with her boyfriend." [Laughs] "Why does that guy hate me?" Well, I spilled a beer on his head! [Laughs] I had to lie to myself in order to continue to see the world in that distorted way. So seeing the truth in black and white, over and over and over again, was really—for me—necessary. After having to write it out and see it, I couldn't lie to myself about it anymore. And through that process, it made me want to not be that person anymore.

I am someone who has always written. I blogged before I got sober. I had a pretty extensive online following. But after rehab, there was a period when the only thing I was capable of writing was inventory. I had absolutely no motivation to write essays, which I had always written. I let my blog lapse. The domain expired and I chose not to renew it. It felt like a good opportunity to let that part of me go. Then, when I finally could write again, it was a different voice. It didn't even sound like I was the same writer. The old voice was really cynical and snarky, and my humor was at other people's expense. I wrote for shock value. It was never blatantly untrue, but I exaggerated a lot. Then, when I started to write again, my voice was more lyrical. There was a different cadence. It flowed differently. It was like I had writer's block for a year. I wasn't ready to write yet. When I was ready—when it was the right time—it just sort of poured out. I felt like God was with me.

I'm working on my memoir, and I still have parts of my life that are really horrible to write about and it feels a lot like writing inventory, but writing is cathartic for me now. It's sometimes uncomfortable, but in general it's not. It feels like I know who I am and I'm okay with it. Although, I've taken a bunch of classes and workshopped material for my memoir, and every time people read my work, they tell me that I don't have enough compassion for my younger self on the page. I'm too hard on her. That is difficult for me because I went through a very tough-love rehab environment. I really don't have a lot of compassion for my younger self because she's kind of a shitty person. I recognize that I was deeply lost and troubled and flawed and genetically predisposed and all of those things, so I'm trying to find a way to both communicate that I was actually a crappy person and still find compassion for the younger me.

Writing this memoir is challenging me to broaden the way I think about who I was. I'm so far removed from that person that I don't need somebody to be harsh with me to try to inspire some kind of change. I can take a wider lens and recognize that I was a really shitty person, but also that I was a good friend sometimes and I loved singing at the top of my lungs in the car—I mean, all of those things are pieces of who I was that are endearing, and they paint me as the person under all the trauma and addiction. No one's all bad, really. We're all complicated, so I think that's a way to complicate my narrative.

How to Write
Big Book Fear Inventory

When Piers first taught me to write fear inventory, he told me to make three columns in my notebook. In the first column, I was to list everything I was afraid of, big or small. My worry about a friend's opinion of me and my terror of global nuclear annihilation both deserved a place on this list. In the second column, I was to answer the question, "Why does this thing I've named scare me?" In the third, I was to ask myself why again, this time, "Why are the things I've listed in the second column such a problem for me?" He said I could continue this process of asking why until I felt that I had reached the root source of each fear.

I wrote fear inventory this way for many years, until I reached a period of anxiety that would not yield to this approach. My girlfriend was pregnant, I had just graduated from college, and I had no idea how to make a living or support a family. I was filled with anxiety, and no matter how many times I got to the "root" of this anxiety—by discovering, for example, that I was afraid of failure, of not being a real "man," of losing my soon-to-be wife and child, and so on—it still preoccupied me constantly. So I made two changes. First, I stopped drinking coffee, which settled my nerves considerably (I was drinking a *lot* of coffee). Second, I turned back to the Big Book's discussion of fear and noticed its comments about self-reliance and God-reliance (quoted in the previous chapter). The book's main point about fear is that it stems from our efforts to control things we cannot control, so the answer to fear is to discover what we need to surrender, then let it go.

My problem wasn't just that my fears had deep roots in my psychology. My problem was that I really believed I had to control my life in order to control the future. Because it's not possible to control things like "my life" and "the future," this belief was causing me a lot of needless stress. But fear is sticky. It's hard to pull out of a fear-based obsession once it takes hold. The only way out was for me to surrender. I had to trust that my higher power would do a better job taking care of my family and my future than I could. In a manner of speaking, I had to put those things in my "God Box," close the lid, and walk away. The result of this discovery was a return of inner peace. And so I've written my fear inventory in these four columns ever since (see table on next page).

To write fear inventory this way:

1. Start by listing all your fears—all the things that cause you worry, stress, panic, paranoia, or terror. These will make up your first column.
2. Fill in the second column by stating why you have each fear. What makes it so scary? And why are those things frightening to you? What might you lose? How might you be harmed?
3. For the third column, look at your thinking and behavior in places where you are relying on your own reason or willpower to do the impossible. What are you trying to control? How are you trying to control it?
4. In your fourth column, ask your higher power to give you insight into how to be different, and write down whatever insights come. What would your life look like without fear? What does surrender look like in this situation?

Fear	Why do I have it?	Where am I self-reliant?	God, what would you have me be?
Raising a family	I don't know how to afford it. I don't want to be a bad parent. If I fail, it means I'm incompetent as a man. I'll lose my wife and kid if I screw this up. I don't know if I could handle that loss and still stay sober.	I'm trying to predict and control my future. I really think I have to figure out how to get the perfect job that solves all my problems. I'm trying to be a perfect parent and our kid isn't even born yet.	Patient, kind. Pay attention to what your wife needs from you in the present and leave the future to me. Trust me that I have good things in store for you, and that you will learn a lot along the way. It really is going to be okay.

"The War Is Over"

PETE B.'s STORY

An early member of Narcotics Anonymous on the East Coast, Pete, describes his efforts to work the Steps in a transitional time for that fellowship. As addicts in NA adapted the Twelve-Step program from AA, they produced their own literature and their own ways of writing inventory.

The second meeting I went to in NA was a Step meeting, where we read from the AA book *Twelve Steps and Twelve Traditions*. I got really involved with that one. I had just had my last relapse, and this guy George told me that the best thing you can do is get involved, so I became the secretary for this meeting and made coffee for another one. At my second or third meeting as secretary, they had a group conscious meeting afterward. George was the General Service Representative. He said that word had come down from Area Services that they wanted NA groups to stop using AA literature in their meetings. This was before the NA Basic Text had been written.

We were like, "What are we supposed to use?"

George said, "Well, there's some talk of an NA book, but until then we can use anything that's written by addicts."

I think George thought we'd just stop having a Step meeting and make it a discussion meeting instead. But the group said: "Well, why don't we meet in Kenny's apartment? We won't call it an official NA meeting, but we'll go through the *Twelve and Twelve*. We'll do a different chapter each week, we'll record people's comments, and Pete can write it all down." I could type sixty-five words a minute, so I was game for it. And that's what we did. We held the meetings, and I would transcribe the recordings. A lot of people came to those meetings, and we went through each Step and we went through the Traditions. We'd read a few paragraphs, then go around the room so people could share what that Step meant to them. I would record what everybody said, and then I'd take it back to my apartment and transcribe and edit it. Then I'd bring the edited transcript to the next Step meeting, and that's what we read in the meeting.

It was a really exciting time, but I was crazy as a bed bug, and there was nobody around who had actually experienced the Twelve Steps. At least nobody I knew in my area. I asked one guy to sponsor me, and we got up through the Fifth Step. After the Fifth Step, he let me know: "That's as far as I've gotten, so that's as far as I can take you." So, you know, that's as far as I got too. For inventory, he said to just read the *Twelve and Twelve* and write whatever I wanted. It was almost like this whole drama of my active addiction all spilled out on the paper. In sharing that inventory, I was able to admit a couple of big, big things that I thought I would carry to my grave. When I learned that we weren't going to go any further—that he hadn't experienced the Sixth Step, and there wasn't anyone else around—it was devastating to me. I was really feeling this powerful spiritual thing, and then I just hit this brick wall.

That was my big problem: finding recovery in NA. To all appearances, I was one of the people who knew more about this stuff, but it was evident my life was not one of somebody in recovery. Especially in my third year. If there was ever a point in my life where I was close to a fully fledged sex addiction, it was then. I was just out of control. It was so painful. And it wasn't even about getting high or not because I didn't really obsess about that too much after the first few months. It was just that compulsive lifestyle. There was a term, "clean and crazy." That was me.

It took me three years before I found an NA group that used the AA Big Book, and that group clearly was different from all the others that I'd seen all over the country. The reason that group was different was that they had actual recovery going on there. They had actually been through the Steps. I made that my homegroup for a while, but they got kicked out of NA. Members would share in meetings that they found recovery through the Twelve Steps and that their sponsors took them through the AA Big Book. That was everyone's experience in that group. When the NA Area Services in Philadelphia said they needed to stop doing that, people said, "Well, we can't alter our experiences," so Area Services removed them from the meeting list. After that, we became "Addicts Anonymous."

My sponsor used the Big Book. We went all the way through it and that was the only reference that was used. I got together with him at his place, and we went through everything in the Big Book that leads up to the Third Step prayer. He guided me like: "Go home. Find a quiet place where you're not going to be disturbed. Get into a humble position, whatever that is for you." He didn't say, "Hit your knees." He said, "Whatever a humble position is for you," and he said, "With all the sincerity you can muster, say that Third Step prayer." He stressed how selfishness and self-centeredness are the key to the problem—the spiritual malady that we suffer as addicts. That Third Step prayer unlocks that and shows you a way out. You're not doing this so you can get better; you're doing this so that you can be in a position to help others. It's not for yourself. It's not for your own aggrandizement. It's so that victory can help you to help someone else. That was a revelation to me. For years, that had been my problem. I was trying to help me, but I didn't understand that I could get well not just to have a great life but so that I could help the next person. That was what I was missing. All this activity that I'd done . . . but I didn't have the spiritual understanding that there were still selfish motives behind what I was doing and that I had to free myself from them.

That prayer led us into the Fourth Step inventory. My sponsor's group at that time used a Fourth Step guide that they had adapted somehow. They had a very firm grasp of what's in the Big Book, but they didn't go through inventory exactly the way it's laid out in the book. They had you read that part, so you got the idea, but they had boiled it down into a much simpler guide. I've learned much later that the guide had been made for one guy who was having a hard time grasping the way it's laid out in the Big Book. I guess the new guide worked with him, so they just started using that.

And it worked for me too. It was very simple, and I think that its simplicity was the key to why it worked. I wasn't encouraged to write a book. I was encouraged just to look honestly and go through the guide. It was pretty revealing for me. I had the realization, going through the process, that a lot of my dramas and everything else were my attempts to run away from who I was. I had this realization that my life had all been an act. It was an act because I was afraid of who I was. After that, everything settled down for me. I met the girl I'm still married to today. I got a job, and I'm still working for the same outfit today. And it all came from just accepting who I was and accepting life on life's terms.

The actual inventory process from that guide was extremely simple. I had written all kinds of stuff before, but I would get lost in it all. I couldn't separate what was ego from what was anything else. It was just all mixed up. They had me write my views of my relationships with the most significant person in my life, family and friends, power, position, money, my job, sex, and God. They had me write in the past and in the present for each, so I had two columns: one for the past, one for the present. And then, under the past column, I wrote the negative aspects of my relationship with each of those different people or things, and then the positive aspects. Then, again, in the present, the negative and positive aspects. Again, it really had nothing to do with what's in the Big Book. It doesn't go into resentment and all that.

At that time, it was right on time for me. It was what I needed. It wasn't a long, involved process. I probably spent two or three weeks on it because he said, "Take your time." I was working, so I would write when I had some time. I worked through each section, and then, when I thought I was done writing, I asked him what was next, and he said, "The Fifth Step."

I was living with my parents in New Jersey at the time. I took the high-speed line into Philadelphia, and he picked me up. We went to his apartment. I started reading, and then it became a conversation. He shared some things about his own experience. He made me feel very at ease. It was so different from my first Fourth and Fifth Step. There was very little drama in this one. It really felt like more of a fact-finding process, like it talks about in the Big Book.

My sponsor wasn't given to hyperbole at all, but when he was driving me back to the high-speed line, he pulled up to the curb, looked at me, and he said: "Peter, the war is over. Peace has been declared upon the land, my friend." And that was exactly the way I felt. I'd had this war in my mind. I was a real headcase. I had a lot of things banging around upstairs, but after that, I just felt no urgency. The desperation was gone. I felt like everything was going to be fine. And it was! No matter what happened. They stressed that the most important thing that you can do is develop a working relationship with your higher power and the Steps were the way to do it. That's exactly what happened for me.

How to Write
Steve's Kitchen Inventory

Pete shared the instructions for his style of inventory writing with me. He still had the paper menu from Steve's Italian Kitchen, where he and his sponsor had met to discuss the process. On the back side of that menu, in pencil, his sponsor had written down instructions and an example of how to write this new form of inventory. To my knowledge, these instructions have never been printed in any official NA literature or regional pamphlets. They were passed down only by word of mouth (and pencil on paper menus) from sponsor to sponsee. Here are the instructions, as they were recorded on the back of that menu:

My view of my relationship with
1. The most significant person in my life right now
2. Family, friends
3. Power, position, money, job
4. Sex
5. God

Answer all topics, past and present, including positive and negative.

(<u>Example</u>)

God

Past	Present
<u>Negative</u> – I hated God. I blamed God for everything. I was also superstitious about God and scared of him.	<u>Negative</u> – Starting to understand and love God more and more, but still don't completely trust Him.
<u>Positive</u> – I hated God but did not want to hate God. I just did not know how to love God.	<u>Positive</u> – I am now gradually trusting and liking of God more and more and I am tired of mistrusting and hating God and now have a desire to love Him more and more.

29

CONDUCT INVENTORY

In Pete's story, we have an example of a relatively new fellowship (early NA) creating its own form of moral inventory. This is a common occurrence in Twelve-Step culture, where the emergence of fellowships is frequent, and each emerging fellowship must interpret the Steps for a new population of addicts. This process often results in new forms of recovery writing.

But the process can go the other way around too. Sometimes, a new kind of inventory produces a fellowship. This is what happened in the case of "conduct inventory," a repurposing of Big Book sex inventory for the examination of a broader set of behaviors. Conduct inventory's growing popularity in a mid-sized New England city led to a new meeting—the first of its kind—that was not part of any other, existing Twelve-Step fellowship.

Conduct inventory, as practiced by the addicts I spoke with, began when Mazie, a heroin addict and recovery professional, was still in her first months of abstinence. She had just finished rehab but was still living on the treatment center's campus, doing odd jobs. Mazie described her state of mind at the time as somewhat fragile, and she found that a new addiction was emerging, now that she was abstinent from heroin: "I was probably a month sober, and I was eating like a crackhead. I couldn't stop eating. There was a quality to it that felt like drugs to me, and I knew there was something more going on, and it scared the living daylights out of me." But Mazie kept her struggle to herself, hoping she would find a way to resolve it without having to tell anyone else.

During this time, Mazie met Anne, an alcoholic and special education teacher, who told a story about trying to quit smoking. Anne was very frustrated that she was abstinent from alcohol but couldn't stop lighting up. When Anne told her sponsor, he said, "Well, why don't you take a look at your relationship with smoking through the inventory process?" And that idea—a second-hand suggestion from Anne's sponsor—excited something in Mazie: "He called it a *relationship*. That is what stuck out to me. It would be like writing sex inventory, but rather than a relationship to a person, she wrote about her *relationship* to smoking." With that insight—that sex inventory could be applied to other kinds of relationships—Mazie felt she had found a possible way out of her disordered eating. Without any further help or instruction, Mazie began to write privately about her relationship with food: "I just used the sex inventory questions, but instead of a person's name, I wrote things like 'squirreling doughnuts in my pocketbook.'"

A few months after Anne's visit, Mazie was hired to the staff of the treatment center where she had been living. One of her clients, Dorothy—an alcoholic and a nurse—showed signs of struggling in the same way Mazie had. Dorothy entered treatment as an alcoholic and got sober only to find that her eating was spiraling out of control. She found herself binging, purging, restricting, and over-exercising: "I got into a really dark space where I couldn't go more than a couple of days without these behaviors. I was absolutely miserable in sobriety. I was suicidal, and so I drank." When Dorothy returned to treatment, Mazie taught her to write what she then called "food inventory," using the Big Book's questions about sex.

Dorothy and Mazie both told me that at first, they were drawn to writing an inventory of their relationship with food because they thought it would give them control over their compulsive eating. Here's how Mazie described it:

I started writing this inventory because I wanted to solve my problem. I wanted the act of writing inventory to make the behavior stop. It has taken me many, many years to understand that that's not how it really works. I can't write my way out of my behavior. The writing just shows me what's in my way, and then how to bring God into all that stuff.

Dorothy came to exactly the same understanding. She told me that after two years of writing food inventory in an effort to control her behavior, she discovered that for the inventory to be effective, it needed to become a means to surrender:

> Before, I had told myself, "Well, what I should really do is write more conduct inventory and stop these behaviors." But now, I was like, "No, what I really need is God's help with the fact that I binge eat whenever I feel insecure, or I'm not happy at my job, or I can't make a decision."

The goal was not control, but *connection*.

The first addict Dorothy sponsored in conduct inventory was Kerry M., a drug addict and treatment professional. Like Mazie and Dorothy, Kerry struggled to recover from drug addiction because, for her, sobering up always meant acting out in other ways: "My many previous attempts at sobriety were characterized by the same sort of downward spiral of events, including my sex conduct and my history with body dysmorphia and eating disorders." Kerry was encouraged by Dorothy to start her conduct inventory process with a formal act of surrender, as she recalled:

> I hit my knees and said a prayer. I just begged God in that moment, like, "I don't care what you do to me, but please just help me get through this so I can help other people to not have to go through what I'm going through."

After this prayer, Dorothy taught Kerry to write conduct inventory and emphasized that this inventory was to be a means of bringing higher power into new areas of her life. From the beginning, Kerry was sponsored to treat inventory as a means of contact rather than control. The results were significant:

> For the first time in my life, after like nine years of trying to get better, I got beyond the inventory. When I read it, nothing dramatic happened. It wasn't until a couple of months down the line when I looked back, and I was like: "Holy shit! I'm okay! I'm alright!" Then I started really doubling down on my efforts in trying to help people and spreading the message. The sponsorship stuff became really important to me and so central to my recovery.

Kerry began speaking about her struggles with behavioral issues in AA meetings, and she found that she was not alone: "People started coming out of the woodwork, saying, 'Me too.'"

Bailey was the first to ask Kerry for help with her disordered eating and issues with spending. Like Kerry, Bailey found that making a surrender and writing inventory about these areas of her life profoundly changed her behavior. With Bailey in recovery, there were now four women writing some version of "sex" inventory to address their relationships with sex, food, body image, and money. When they shared their experiences in meetings and made themselves available as "conduct sponsors," other addicted women reached out to them for help, many of whom then served as conduct sponsors to still other women. Before long, conduct inventory was not just the practice of a small group. It had spread well beyond Mazie, Dorothy, Kerry, and Bailey. Women they had never met were writing and teaching others to write repurposed sex inventory for all kinds of relationships and behaviors.

Kerry told me that she and the other women I interviewed noticed a trend in the now loosely organized conduct-inventory community: women new to the writing practice often used it as Mazie and Dorothy did at first, that is, as a means of self-control rather than as a way to surrender. As Kerry put it:

The more people who reached out for help, the more we saw a need to standardize the process. We realized that people were referring to conduct work as inventory—just inventory. And so all these people were shuffling all these other people through an inventory, and then they wouldn't take it any further. We realized that everybody's doing these Fourth Steps [i.e., writing inventory], but nobody's really taken a Third Step [i.e., making a surrender and entering relationship with a higher power]. So when I say "standardize the process," I mean we are more deliberate about it, and the questions that we ask are pretty specific: "Are you powerless around this? Are you sure you need to surrender? And how do you know?"

Kerry told me that she, Dorothy, and Bailey decided to further standardize the process by starting a meeting, and that meeting is now a hub of activity for women in need, who write—and teach each other to write—conduct inventory as a means of surrender.

How to Write

Conduct Inventory

Even though the addicts who invented and popularized this kind of writing are all women, conduct inventory can be a useful exercise for anyone. Conduct inventory is a creative adaptation of Big Book sex inventory for the purpose of examining relationships more broadly as opposed to just sexual relationships. In fact, we can use this inventory to examine more than just our relationships with other humans. It can also reveal things about our relationships with substances (like Anne's relationship with smoking) and behaviors (like the others' relationships with disordered eating). To give a sense of the scope of conduct inventory, Bailey shared a list with me that covers all the different kinds of relationships their meeting was meant to address:

- Body Image
  - Overeating
  - Over-exercising
  - Restriction
  - Bulimia
  - Anorexia
  - Supplements
- Relationships/Sex
  - Codependency
  - Balancing of relationships

- Money
  - Overspending
  - Frugal
  - Gambling

As you can see, this format can be applied to a wide range of problematic relationships—with humans, behaviors, and substances.

Each of the addicts I interviewed about conduct inventory had a slightly different interpretation of the Big Book format. Here is the one Dorothy described to me, with her example, on the opposite page.

To write conduct inventory:

1. First, identify a problematic relationship in your life in the area(s) of body image, human relationships (including sex), and/or money.
2. Then, list all the problematic behaviors that emerge from that relationship for you. Anything you do in that relationship that is unhealthy physically, spiritually, or emotionally should go on the list. This list will become the first column of your conduct inventory.
3. Fill out the rest of the columns in Dorothy's format above for each item on your list.
4. As always, prayer and meditation will be helpful in an inventory process like this. The goal here is to surrender and make contact with a power that can guide you into a new relationship with whatever person, substance, or behavior you are writing about.
5. And, as always, it is best if you have a sponsor or otherwise a trustworthy, understanding friend to share your discoveries with. Recovery writing is always a way of preparing to take action, including the action of talking to others about what we've learned.
6. If Dorothy's format doesn't quite work for you, you may instead try these questions, which Bailey said are used in conduct inventory meetings (her example is included on page 216).

Food behavior	Selfish, Dishonest, Inconsiderate	Who else was affected?	Suspicion, Bitterness, Confusion	What is this really about?	How can I become God-reliant?
Told husband we needed a scale because "I was worried I was losing weight."	Selfish: Obsessively thinking about my weight makes me not available to anyone. Dishonest: Lied to husband. I've never been worried about losing weight in my life. Inconsiderate: Having a scale in the house causes husband to worry that I'm obsessing about my weight.	Husband, co-workers, sponsor, sponsee, friends, other members of conduct group	Suspicious: Husband questioning my motives and wondering why I'm in the bathroom so much. Bitterness: Once husband realizes I lied, sponsees because I lied, sponsees because I'm talking about transparency but lying. Confusion: Husband because I told him I can't have a scale in the house, sponsees when I say I'm recovered from food issues but still struggle.	Feeling loss of control with my fertility issues. If I can control a number on a scale and that provides relief. Needing a secretive behavior to focus on so I don't feel pain and loss of being unable to get pregnant. Wanting inward pain to show outwardly.	Pray to tell husband the truth about the scale and throw the scale out. Ask for support for the loss I am feeling. Attend infertility support group. Write more inventory about small behaviors around food before acting out.

215

What happened?	Who was affected?	Arousal of suspicion/ confusion?	Selfish, Dishonest, Self-seeking, Inconsiderate	What is this really about?	What to do differently?
Purged at lunch break at work.	Co-workers Patients	Took longer than 30 minutes on lunch break.	Selfish: Need to feel that compulsion and feel thinner instantly. Dishonest: Lying about why I took so long. Self-seeking: I want to be seen as healthy, thin, and beautiful. Inconsiderate: Leaving my covering nurse longer than I should and putting patients at risk being away longer as a primary nurse.	Needint to undo the damage of starting to eat and not being able to stop. Not being able to sit in discomfort.	Pray through discomfort. Pray before meals. Meal planning. Not relying on what's available (or unhealthy foods).

30

READ AND PRAY, THEN WRITE AGAIN

When I finished writing my inventory—of resentments, fears, and sex—Piers and I set a date for me to read it to him. This was an anxious wait for me. Not that I was particularly excited about making a confession, but I had two or three notebooks full of the worst things about myself—all my selfishness in one place—and I began to worry that I would die and someone would find my notebooks. My last message to the world, to everyone named on one or more of my lists, would be a frighteningly vulnerable testimony. I started carrying my inventory with me everywhere I went. This way, there were at least some scenarios in which my death would destroy my inventory too. But the weeks leading up to my meeting with Piers were completely uneventful, and when the day came, I had my inventory at hand.

Piers came over with an apple and reclined on the spare bed that I had wedged into the kitchenette of my two-room apartment. I sat across the room at my little table with my notebooks. He told me just to read everything verbatim from the page, without any deviation, explanation, or storytelling. Just read what I'd written. No embellishment. He wanted the facts.

While Piers crunched on his apple, I spilled my guts. Every resentment, fear, and sexual foible, every moment of selfishness, and every lie . . . I just read straight through it all without stopping.

Several hours later, when I was finally done, Piers told me a few things from his own inventory. I think he wanted to let me know that I wasn't alone in keeping the weird and horrid secrets

I'd been keeping. I was just another addict, who did a bunch of stupid, selfish, hurtful things like all the rest of us.

Piers told me to spend the next hour alone in quiet meditation. I could take a walk or a bath or whatever. But the point was to focus on what I'd read, and to pray about it. If I had left anything out, on purpose or by accident, I should call him and get it off my chest. After the hour was up, I was to read a specific prayer from the Big Book and ask my higher power to remove the things that were keeping me from being useful to others.

I did take a bath. And I did have a think. Somehow, I was expecting to feel *really different* after I read my inventory—like eat-a-sheet-of-acid different, or Buddha-attains-enlightenment different—but I didn't. The sky didn't part. The face didn't fall off reality, and no cosmic secrets were revealed in their full, ineffable awesomeness. I did not become a perfect being with a perfect mind. Instead, I just felt grounded, lighter, comfortable.

Nothing else came to mind that I should confess, so when the hour was up, I read the prayer from the Big Book out loud, and that was that.

The next morning, I woke up a bit earlier than usual and went to the kitchen to start my coffee. While it brewed, I sat at my kitchen table. The birds were singing outside. A very pleasant early morning light filtered through the branches of the tree outside and played over my kitchen floor. I poured my coffee and waited for it to cool down. The birds sang. The light played. Steam rose from my cup. It was beautiful.

I don't know how long I sat in that state of absorption in the beauty of everyday things, but it all came to a sharp halt when I suddenly realized what I was doing: I was just sitting there! I wasn't thinking about anything at all. I was just *happy*. I couldn't remember having a morning like this ever before in my entire life. I had long grown accustomed to waking up and wishing that I'd died in my sleep. Eventually, I would drag myself from bed when my depression was overpowered by my craving for caffeine. As I slowly returned to full consciousness, my mind would flood with all of the many, many things I loathed about the world and the people in it. I would remember everything I had to do that day, and all the people I had to see. It was all so painful to me.

But not this morning. This morning, it was all birds and sunbeams and coffee steam, without a thought or a care in the world. I started to think over my responsibilities for the day, but nothing stood out as particularly burdensome. I thought about the people I would probably see. I no longer resented any of them, and I no longer feared their opinion of me. They were just people, stuck in their own struggles in life. Same as me. It would not be a chore to see them.

That morning initiated a period of about three months when I felt no fear and could not cop a resentment if I tried. You could have stepped on my foot and spit in my face, and I would have thanked you for the opportunity to deepen my capacity for compassion. Most days, thoughts came and went in an even flow, without ever pulling me into inner turmoil. When I did get stuck on something, it wasn't long before I realized what was happening and let it go again.

Once, I was walking to the bagel shop and started worrying about what people might think about my hair. I got really wrapped up in that worry for a minute and became oblivious to my surroundings. *Man, I must look so dumb*, I thought. *Those bagel shop people sure are going to have a laugh.* I hadn't even had a haircut or anything. I just suddenly felt sorry for myself because of my hair for some reason, and this new focus completely hijacked my mood.

I kept plodding along, completely distracted, when a bumble bee flew smack into my forehead. It bounced off and hovered in front of my face for a second. We made eye contact. Then it bumbled off again. Just like that, I was out of my head and in the world again. And I could see how silly it was of me to get wrapped up in a petty fear like that. Life was hard for everyone, I reasoned.

At least if my hair was funny, it would take people's minds off their suffering for a minute. And anyway, people were usually so busy with their own worries and pain that no one would even think twice about my appearance. Probably, my hair was just fine.

Those months were so tranquil, no matter what was going on around me. But—and I still feel the loss as I write this—as time passed, my bliss faded. Normal life returned, and eventually, I got hung up on fears and resentments all over again. The girl I liked wasn't treating me the way I thought she should. So I wrote some more inventory about my resentment. The resentment inventory uncovered some fears, so I wrote about those too. And because I wanted a sexual relationship with this woman, I wrote a bit of sex inventory as well. I prayed, I wrote, and I saw where I was being an asshole. I called up Piers, and he came over. It turned out he'd had an argument with his girlfriend too. We read inventory to each other, and peace of mind returned once again— not perfect-mental-tranquility peace, not bee-flies-into-your-forehead peace, but an everyday peace. A solid peace. A workable, grounded peace.

And I could return to that peace of mind anytime I needed to. Just by writing a few things down.

"Allowing It to Bubble Up"

Samuel F.'s Story

Samuel describes the difference between his first moral inventory and his second, under new sponsorship. He also describes the benefits and the challenges of using school writing to research the historical and theological context of his own inventory experience, as well as a potential remedy for perfectionism in the form of automatic writing.

The second time I went through the Steps, it was as per *Big Book Awakening* by a guy named Joe Hawk. He developed this form of the Steps that is basically a companion workbook to the Big Book, and basically, its main device is that it turns all the statements of the Big Book into questions and asks you to, like, apply them to yourself, in your own life. It's very writing-intensive. The first part of it is to write out your story, and then later there are other writing practices like making a list of character defects, which involves looking up the definitions, looking up the antonyms, and just keeping that on record for use in your inventory writing. It's like a hundred and fifty adjectives, basically. It's really trying to be as precise as possible with the defects and with their antonyms, so you can pray for the opposite of each defect you have. There is also an exercise that is to identify what your higher power used to be, what it's like now, and what you would like it to be.

Then, the way they have you write inventory is different from what I did the first time I went through the Steps from the Big Book. You write a prayer, you write the name of the person you resent, you write the details of the resentment, and then there's this technique in the third column: Each of the categories in the Big Book—pocketbook, personal relations, pride, self-esteem, and so on—correlates to what he calls "absolutes" that we hold about the world. For example, if a resentment affects my pride, the absolute might be: "I know I need to be loved and adored everywhere I go, and if I'm not and if people aren't fawning over me at every second, then I'm going to be a mess. I'm miserable." And then a self-esteem absolute would be, like, "I really know everything about the world, and it's unfortunate that other people don't know that." [Laughs] The idea is that it's like "king baby mode." It makes you realize how entitled you are and how you are guided by all these misconceptions about the world that are nonetheless formative of your experience. When you start to write them down, you start to realize how silly it is, and it's supposed to inspire laughter at the fact that you take yourself so seriously and that you go through life this way.

I actually find this really difficult to do because I actually don't really like it. [Laughs] I have been having a hard time with it because I don't want to be a "bad sponsee," quote unquote. I want to be able to set aside my anticipation of what the outcome is going to be and just allow myself to have a new experience with inventory, but I've never been comfortable with it because I don't think it's specific enough. I feel like the way that I first learned inventory was very, very specific and it taught me things about myself that this form of inventory seems to . . . it just makes me feel like an asshole, basically. So I've made an adjustment: I make the absolutes more targeted to the specific resentment. I write them out as more like mistakes in my thinking, like, "I need to punish this person for what they did to me," or, "If I don't have a perfect girlfriend, I'll never be happy." So, in the way I do it, they're not really absolutes that I hold about the world. They are mistaken thoughts I have about other people, which I actually find really helpful because they refer to my own specific situation and my particular resentment. The other strategy is so general that it just paints the story of a big baby who's mad at the world in general.

The most powerful thing about my recovery has been the inventory-writing process as I first learned it, and I will never stop writing inventory that way, so I've basically taken what I need and left the rest behind with respect to this new style. My relationship with inventory for a long time was that I would have a lot of static in my head after I hadn't written inventory for a while, and then I would just write it all down and then feel this surprising calmness. That was really, really interesting because I was like, "Oh my god, the static is gone!" As I was writing inventory, I was writing out things that I already knew but were just below the threshold of consciousness and were being interpreted in my head as static, as this vague anxiety. But as soon as I wrote them down, it was like, "Oh, this is exactly what's going on!" It was so precise that it was really interesting. In many ways, I've been trying to get back to that level of enthusiasm that I had when I first wrote inventory. I mean, I saved all my inventory from that period, and I have suitcases full of it. I think one of the funny things about the rehab I went to was that it *so* emphasized writing. It was like: "Have you written about this? No? Well, don't talk to me, asshole! Go do your writing!" [Laughs] It was a little extreme in a way, but it was this technique to help me be able to unforget or to reveal what I already knew about myself *to* myself.

Although, philosophically and metaphysically, the question about inventory is this: Am I just raising my awareness to such a degree that I am now able to see things whereas formerly I was blinded by routine and ordinary patterns of thought? Or is there really some sort of intervention on the part of a deity, however it is conceived—like the divine as consciousness or some kind of reservoir of consciousness that I'm tapping into or something? I don't know. Early in recovery, I was exploring the latter option really seriously. I was taking the God option really seriously, and in recent years, now that I'm getting a divinity degree, I've sort of walked back from that and become more disenchanted.

My schoolwork has been an exploration of my conversion experience or my recovery as an event. So I consider my professional life to be pretty intimately tied to my recovery that way, in that I've been basically just writing papers that have been trying to unearth the history of that experience and to trace a genealogy that explains the lineage I am in. All my papers were about Alcoholics Anonymous—AA history, the Oxford Group, all about the links with New Thought and therapeutic culture. I really dug into that literature.

So, my studies have been really great, but they have also made some things much harder. For example, when I first learned that God could be an experience and not an entity, that idea really, really worked for me. And then I read this whole genealogy of people turning to experience to sort of find some sort of religious legitimacy amidst Enlightenment rationalism, and everything became historicized and couched in this academic distance that loses a lot of the spirituality. It makes it much harder to have a really rich prayer life. I'd be in meetings, and people would say things, and I'd go, "No, that's not true," in my head. It was this grad-school, shitty, snarky internal monologue where I think I'm better than people and I think I know everything. It sucks. It's so isolating. It just means that I'm putting up more barriers between myself and other people. At this point, I've decided I can't write about AA anymore because it's too close to home.

I joined a bunch of people in recovery who meet up every week and go through the book *The Artist's Way*. We read through the book together, and we talk about our progress, but the main exercise is called "morning pages." I wake up in the morning and write four pages of automatic writing. You just try to turn off the censor part of your mind and write something that's unfinished. It's not bad writing. It's actually good because that's how things get written. The first thing that comes out doesn't need to be perfect, but I have this desire to have every line be brilliant, which really hampers my creativity and makes me not write until the very last minute. The funny thing is that whenever I start writing, I get really excited and enjoy it, but staring at the blank page fills me with dread. I just wish I could get to that state of play right away, and that's what those morning pages are meant to allow you to do. They're also connected to moral inventory because they're about bringing up to the surface that which is subconscious or buried in a way that's unmediated. When you write resentment inventory, the truth gets written on the paper just like you prayed for. In the same way, with morning pages, you're trying to create this automatic writing where you're not crafting the sentence or the phrase. You're just allowing it to bubble up from the unconscious.

31

SHARING INVENTORY

Good sponsorship—sponsorship from addicts with in-depth, first-hand experience with the Twelve Steps, who do not abuse their sponsees—is an essential ingredient for effective recovery writing. In the inventory process, a Twelve-Step sponsor acts both as a writing instructor, teaching their sponsees how to write, and as an audience, listening attentively to their sponsees when they share their writing. Sharing inventory is a vulnerable experience. You have to tell someone else all the worst things about yourself. For that experience to be effective and healing, you have to write under the guidance of someone who has written and shared their own inventory—so that they can help you arrive at valuable insights—and who isn't going to abuse you or judge you. Ideally, a sponsor is someone who has seen and shared their own brokenness and can meet your vulnerability with compassion.

At the same time, every sponsor works differently, and different traditions of Twelve-Step sponsorship pass on different practices to their sponsees. When it comes to sharing and hearing inventory, some, like Piers, listen quietly as their sponsees read word for word what they have written. They believe that a prayerful inventory-writing process will provide all necessary discoveries, so no further input is required from the sponsor. Others take a more conversational approach to hearing inventory, playing a more active role in the process. They believe that inventory writing provides some initial insights that need to be deepened through dialogue, which requires input from the sponsor, sometimes in the form of further questions and sometimes in a mutual exchange of confessions.

The addicts I interviewed who had sponsors like Piers told me that they read their writing verbatim, just like I had: "What my sponsor did . . . he just quietly listened," said one respondent. "He was pretty adamant that I just read," said another. "He just lay back and chewed on ice the whole time," said a third. One addict explained that reading inventory requires "not doing any type of editorial—it's just what's on the page." He said that adding any commentary is generally a means of avoiding a full, unvarnished confession: "When I see folks go off-script, more often than not, it really is about a softening of the truth. It's the addiction trying to explain itself."

In other words, the value of just "sticking to the facts" is that it maximizes the power of writing to work against our addictive tendency to rationalize, minimize, and otherwise deceive ourselves. One addict compared writing a resentment to fixing a thought in place, thus making it more real: "If I just contemplate it, it can wiggle around in all kinds of ways. Once it leaves my brain, it becomes what it is. Once it's on the paper, it becomes unchangeable, and so writing it keeps it from squirming around in my brain. My rationalization stops." Others agreed, saying things like: "Until I sit down and write the inventory and share it with another human being, it isn't real. It's just whatever might be floating around in my head. It becomes real when I put pen to paper and get it in black and white." These addicts told me that having the "truth" on paper meant they had to deal with the reality of what they had written: "It's like you can't hide behind it anymore," said one. "I can't just slough it off once it's on paper," said another.

For these addicts, sharing inventory in a way that deviated from what they had written down "in black and white" was seen as a return to the mental "squirming," "rationalization," "truth softening," and dishonesty that had preceded the writing process. And so they placed a high value on maintaining a fidelity to the written word as they shared their inventory.

For addicts who took a more conversational approach to sharing inventory, the act of sharing was seen as an opportunity to expand on the partially developed insights that inventory writing produced. Owen, for example, told me that he sometimes struggled with the discovery process as he wrote the fourth column of his resentment inventory. When I asked him how he got through that struggle, he said: "Well, in a lot of cases, I half-assed it. I put down whatever I could think of at the time. Putting a finger on the exact nature of my wrongs came later, when I shared my inventory with my sponsor." Owen told me his sponsor asked him to read his inventory aloud:

> When I got to the fourth column and I had half-assed it—or in some cases, left it blank because I didn't know—he would say: "Alright, let's talk about this. What makes it so hard for you to figure out what goes in that column?" And that was the process. When I finally was able to figure out what my role was, I didn't go back to revise the inventory because it didn't feel like it mattered to write it down. The crux was in talking it through.

For Owen and his sponsor, sharing inventory meant sharing the discovery process. Where Owen had met the limits of his own insight, he and his sponsor worked together to find the truth. Writing provided a useful context for this discussion: it zeroed in on those places where Owen needed help to make an important discovery. But a completed, written inventory was not the end goal of the process. Instead, the goal was the experience of discovery and the insights and changes it afforded.

Jerry and Anne had similar experiences with sharing their inventories. Their sponsors also felt that the "crux was in talking it through." In fact, their sponsors didn't even ask them to open their notebooks or do any reading at all. Jerry told me he pushed his notebook across the table to his sponsor when they met:

> He said, "Well, what do you want me to do?"
> I said, "Look it over and see if I got it right."
> He said, "Jerry, why don't you tell me what's in there? There is no right or wrong to this. Just tell me what you found."

After that, Jerry didn't read from his moral inventory. Instead, he and his sponsor had a long discussion, facilitated by Jerry's memory of what he'd discovered in his writing process.

When Jerry sponsored Anne, he asked her to share her inventory in the same way: "I don't think I read anything to him," she told me. "We were together for eight or nine hours, and I don't know if I ever actually opened a notebook." Anne was clear that sharing inventory is not meant to be a "recitation" of wrongs or a chance for "correction" by the sponsor. Instead, she said: "[As a sponsor] you encourage people to tell their story. It's not, 'What did you write down?' but, 'What have you *learned*? What have you *uncovered*?' And then it really becomes their experience."

For sponsors like Jerry and Anne, sharing inventory relies more heavily on discussion with the sponsor than on the written word. Writing prepares addicts to tell the truth about themselves by helping them make important discoveries, but the value of sharing inventory lies in how it enables sponsor and sponsee to relate to each other in a new way. The sponsor can tell personal stories to let the sponsee know they are not alone, and the sponsor can help the sponsee share the truth of what they've learned without sticking strictly to what they've written. The goal here is to make sure not that every word is read but that every truth is named.

Even though the addicts I interviewed had different ways of sharing their inventory, they all did share it, and they all told me that sharing inventory was an essential part of the process.

When they shared their inventory, they felt a great sense of relief that came from feeling fully known and fully accepted by another person. Sometimes, they described the experience of sharing as "embarrassing" or "humbling," but they also used phrases like "freeing," "a weight lifted up off me," "like taking a deep breath and letting out a big sigh," and "finally, I can move on." One addict told me: "When I got through, I remember thinking something I'd never thought before, *Here's a person who knows who I really am.*" Another said, "For the first time ever, there were no secrets in my life."

Several addicts told me about moments when they shared something particularly shameful and found that their sponsors completely understood and accepted them. For example, Joe C. said: "There were parts of my inventory I didn't want to ever share, but the response I got was, 'Yeah, me too.' All of a sudden, I didn't feel so alone or ashamed." Maureen D. had a similar experience with her sponsor: "I told her this big thing that I wasn't going to tell anyone. Not only did she not judge me, she also had that same experience herself. All the shame just kind of left."

Piers described the process as "cathartic," saying: "It makes you feel different, and not just on the level of emotions—you feel biologically different. You are releasing tension in a different way somehow." This deep release came from "the writing and the reading together" and "not one without the other."

No matter how you share your inventory, the key is to share it. Making discoveries without telling someone else what you've found just doesn't do the trick.

"You Can't Be Loved That Way and Not Believe in God"

ANNE'S STORY

Anne started her Twelve-Step process with a Big Book Step Study group and then transferred to another form of sponsorship while she was in the middle of writing her inventory. Her story offers a sense of how different groups can present the same inventory instructions in different ways.

I first learned about the Twelve-Step process when I saw it printed on a banner on a wall at a meeting. Seeing the Steps that way, you get the sense this is something you can think your way through. At the time, I thought it looked like a good process for psychological healing if they'd just left out some of that antiquated language that included God. I could see how it would allow someone to reintegrate themselves back into the world. I'd had twelve years of Catholic school, so I was familiar with the idea of confession and penance, and it looked a little bit like that to me at the time.

Later, I was introduced to the Big Book Step Study process, which is very directive and matter-of-fact. It also involves a lot of writing. People would get up in front of the meeting and tell you, "I had a stack of notebooks three feet off the ground and it took me two years of writing." People in that group were being directed to make lists of every address they'd ever lived at to prepare for writing an inventory of their entire lives. It was a lot, but I was still willing to do it because I'd come to the conclusion that my best thinking had destroyed every good thing in my life.

At the same time, I was experiencing a lot of confusion and loss. My doctor put me on some medication, but all that did was lift me up out of depression enough that I wasn't being diligent about my writing. I had become aware of things about myself that weren't quite right, but I didn't have the impetus or the spiritual connection to go forward. I landed on the rocks. I was having suicidal ideation. Someone suggested that I go to another meeting. I didn't think meetings would do any good, but they said: "Oh, you gotta go to this one! This is Jerry's meeting." And now, here I was with suicidal ideation, but I said: "I'm not going to any meeting with somebody's name on it. That's not AA." But, in the end, I was desperate enough and agreed to go.

What I heard at this meeting was a completely different tradition of talking about the Steps and looking at the Big Book from before. I was sitting on a dirty shag carpet in the religious education building of a church in Plainville, Massachusetts, and trying to figure out what this man's angle was. He was saying things I'd never heard before. He had such a way of drawing everybody in that I really wondered if it was a con. It had to be too good to be true, so I watched him. I would sit there and listen, and tears would stream down my face. I couldn't control it. For the first time, I was hearing someone speak with depth about the same things that I recognized about myself. There was hope.

When I look back on the Big Book Step Study process now, I see a worshiping of the process. It has a real appeal for people who like to get check marks and A-pluses and who like to know exactly how to do things. I was a Catholic girl, so A-pluses and check marks and "you're doing it right"—that kind of writing should have been the perfect fit for me. But what I heard from Jerry and from his sponsor Don was a whole lot less about how inventory should look—when it should be done, how many notebooks, and so on—and a whole lot more about giving my life to the Spirit. One thing Don said that stuck with me was that the Steps are a spiritual process, and you can't do a spiritual thing perfectly. You're too human. That idea relieved the pressure I felt to do things perfectly. It helped me open myself to really looking at my life. No one was going to tell me my inventory was wrong, and that allowed me to have my own spiritual experience rather than just doing an exercise in writing.

In short order, I asked Jerry to sponsor me. I had about two hundred and thirty names on the resentment inventory that I'd started with Big Book Step Study. I think I had finished about fifty names or so in a style that I would describe as "journaling in confusion." Like I said, I was not very motivated, but once I started working with Jerry, I wrote with a vengeance.

The process of writing inventory became about seeing what was happening in my thinking and in my processes. In the past, I would pray, "Dear God, please don't let me yell at the kids, and make me better and shine up the outside," but through inventory, I uncovered the reasons why that kind of prayer wasn't changing me. My thinking—my fear-driven thinking, manifested as selfishness—was not going to allow that change. If I don't change what I think, I'm not going to change what I am or what I do.

I wrote down everything in my deepest thoughts that I would never want anyone to know, and I was amazed that I could see the truth. What shocked me was that the things I wrote didn't really surprise me, like, "Oh, where did that come from?" or, "Oh, I've been repressing that memory." It was things I knew already. But when I say I "knew" them, it was a sort of subconscious thinking where you have thoughts but then say: "Shhh! Good people don't think that shit!" So, there was some tremendous power in this thing that allowed me to actually write these thoughts down, and it came with a level of belief that I could be relieved of all this stuff and recreated.

But then there were times when what I wrote was so heartbreaking . . . the shabbiness and the selfishness of my behavior. I was convinced that if anyone really knew the depth of my shabbiness, I would get kicked out of the club. I would not be able to hang out with Jerry or Don or any of the folks who were so spiritually fit. So I had to confess it right away. I would pick up the phone, and I would call Jerry, and I would tell him what I had just uncovered about myself. Every time that happened, he would share an experience of his that was similar to mine, and it proved to me that I was safe and I was loved and I could go forward.

I wrote my inventory and then I read it to Jerry. Well, when I say "read," I don't think I actually read anything to him. We were together for eight or nine hours, and I don't know if I ever opened a notebook. He asked me what I'd found out, and I told him. It was amazing because I wasn't just reciting junk I wrote off the top of my head. I really talked about what the experience had been like for me. I wasn't looking for his A-Okay. This was *my experience*. I think that's one of the reasons why it's important not to get too technical with this thing. We have to give people the dignity of having their own experience. When I asked Jerry later why he didn't have me read my inventory, he said: "You were so fragile, I don't think you could have managed it. It just seemed like the loving thing to do."

That doesn't mean we are always gentle with our feedback. Six weeks later, I called Jerry to read him a resentment against a person, but I really just wanted him to hear what a shit this other person was, right? So I read him the inventory, and he said, "Anne, this is bullshit." This is the guy who said I had been too fragile to read my inventory six weeks earlier! He said, "Why don't you go back and read the part of the Big Book that's between the third and fourth columns, then call me back after you've looked this over again?" He wasn't being directive—he didn't tell me exactly what I should have written—but he was *direct*. He told me the truth. Love is direct sometimes.

What I learned from this tradition of following the Steps is that we have to feel safe and understood and loved before we can submit ourselves to the grueling process of looking at our lives and our faults. It's about the spiritual connection that you make through your writing rather than the mechanism of writing itself. Writing is just a means to an end. It's a concrete way that I demonstrate surrender. Inventory is about deciding what works in my life and what does not, and then offering it all to the Spirit because I haven't done such a damn good job with it myself.

I'm not a practicing Christian, but I believe this applies at the level of the crucifixion: the whole experience that we go through, and all this pain and uncovering of our faults and flaws—this is the level of resurrection or renewal or recreation that we can achieve. It's an act of faith to just write down this shit that I never want anyone to ever see or know. I have faith in the people who came before me. They're saying that if I do this, I might be different on the other side, and they're promising that they will walk with me through this thing. When I'm horrified by what I find, they tell me: "It's okay. It was the same for me. Keep going." You can't be loved and accepted that way and not believe that there is a god.

32

WRITING FOR AMENDS

Writing inventory and sharing it with a sponsor are important parts of the Twelve-Step process, but they are not the end of the road. It's not enough just to see and say the truth, we have to *act* on it as well. Most of the addicts I interviewed understood amends to be a natural extension of the inventory process. By writing and sharing inventory, we discover our moral shortcomings and we see how those shortcomings have caused harm to others. By making amends, we take action on this information. We go to the people we've harmed, admit our mistakes, and offer to help them heal from the harm we've caused.

Amends are almost always made in person, without any writing involved. In fact, among the addicts I know and those I interviewed, there is a common feeling that writing is great for inventory but strictly secondary for amends. The addicts I spoke with wrote amends *lists*—meaning that they wrote down the names of people they had hurt, and sometimes a few details about how they had hurt those people. But they wrote amends *letters* only when a face-to-face meeting was impossible or inadvisable, usually when a name on the amends list belonged to someone who was far away, who didn't want to meet in person, or who was deceased. In these cases, writing a letter of amends was seen as the appropriate response.

When they wrote amends *lists*, the addicts I interviewed told me, they found the experience "scary," "intense," "overwhelming," and "shitty," but also enlightening and liberating. Joe C. explained that his experience with Step Eight was surprising and revealing: "I put all these people's names down on a list. For the first time, I got to see all the people I'd hurt on a piece of paper. And I went, 'Holy shit, that's a lot.'" Leah had a similar experience. When she saw the full extent of the harm she had caused others, she wanted to run away: "I didn't want to talk to these people. I'd stolen stuff from them! I didn't want to give back the money. I didn't want to admit where I had been wrong. It was uncomfortable, embarrassing."

Along with this discomfort and embarrassment, respondents also experienced a deep shift in their life focus from their own selfish concerns to the needs of others. As Julie B. put it: "Up until I wrote my amends list, the Steps had all been things that I did for myself. Writing an inventory was a very personal thing, and then reading it to someone was like . . . it was all about me. Writing my amends list meant I needed to find a way to approach these people in a way that might be helpful for them and not just for me." Mark A. made a similar point when he told me that writing moral inventory had generated "some genuine remorse" in him for the people he had harmed. Writing an amends list, he said, became an opportunity for him "to cultivate compassion—not pity but compassion—a genuine effort to put myself in their shoes to see what it must have felt like for them." He continued, "I don't think you can make real amends unless you've done your best to identify and share in the pain that person has."

When they wrote amends *letters*, the addicts I interviewed said that their writing sometimes worked just like face-to-face amends: they admitted their wrong to someone, and the person responded in ways that enabled them to heal some of the harm they had caused.

Bob P., for example, told me a story about an amends he made over social media to a woman he had "made fun of a lot in eighth grade." The woman lived near him, but Bob had not had any communication with her since middle school, so he felt that she would probably not want him knocking on her door one day, completely out of the blue. So Bob reached out to her online:

> I reached out to her on Facebook, and I made the amends. I told her that I was in recovery and was making amends to people I had hurt, and I told her that I knew I had hurt her. I said: "Do you have any suggestions? Are there things that I can do to make you more comfortable with what happened?" And she said: "You have two daughters. I hope that you're raising them to be more sensitive than you were at this age." I said, "That's fair advice." We haven't spoken since then, but we're friends on Facebook, and, you know, at the end of it, she said, "I can't believe you messaged me!" That was pretty amazing—to be able to make amends and have her respond like that.

Bob's Facebook amends worked kind of like face-to-face amends because instant messaging allows people to respond quickly to each other, sort of like in a real-life conversation. Bob could say his piece, and the woman could respond directly, with the added feature that she had more privacy and could take her time to think about her response more easily than if Bob were standing on her doorstep, waiting for her reply.

More often, written amends are used when addicts don't necessarily expect a reply, often because the harmed party is deceased. But even these cases can produce moments of discovery when addicts find a suitable way to take concrete action for their amends. Jen M., for example, told me about how she made amends to her deceased parents. She struggled to come up with any meaningful action that would even symbolically amend the harm she had caused them. Jen's sponsor suggested that she write a letter and read it at her parents' graveside. A day after she did, she had a moment of contact:

> I was at their cemetery, and I read the letter. I didn't have any big "aha" moment or spiritual experience or anything like that. Then, maybe a day later, something was on the radio about praying the Rosary, and I went: "Duh! Mom and Dad were incredibly Catholic." If my parents were here right now, my mother would be like, "Jen, would you say the Rosary please?" And I'm sure they would love for me to have a mass said for them. I had been thinking and thinking and thinking, like, "What could I do?" And then, all of a sudden, after I wrote this letter and went to the graveside and read it out loud, the next day I was like: "Okay. Yeah. Thanks, God."

Jen's letter shifted something for her. Where she was stuck and unable to discover a means to amend the harm she had caused her parents, writing and reading a letter opened her up and allowed her to discover the answer she was looking for. In this way, writing can help addicts take action in the amends process.

I don't want to make too big of a deal about writing's role in amends, since so much of the work happens in conversation and action. But writing does come in handy when the normal means of amends are not available. In that case—like for Bob and Jen—writing can act as a substitute for conversation, even if your conversation partners have already passed on.

"What Am I Going to Do Differently?"

JESSE S.'S STORY

Jesse describes how he writes in order to connect with his higher power throughout long-term recovery. Jesse's writing practice puts great emphasis on moving from contact into action.

I would say that writing is a way to grow spiritually. It helps me get in touch with the prayerful moment. I've been in recovery for thirteen years now, and over the past year or so, I've been having a hard time where my mind has been too busy for prayer. I got away from regular inventory writing, and so my mind has gotten much busier. I started to notice that I'm not embodying my spiritual practice in the way that I'd like, and I feel a need to deepen my practice and clear out the mental clutter. I'm interested in growing again, because I've seen what not growing looks like. So now I'm working on that.

At first, I tried thinking my prayers, saying them out loud, or doing something with my body—like getting on my knees—just to be able to feel that prayer was working and to believe in it. But I was having a hard time doing it that way, so I was just like, "Alright, I'll write it out." Writing cleared my mind of distracting thoughts. In that way, writing allowed me to be more present to my prayer, to believe it, and to feel it. So writing clears me. It is a meditative practice in that it allows me to be more open to the grace that I'm asking for in a prayer. If I just say the prayer out loud or think it, I don't feel it. Maybe I'm going through the motions, but I'm not actually having a spiritual experience. Writing allows for that spiritual experience to happen for me.

I would say that spiritual growth means deepening your relationship with a higher power, and a lot of things come from that. As a result of my relationship with God, I am a better person. I am a better partner. I am a better community member. I am a better teacher. I am a better colleague. I am a better mentor. I'm a better friend. I'm a better son. I'm a better sibling. I'm a more generous person. I would say all those changes came from my spiritual life, because those are things that I would not be especially capable of growing into otherwise. Writing is connected to that growth because in my life, for an overwhelming majority of the time, growth has come from some kind of hardship or difficulty, and writing—specifically the inventory process—is the most structured kind of writing I have done that allows me to get myself out of the way and connect with my higher power. When I say "get myself out of the way," what I mean is that without inventory, I would be on a progressively worsening path in all of those roles that I mentioned. I would be progressively less generous and less loving in all areas. Apart from inventory, the way I deal with negative feelings is extreme head-in-the-sand avoidance. I also have a really well-developed coping mechanism that is my ability to put on a really great face like everything is fine. So to the outside world—to virtually everybody, including my therapist and even myself—I present this narrative that is not well grounded in the truth of whatever is actually happening in my life. So without inventory, I can't even be honest in therapy.

But those mechanisms can only last so long before I start to feel uneasy, and then things blow up to a point where I can't handle it anymore. It all kind of comes flooding back, and I feel those feelings pretty strongly. So when those feelings do pop up, writing makes me feel better. But its value is not just in enabling my ability to express negative emotions. I mean, that's certainly helpful, right? But its more significant effect comes from the fact that inventory writing allows me to shed that self—the pride and ego—so I can be clearer in my mind and a better person in my life.

Writing helps me get honest. I can't be honest with myself if I don't genuinely look at myself on a regular basis. What I mean is without inventory, I don't really take responsibility for my behavior. In the fourth column of resentment inventory is where I can be like, "Oh yeah, I'm reacting to my feelings, getting hurt and acting out in this way," or like, "Oh, I'm doing the wrong thing in this relationship," and then it becomes, "Okay, so what's the next right action to take?"

Ideally, you change in the process and you don't have the same resentments anymore, but it doesn't always happen that way. For one thing, there are some relationships with layers that you just keep peeling. So, for example, the first time I ever wrote resentment inventory about my mother, it was an opportunity to clear away the big shit and have a better relationship with her. But later, I wrote more inventory about her. That relationship wasn't totally resolved to the point where I would never feel resentment again. Sometimes, the same reasons that we write resentment inventory in the first place might still be there. We can't just wish those things away.

I've also noticed the ways that my resentment toward my mother takes a different form today. It's a new kind of resentment. I just wasn't able to feel it before. I had to write about the first layer first, so that these other resentments could surface. Writing about a deeper resentment provides me with an opportunity to have a better relationship with my mother and to become more aligned with God.

On the other hand, sometimes I'm just writing the exact same inventory because I copped a resentment, wrote about it, and then let it ride for a while without changing my own behavior. I didn't change, so therefore I'm going to have the exact same inventory.

One of the most important parts of inventory is asking: "Okay, what am I going to do differently? How am I going to change in the future with regards to this relationship? Is there any kind of action that is called for as a result of writing this inventory?" That action could be an amends or any number of things. It could be that I have to do something at work that I've been putting off, for example. Action is part of the process, and I'll actually write that out too. I write the questions: "What can I do differently? What action needs to be taken?" Then I write the answers down. Oftentimes, I'll do part of that reflection when I read the inventory to someone. I'll tell them this is part of my process and say: "I'm interested in changing. Here's what I'm thinking. What do you think?" Sometimes, I'll get a suggestion from them, or at least an idea of whether they would recommend doing what I'm thinking of doing.

I also do some writing before and after inventory. It's like a free-form, prayerful writing. I just write. Before inventory, I need to be able to get into the space to connect to my higher power, and in order to do that, I need to pray. So writing prayers is the thing that actually gets me to that place. It usually takes the form of a big ask to God, like: "God, please help me. Please clear me from my distractions. Please help me to see you. Please help me to be honest, so that I might serve you."

Actually, I pray to my guardian angel in the same way. I write out her name and ask for her care and protection because the process can be really difficult for me. The feelings I have are really physical things that happen. When I feel anxiety or restlessness, those are negative physical things happening to my body, so my guardian angel is a person who will take care of me in a motherly way or in a way that's very caring and gentle. So I'll write: "Rachel, please surround me in golden light. Rachel, please help me be able to be at peace with myself. Please take care of my physical wellbeing, so that I might be able to do this inventory." After I write inventory, I'll sometimes write, "Thank you for the care and protection you gave me." I won't always write these out. In prayer, I extend myself to be able to feel God or Rachel, but when I'm not feeling it, then that's when I would go to writing to be able to feel that connection.

How to Write

Practice Amends

Making amends is a delicate act that requires great care. If we do not approach the people on our list with empathy and pay close attention to their needs, we run the risk of doing further harm. Rushing into amends, hoping to rid ourselves of guilt or embarrassment—or worse, hoping to "prove" to someone that we are all better now—is a recipe for disaster. Unfortunately, these are easy mistakes to make. In early sobriety, many of us experience the sudden return of repressed emotions, including shame and guilt, and we naturally want to resolve these uncomfortable feelings as quickly as possible. The irony of our position is that in our self-centered attempts to assuage these feelings, we only do more harm, and as we do more harm, our feelings of guilt and shame grow.

The guidance of an experienced sponsor is critical in the amends-making process. While this guidance normally takes the form of a conversation, writing can play an important role. Owen told me about a writing exercise he developed to help sponsees who were facing difficult amends:

> I had a guy who wanted to make amends to his partner, and he was all over the place because he wanted to make the amends, but he was worried about how it would come across,

and he had already apologized a million times in the past. It just looked like it was going to be a train wreck. So I said to him: "Why don't you just write it down? Write down what you think you want to say to her. Call me up in a day or two and read me what you've written, and we'll talk about it." He did. And it was a mess. So we talked about it. The conversation was around the questions of how you make an amends, not an apology; and how you make it about your behavior, not hers; and how you make clear what you're going to do without making promises you're not going to keep. I think we must have gone through a couple of different drafts on that one.

Owen's practice amends method represents one of the few instances in my interviews when an addict reported making use of writing's power of *revision* to complement its power of discovery. By having his sponsee draft, discuss, revise, and redraft his letter multiple times, Owen was able to help him discover a way to approach his partner without causing further harm to the relationship. Note that the final draft of the letter was not delivered to the man's partner. It simply served as a guide for the kinds of things he might say when they spoke.

To write practice amends:
1. Have a sponsor you trust who can guide you through the amends process.
2. Make an amends list by writing down the names of all the people and institutions you have harmed.
3. Discuss this list with your sponsor, telling them the harm you think you caused in each case and getting their insight on how best to approach that case.
4. Identify the amends that you are most eager, or most hesitant, to approach. Or, ask your sponsor to identify which amends they think you might need to practice first.
5. Draft a statement that you would like to make to that person. Say whatever you want in this statement.

6. Read your statement to your sponsor and be prepared to take notes. Ask them to correct you by pointing out any aspects of your statement that could cause harm or otherwise be unproductive.
7. Take your notes and start over. Draft a new statement (or adjust the first draft) to account for the advice your sponsor gave you.
8. Read the new draft and take notes again; repeat as many times as your sponsor deems necessary.
9. When you've arrived at a final revision, your understanding of how to make this amends will also have been revised. You can take the letter with you, and maybe even read it verbatim if your sponsor thinks that would be appropriate. The important thing is that you approach the person in the spirit of your final draft.

"It Has to Be Nourished"

STEVE H.'S STORY

Steve describes a unique way in which writing can help addicts take action in their relationships. His Step work in Recovering Couples Anonymous allowed him and his wife to build greater intimacy by recovering together.

For me, recovery started when my wife went into treatment. During family week at the treatment center, I started to write about what was going on in my marriage. After that, I started going to Sex and Love Addicts Anonymous (SLAA) meetings and eventually got a sponsor and started working the Steps. Then my wife and I started going to Recovering Couples Anonymous (RCA). Eventually, we got a sponsor couple. They were really big on the Steps, so we worked the Steps together.

In RCA, people do their first three Steps at meetings. You write them ahead of time and then read them to the group. Each Step has a series of questions. Each of us recorded answers for the other person. So, if I answered the question, my wife was writing down what I said and vice versa. It's powerful that you write what your partner is saying, and then you read what you said but it's in their handwriting. We did that all the way through the first three Steps. The steps in RCA are focused on the coupleship rather than individuals, so you talk about your own stuff, but you talk a lot about how your past and particularly your family of origin affect your partner and your family.

Basically, the idea is that we were powerless over our relationship and it had become unmanageable, and as a result, we were headed for separation or divorce. We realized no human power could help us and believed that God could and would if sought. It's the same Twelve-Step principles, just applied to your coupleship. It turns out that in most cases, the coupleship has been broken by addiction and co-addiction. Recovery usually involves an identified addict who has screwed up in some way or whose addiction has become problematic. So people often come into RCA because the addiction has become unmanageable, but the key to ongoing recovery is that the other person—the identified victim, if you will—has to realize that they need to be in recovery too. They've got a role as a co-addict, and they have to work their own program for the coupleship to really work.

A lot of the first three Steps is about developing intimacy through just learning about each other. A lot of times, when people first come to RCA, intimacy is understood pretty narrowly as sexual intimacy, and so if you have a couple that's struggling with intimacy, all the energy seems to be aimed at that point. What's hard for people in the midst of that to realize is that sex is the end result of the larger process of intimacy building. A lot of times, you're focusing on the wrong end of the problem. But when you can start talking about money and kids and time and household chores and things like that—or having fun together— then intimacy is much easier to achieve on a physical level as well.

People say all the time when they work these Steps that they learn things about their partners that they didn't know, stuff from childhood that modeled things for them, like marriage and the sharing of feelings. For example, in the second Step, you write about your history with higher power. You are supposed to describe what your higher power looks like, and your partner describes theirs. These don't always match, but it's important to understand and respect the other person's spiritual identity and history. Then there's an emphasis on the coupleship together invoking a higher power to support it, and so you pray together. There are other exercises to build intimacy, but that's one of them.

Sharing your writing in the first three Steps with the group feels pretty vulnerable. You have to be at a point where you trust the group not to judge you but to really listen and hear you. It's very powerful because there's a real appreciation from the group members that what you have done is not something couples do very much. I've been in the church for a long time and I've never experienced anything like this, where couples reveal their struggles and their failures in such an honest way. It's very freeing. When things aren't going well with a couple, there can be a lot of shame. When you realize that there are other people who have experienced the same thing, it mitigates that shame, and you're able to acknowledge that your failures aren't so unique. It builds that sense of experience, strength, and hope. To be seen and known by other people is deeply bonding. Typically, couples will go out to dinner after meetings. It's a unique thing. I've never experienced anything like it. It's not for everybody, but it can be very transformative.

Every time we did a Step, my wife and I would write either together or separately, and then we'd share it with our sponsor couple at a coffee shop, and then we'd get feedback. At Step Four, it became an inventory of the relationship. The idea is that the coupleship is its own breathing, living entity. It has to be nourished. It has to be paid attention to. That doesn't mean that we don't have our own lives or our own recovery processes, but the coupleship requires its own attention. It has also done its own harm, and so we make an amends list for the harms the relationship has caused. It's not easy to think about how a coupleship has created problems or injured people or other relationships. One of the ways to think about that is in terms of collusion: how two members of the partnership colluded to ignore something or to cause harm, for example. It's a different way of thinking. Usually, when we think of amends, we think of individual things—that I've done or that you've done—so there also is a place for making amends to each other.

It's an interesting application of the Steps—very powerful. I'd say I've seen the promises of recovery come true in RCA more than anywhere else. A lot of the couples that come into RCA are those in which both people have been in recovery for a long time but haven't built any intimacy because their programs are so separate. They come in, and they say: "Wow, we never thought that our recoveries had anything to do with each other! We were just sort of glad the other person was sober, but the idea that we might have something to work on together never really dawned on us."

There are also aspects of the process that are for sustaining the coupleship. There's a fighting contract, which includes taking a moratorium on certain subjects and making an agreement about what it means to fight fairly, and so on. There are contracts around everything from sex to housework to finances, all of which require that couples work together to learn how to be in a relationship in a healthy way.

It's not an easy process. We had a lot of issues and had to work through a lot of pain. We called our sponsor couple up all the time. One example I recall had to do with finances. I have two kids from a previous marriage, and I think we were having a disagreement over spending money on things for the kids. We talked to our sponsor couple—also a blended family—and they said, "Here's our experience: you need to do a real Fourth Step around your finances." That meant really thinking about what money means to us, what it brings up for us, and what resentments we have that are tied to money. That was really helpful because once those fears and resentments get expressed, it becomes a lot easier to negotiate and trust each other and to be aware of the other person's sensitivities.

That inventory was a four-column thing. We both reflected on what came up for us around money and why, and we both did that privately. Then we got on the phone with our sponsor couple. I don't remember if we had shared the inventory with each other first or if we shared it for the first time with our sponsor couple on the phone, but either way, we read that stuff and they gave us feedback.

The process of doing the work was really what changed the dynamics for us. It's kind of magical, really. Don't know how to describe it. If I had to guess, I'd say that in a marriage, there are a lot of issues that have historical connections and subtext. For example, I might be pissed about the fact that my wife spent five hundred dollars on something that she hadn't talked to me about, but it's inevitably about more than that particular event. It's about what money means to me emotionally. I may even be able to trace it back to some episode earlier in life. It may be fear of running out of money. It may be a sense of betrayal. When one can identify those things and a partner can hear them and realize, "Oh, this really is about something deeper and more primal to this person," then that is really intimacy building. That's really what the Steps in RCA do. They allow couples to build intimacy because you develop empathy for each other and learn each other's histories in revealing ways.

HOW TO WRITE
A Coupleship First Step

Recovering Couples Anonymous practices a social form of recovery work. Its Steps are designed for two people in a committed relationship to work through together in order to build intimacy. If you are looking for a way to practice Twelve-Step principles in your intimate relationship(s), it might be worth giving the RCA's Step guides a look. Here is an abbreviated version of their First Step writing practice from their basic text.[64]

1. Take one pencil and one piece of paper and begin the process together.
2. Divide the paper in half with a vertical line down the middle.
3. On each side, make lists of the coupleship issues over which you each feel powerless.
4. Divide the duties of writing and dictating, as you each answer the following questions:
   1. What dysfunctional roles have you brought from your family of origin?
   2. What have your family-of-origin models taught you about relationships?
   3. If you have had experiences of abuse, how have those affected your ability to relate, to be intimate, and to be sexual?

4. How do your individual addictions or dysfunctions affect your coupleship?
5. What are recurring issues you never seem to resolve (e.g., how you spend money, how you spend your time together, parent, divide household duties, celebrate holidays, etc.)?
6. How do these issues bring you to anger and what are your patterns of expressing anger?
7. In what ways do you feel hopeless about your coupleship?
8. In order to save your coupleship, what measures have you tried that haven't seemed to work?
9. How do you fight unfairly?

In RCA, your answers to these questions would be shared with your "sponsor couple," another couple in recovery who have already done this process and can guide you through. If you are not able to find an RCA meeting, you might consider working these Steps together with other couples and/or sharing your answers with a neutral, understanding party whom you both trust.

33

THE OUTLIER

One addict I interviewed—I'll call him Wallace—was not a member of any Twelve-Step fellowship. Wallace attended AA briefly but soon stopped attending meetings over his disagreement with the notion of "powerlessness" or, as he put it, "the AA concept that you have within you a weakness to alcohol and that this weakness is going to be with you forever." After a period of abstinence, Wallace felt that he was gaining control over his alcohol consumption: "Yes, I had abused alcohol in the past, but I was no longer in a position where it had control over me. I was in a position where *I* had control over *it*, and that's when I stopped going to those types of meetings." For Wallace, leaving meetings did not in any way mean giving up his commitment to sobriety. In fact, at the time of our interview, Wallace was preparing to celebrate twenty years of sobriety.

Instead of meetings, Wallace found himself a temporary, long-distance sponsor who supported the notion that he could control his drinking through willpower. The trick, though, was to find a way to focus the will and train it to withstand the pressures of early sobriety. They settled on the idea of journaling:

> In my career, I had taken a number of courses and read a lot
> of books on self-help, so sitting down and trying to establish

goals and determine how to accomplish them was second nature to me. I found that if I attacked this challenge the same way I would attack any problem in the business world, I could draw upon the skills I had to analyze the situation, develop a plan, determine the progress I was making against the plan, determine any alterations that needed to be made to the plan, and go through that iterative process of starting something and accomplishing it. I would say the more that I wrote to myself, the easier it became, and it encouraged me to write even more. It just built on itself.

In other words, Wallace's journal became a focal point for his efforts to exert control over his alcoholism. In its pages, he worked out his plans and strategies for staying sober. For example, Wallace told me that early in sobriety, he found himself in a crisis. He was about to go on an annual camping trip with old drinking buddies. Wallace felt under pressure: his friends would expect him to drink with them, which he didn't want to do. But he didn't feel ready to out himself as a sober alcoholic either. Struggling to find a way to get through the weekend without taking a drink, Wallace turned to his journal:

> I determined I was going to have to ask for help, so I reached out to one of the other dads who is a social worker and told him my problem. I said, "The peer pressure on me to have to drink—I'm going to crumble, and I don't want to do that." He said, "I will give you the air cover you need to get through this." He got me through a couple camp-outs that way, and after that, I was able to be honest with the guys and just say I had quit drinking.

The way Wallace told his story makes it clear that he thinks of his discovery process as something that *he* did. He analyzed his situation, came to a determination, and acted on it. At no point did his hand move of its own accord, nor did any extra-egoic voice whisper wisdom into his ear. Instead, as told by Wallace, the whole process was simply a demonstration of "some real higher-order thinking" on his part. He—all by himself—arrived at the idea that he needed to ask his social-worker friend for help. Wallace feels this way even though at the time of our interview, he felt that he was "getting better at asking for help" though "not quite there yet." The very idea of asking for help would have been uncharacteristic of Wallace at the time of that first sober camp-out—it was not the kind of thing that would have occurred to him normally. And in fact, it did not occur to him *normally*, not until he put his pen to paper.

Over time, Wallace's journaling moved from immediate problems to deeper reflections on the origins of his addiction:

> So you say to yourself, "Okay, if you're a smart individual and you know that drinking to the point where you're unaware of what you're doing, drinking to the point where you may be offending others, drinking to the point where you know if you get behind the wheel of a car, you're a danger to yourself and society—if you're aware of those types of things, why do you continue to drink? What is wrong internally, within me, that I would do this?" That was a very long conversation with myself that was not just one night of sitting around writing. The problem is so much deeper than just "I drink too much." Okay, fine. Anybody can figure that out, but what is in me that gets me out of control? I had to go into depth about what made me tick and why I was the way I was. I got extremely introspective. I had extensive material in there about my relationship with my father and things like that, things I had never shared with anybody else in the world and I probably hadn't realized about myself.

In spite of Wallace's resistance to fundamental Twelve-Step principles, his journaling led him into a self-reflective process similar to the kind of intensive soul-searching typical of moral inventory. Just like addicts who wrote moral inventory, Wallace found that writing helped him to become introspective and to make discoveries about his life:

At times, it was a painful process, a very, very difficult process, because I was unveiling things about myself that I was very ashamed of, things that made me disappointed in myself. At first, I resisted that. I was reluctant to be honest, even with myself. But I realized that as long as I was reluctant to be honest with myself, I was not going to be able to successfully create a life where I didn't drink, so that's when the intensity and the introspection and the time invested in talking to myself through the written word grew. I think in general, I'm a lot more honest now. I'm willing to listen a lot more to other people's points of view. Over time, I'm evolving into a much gentler, warmer person.

What I learn from Wallace is that there is power in writing, no matter how you think about it. Even if you don't go in for all the ideas I've been pitching over the course of this book, there's still real value in sitting down somewhere and getting quiet with paper and pen. You don't have to pray, you don't have to believe in a higher power, and you don't have to let the voices in your head do your writing for you. You can believe that all your ideas are your own if you want to, just so long as you write.

By writing, you will make discoveries. By making and sharing these discoveries, you will change and grow. Through this change and growth, you will recover from addiction.

Conclusion

Over the years, I've written a lot of inventory. Now and then, I'll get resentful or scared, so I'll write about it using the format I learned from Piers. Doing so has made it possible for me to stay clean and sober all this time. I got married, had kids, and went to school—all the way through my PhD. In the process, I was able to restore my relationships with my parents and my brother. I've even been able to write and publish creative work in different genres. I would not have been able to do any of these things while I was getting high, or even when I was sober but still miserable. Stoned or sober, I'm the kind of guy who sits on his anger, letting resentments pile up until I sink into a deep depression. I sit on my fear, too, until it grows into paranoia. But with inventory, I can deal with each resentment or each fear as it comes up. I can work through these feelings, let them go, and have better relationships with the people in my life. In this way, recovery writing enables me to function in the world as a person.

In recovery writing, we move from desperation to surrender, from surrender to contact, and from contact into action. This movement describes the process of recovery, and it also describes the process of discovery. As we write, we must discover the truth about ourselves and our addictions. Making this discovery requires acknowledging our lack of power and insight, so we turn to a source of ideas beyond the limits of our egos. In making contact with that source, we are given new ideas, new knowledge about ourselves. As a result, we also discover a whole new way of living. We find ourselves in healthier relationships with other people and things, including our addictions. We find we don't have to make ourselves suffer anymore.

Recovery writing isn't about getting the right answers or producing perfect prose. You don't have to be super smart or creative to benefit from this stuff. You don't need to be a professional writer or a writing expert. You just need to get yourself a pencil and some paper, say a quick prayer, and start telling the truth.

The truth is painful to see and share. Recovery writing is not easy. We need help from other addicts and from a higher power. Other addicts show us how they write, and they hear us out without judgment when we speak the truths we've discovered. Our higher powers make that discovery possible by showing us things about ourselves we weren't willing or able to see until we sat down with a blank page and prayed for answers to come.

May the Spirit write with you always and show you what you need to see.

LEARN MORE ABOUT RECOVERY WRITING

If you do any writing as a part of your recovery, I would love to hear from you, especially if you have helpful ways to write that were not covered in this book. I'm always interested in hearing about and sharing new recovery writing practices. If you'd like to share your writing experiences with me and others, please join us at recoverywriting.org.

NOTES

1   At the time of this book's publication, you can download the app from the Apple App Store. It's called "Free Tenth Step Nightly Inventory App" from the developer *Twelve Step Apps*.

2   I relied on the AA Big Book, p. 86, to write this list of questions.

3   AA Big Book, p. 29.

4   AA Big Book, p. 25.

5   "First Step to Recovery: A Guide to Working the First Step," International Service Organization of SAA, Inc., 2018.

6   Nathan told me this exercise came from the basic text of *Sex Addicts Anonymous*, also known as "The Green Book." For this exercise, I relied on Nathan's report rather than the text he was using.

7   Writing experts use the terms "invention" and "discovery" more or less interchangeably. For an overview of this scholarship, see Lauer, Janice M. *Invention in Rhetoric and Composition*. Parlor Press, 2004.

8   See Lauer, pages 76–78, 88–91, and 109–10, on theories of "epistemic rhetoric." "Epistemic" means that a practice generates new knowledge or ideas and "rhetoric" refers broadly to the processes involved in writing and speechmaking. These theories describe how writing produces new knowledge.

9   For example, see Flower, Linda and John R. Hayes. "The Cognition of Discovery." *College Composition and Communication*, vol. 31, no. 1, Feb. 1980, pp. 21–32.

10 See, for example, Bartholomae, David. "Inventing the University." *Journal of Basic Writing*, 1986, vol. 5, no. 1, pp. 4–23. Bartholomae argues that college writers invent internal representations of entire social contexts, like departments and universities, in order to discover workable prose within those contexts.

11 See, for example, Vitanza, Victor. "Three Countertheses: Or, A Critical In(ter)vention into Composition Theories and Pedagogies." *Contending with Words*. Eds. Patricia Harkin and John Schilb. New York: MLA, 1991, pp. 139–72. Vitanza argues: "What appears to be writing as discovery is only—unbeknown to its unself-conscious mystified self—writing that uncovers what had already been predetermined by the modes, or the social codes, or production and representation" (150). In other words, even when we think we are discovering something new, we are really just unknowingly reproducing the stuff of our social environment.

12 See, for example, Bawarshi, Anis. *Genre and the Invention of the Writer: Reconsidering the Place of Invention in Composition*. Utah State University Press, 2003. Bawarshi argues that the genre of writing shapes the kinds of things we discover when we write.

13 See, for example, Young, Richard, Alton Becker, and Kenneth Pike. *Rhetoric, Discovery, and Change*. New York: Harcourt, Brace, Jovanovich, 1970; Kneupper, Charles. "Dramatistic Invention: The Pentad as Heuristic Procedure." *Rhetoric Society Quarterly*, no. 9, 1979, pp. 130–36. Young, Becker, and Pike recommend something called "tagmemic invention," which asks writers to think about a subject from different perspectives. Kneupper adapts Kenneth Burke's five aspects of motivation for the purpose of helping writers come up with ideas.

14 See Berthoff, Ann E. *The Making of Meaning: Metaphors, Models, and Maxims for Writing Teachers*. Portsmouth, NH: Boynton/ Cook Publishers, 1981.

15 See Britton, James. "Shaping at the Point of Utterance." *Reinventing the Rhetorical Tradition*. Eds. Ian Pringle and Aviva Freedman. Conway, AK: L and S Books, 1980. 61–66. Britton recommends a method that involves writing without ever looking back to see what you've already written. Writing "at the point of

utterance" means always writing from the point of searching for language rather than expanding on existing writing.

16 James Merrill, *The Changing Light at Sandover*, p. 113. Misspellings are from Merrill's text.

17 Merrill, pp. 117–18.

18 Merrill, p. 117.

19 Merrill, p. 127.

20 See Stevenson's "A Chapter on Dreams" from his collection *Across the Plains* for his description of gaining ideas for stories from the figures who act out his dreams.

21 See Toronto, Richard. *War over Lemuria: Richard Shaver, Ray Palmer and the Strangest Chapter of 1940s Science Fiction.* McFarland & Company, 2013, especially chapters 13–19.

22 For more on Bill W.'s use of occult practices, see, for example, Cheever, Susan. *My Name Is Bill: Bill Wilson—His Life and the Creation of Alcoholics Anonymous.* Washington Square Press, 2005, especially chapter 32, "The Spook Room," pages 201–209.

23 See Foxwell, John, Ben Alderson-Day, Charles Fernyhough, and Angela Woods. "'I've Learned I Need to Treat My Characters Like People': Varieties of Agency and Interaction in Writers' Experiences of Their Characters' Voices." *Consciousness and Cognition*, vol. 79 (2020). Foxwell's research reveals the variety of ways in which fiction authors relate to the imagined figures of their own characters, affording them different degrees and kinds of agency. For a broader discussion of voice-hearing, including its presence in creative writers, see Fernyhough, Charles. *The Voices Within: The History and Science of How We Talk to Ourselves.* Basic Books, 2016.

24 See Toronto, Richard, *War over Lemuria,* especially pages 204–22.

25 For a discussion of automatic writing in various forms, see Thompson, Rachel Leah. "The Automatic Hand: Spiritualism, Psychoanalysis, Surrealism." *Culture: An Electronic Journal for Visual Culture*, No. 7, 2004, pp. 1–14. For a broader discussion of the relationship between psychoanalysis, surrealism, and creative writing (but unfortunately missing spiritualism), see Brophy, Kevin. *Creativity: Psychoanalysis, Surrealism and Creative Writing.* Melbourne University Press, 1994.

26 O'Connor, Flannery. *The Habit of Being: Letters of Flannery O'Connor.* Farrar, Straus and Giroux, 1988, p. 5.

27 For an in-depth discussion of the difference between "compliance" and "surrender," see Tiebout, Harry. *Harry Tiebout: The Collected Writings.* Hazelden, 1999.

28 AA Big Book, pp. 60–61.

29 AA Big Book, p. 63.

30 NA Basic Text, p. 28.

31 See Keating, Thomas. *Open Heart, Open Mind.* Bloomsbury Continuum; Anniversary edition, 2019. Keating's description of Centering Prayer relies on the metaphor of boats passing by on a river, but its purpose and details are different from those of the thought experiment I propose.

32 See the AA Big Book, pp. 35–37, for the story of "Jim."

33 See Pennebaker, James. *Opening up: The Healing Power of Expressing Emotions*, 3rd ed. The Guilford Press, 2016. On pages 13–26, Pennebaker tells his version of this story.

34 Pennebaker, pp. 16–17.

35 Craft, Melissa A., Gail C. Davis and René M. Paulson. "Expressive Writing in Early Breast Cancer Survivors." *Journal of Advanced Nursing*, vol. 69, no.2, 2013, pp. 305–15. Print.

36 Koschwanez, Heidi E. et al. "Expressive Writing and Wound Healing in Older Adults: A Randomized Controlled Trial." *Psychosomatic Medicine*, vol. 75, 2013, pp. 581–90.

37 Smith, Helen E. et al. "The Effects of Expressive Writing on Lung Function, Quality of Life, Medication Use, and Symptoms in Adults with Asthma: A Randomized Controlled Trial." *Psychosomatic Medicine*, vol. 77, 2015, pp. 429–37.

38 Baikie, Karen A. and Kay Wilhelm, "Emotional and Physical Health Benefits of Expressive Writing," p. 340.

39 See Pennebaker, pp. 10–11.

40 Heidegger, cited in Rickert, Thomas. *Ambient Rhetoric: The Attunements of Rhetorical Being.* University of Pittsburgh Press, 2013, pp. 239–40.

41 Rickert, p. 240.

42 Rickert, p. 8.

43 Ong, Walter. "The Writer's Audience Is Always a Fiction," p. 61.
44 Flower, Linda and John R. Hayes. "The Cognition of Discovery," p. 30.
45 For a discussion of these "types" of audiences, see Lundsford and Ede's distinction between audience "addressed" and "invoked": Ede, Lisa and Andrea Lunsford. "Audience Addressed/Audience Invoked: The Role of Audience in Composition Theory and Pedagogy." *College Composition and Communication*, vol. 35, no. 2, 1984, pp. 155–71. See also their follow-up article, critiquing their first: Lunsford, Andrea A. and Lisa Ede. "Representing Audience: 'Successful' Discourse and Disciplinary Critique." *College Composition and Communication*, vol. 47, no. 2, 1996, pp. 167–79.
46 See, for example, Field, Victoria, Gillie Bolton, and Kate Thompson. *Writing Works: A Resource Handbook for Therapeutic Writing Workshops and Activities*. Jessica Kingsley Publishers, 2006, pp. 224–26; and Pennebaker, James and John Evans. *Expressive Writing: Words That Heal*. Idyll Arbor, 2014, pp. 122–28.
47 AA Big Book, pp. 87–88.
48 Batterson, John. "How to Listen." Available from Hindsfoot Foundation, www.hindsfoot.org/batterson.doc.
49 See, for example, Bradshaw, John. *Coming Home: Reclaiming and Healing Your Inner Child*. Bantam, 1992.
50 For more information on Father Bill W.'s approach to the practice of two way prayer, see twowayprayer.org.
51 Johnson, Robert. *Inner Work: Using Dreams and Active Imagination for Personal Growth*, p. 138.
52 Johnson, pp. 143–47.
53 Johnson, pp. 185–86.
54 Johnson, p. 183.
55 Johnson, pp. 138–39.
56 Johnson, p. 140.
57 Johnson, p. 197.
58 Johnson, p. 98.
59 Batterson, John. "How to Listen." Available from Hindsfoot Foundation, www.hindsfoot.org/batterson.doc.

60 Johnson, p. 192.
61 AA Big Book, pp. 64–65.
62 AA Big Book, p. 64.
63 AA Big Book, pp. 64–65.
64 Recovering Couples Anonymous. *Recovering Couples Anonymous: A Twelve-Step Program for Couples*, 4th ed. World Service Organization of Recovering Couples Anonymous, 2011.

WORKS CITED

Alcoholics Anonymous. *Alcoholics Anonymous: The Story of How Many Thousands of Men and Women Have Recovered from Alcoholism*, 4th ed., New York City, Alcoholics Anonymous World Services, INC., 2001.

---. *Twelve Steps and Twelve Traditions*. New York City, Alcoholics Anonymous World Services, INC., 2004.

Baikie, Karen A. and Kay Wilhelm. "Emotional and Physical Health Benefits of Expressive Writing." *Advances in Psychiatric Treatment*, vol. 11, no.5, 2005, 338–46.

Bartholomae, David. "Inventing the University." *Journal of Basic Writing*, vol. 5, no. 1, 1986, pp. 4–23.

Batterson, John. "How to Listen." Available from Hindsfoot Foundation, www.hindsfoot.org/batterson.doc.

Bawarshi, Anis. *Genre and the Invention of the Writer: Reconsidering the Place of Invention in Composition*. Utah State University Press, 2003.

Berthoff, Ann E. *The Making of Meaning: Metaphors, Models, and Maxims for Writing Teachers*. Portsmouth, NH: Boynton/Cook Publishers, 1981.

Bradshaw, John. *Coming Home: Reclaiming and Healing Your Inner Child*. Bantam, 1992.

Britton, James. "Shaping at the Point of Utterance." *Reinventing the Rhetorical Tradition*. Eds. Ian Pringle and Aviva Freedman. Conway, AK: L and S Books, 1980, pp. 61–66.

Brophy, Kevin. *Creativity: Psychoanalysis, Surrealism and Creative Writing.* Melbourne University Press, 1994.

Bullitt-Jonas, Margaret. *Holy Hunger: A Woman's Journey from Food Addiction to Spiritual Fulfillment.* Vintage, 2000.

Cameron, Julia. *The Artist's Way: 25th Anniversary Edition.* TarcherPerigee, 2016.

Cheever, Susan. *My Name Is Bill: Bill Wilson—His Life and the Creation of Alcoholics Anonymous.* Washington Square Press, 2005.

Craft, Melissa A., Gail C. Davis and René M. Paulson. "Expressive Writing in Early Breast Cancer Survivors." *Journal of Advanced Nursing*, vol. 69, no. 2, 2013, pp. 305–15. Print.

Ede, Lisa and Andrea Lunsford. "Audience Addressed/Audience Invoked: The Role of Audience in Composition Theory and Pedagogy." *College Composition and Communication*, vol. 35, no. 2, 1984, pp. 155–71.

---. "Representing Audience: 'Successful' Discourse and Disciplinary Critique." *College Composition and Communication*, vol. 47, no. 2, 1996, pp. 167–79.

Fernyhough, Charles. *The Voices Within: The History and Science of How We Talk to Ourselves.* Basic Books, 2016.

Field, Victoria, Gillie Bolton, and Kate Thompson. *Writing Works: A Resource Handbook for Therapeutic Writing Workshops and Activities,* Jessica Kingsley Publishers, 2006.

Flower, Linda and John R. Hayes. "The Cognition of Discovery." *College Composition and Communication*, vol. 31, no. 1, Feb. 1980, pp. 21–32.

Foxwell, John, Ben Alderson-Day, Charles Fernyhough, and Angela Woods. "'I've Learned I Need to Treat My Characters Like People': Varieties of Agency and Interaction in Writers' Experiences of Their Characters' Voices." *Consciousness and Cognition*, vol. 79, 2020: 102901. doi:10.1016/j.concog.2020.102901

Hicks, Esther and Jerry Hicks. *The Law of Attraction: The Basics of the Teachings of Abraham.* Hay House, 2006.

Johnson, Robert. *Inner Work: Using Dreams and Active Imagination for Personal Growth.* HarperOne, 1986.

Keating, Thomas. *Open Heart, Open Mind.* Anniversary edition. Bloomsbury Continuum, 2019.

Kneupper, Charles. "Dramatistic Invention: The Pentad as Heuristic Procedure." *Rhetoric Society Quarterly*, vol. 9, 1979, pp. 130–36.

Koschwanez, Heidi E. et al. "Expressive Writing and Wound Healing in Older Adults: A Randomized Controlled Trial." *Psychosomatic Medicine*, vol. 75, 2013, pp. 581–90.

Lauer, Janice M. *Invention in Rhetoric and Composition*. Parlor Press, 2004. WAC Clearinghouse. https://wac.colostate.edu/books/referenceguides/lauer-invention/

Lean, Garth. *On the Tail of a Comet: The Life of Frank Buchman*. Helmers & Howard Publishers, 1989.

Maté, Gabor. *In the Realm of Hungry Ghosts: Close Encounters with Addiction*. North Atlantic Books, 2010.

Merril, James. *The Changing Light at Sandover*. Knopf, 2011.

Narcotics Anonymous. *Narcotics Anonymous Basic Text*, 6th ed. NA World Services, Inc., 2008.

O'Connor, Flannery. *The Habit of Being: Letters of Flannery O'Connor*. Farrar, Straus and Giroux, 1988.

Ong, Walter. "The Writer's Audience Is Always a Fiction." *PMLA*, vol. 90, no. 1, 1975, pp. 9–21.

Pennebaker, James. *Opening up: The Healing Power of Expressing Emotions*, 3rd ed. The Guilford Press, 2016.

Pennebaker, James and John Evans. *Expressive Writing: Words That Heal*. Idyll Arbor, 2014.

Recovering Couples Anonymous. *Recovering Couples Anonymous: A Twelve-Step Program for Couples*, 4th ed. World Service Organization of Recovering Couples Anonymous, 2011.

Rickert, Thomas. *Ambient Rhetoric: The Attunements of Rhetorical Being*. University of Pittsburgh Press, 2013.

SAA (Sex Addicts Anonymous). "First Step to Recovery: A Guide to Working the First Step," International Service Organization of SAA, Inc., 2018.

---. *Sex Addict Anonymous* (commonly called "The Green Book"). International Service Organization of SAA, Inc., 2005.

Smith, Helen E. et al. "The Effects of Expressive Writing on Lung Function, Quality of Life, Medication Use, and Symptoms in Adults with Asthma: A Randomized Controlled Trial." *Psychosomatic Medicine*, vol. 77, 2015, pp. 429–37.

Stevenson, Robert Louis. "A Chapter on Dreams," *Across the Plains*. New York: Charles Scribner's Sons, 1892.

Schucman, Helen. *A Course in Miracles: Based on The Original Handwritten Notes of Helen Schucman*. Circle of Atonement, Inc., 2021.

Thompson, Rachel Leah. "The Automatic Hand: Spiritualism, Psychoanalysis, Surrealism." *Culture: An Electronic Journal for Visual Culture*, no. 7, 2004, pp. 1–14.

Tiebout, Harry. *Harry Tiebout: The Collected Writings*. Hazelden, 1999.

Toronto, Richard. *War over Lemuria: Richard Shaver, Ray Palmer and the Strangest Chapter of 1940s Science Fiction*. McFarland & Company, 2013.

Twelve Step Apps. "Free Tenth Step Nightly Inventory App." www.12stepapps.org/10th-step.html.

Vitanza, Victor. "Three Countertheses: Or, A Critical In(ter)vention into Composition Theories and Pedagogies." *Contending with Words*. Eds. Patricia Harkin and John Schilb. New York: MLA, 1991, pp. 139–72.

Young, Richard, Alton Becker, and Kenneth Pike. *Rhetoric, Discovery, and Change*. New York: Harcourt, Brace, Jovanovich, 1970.

ABOUT THE AUTHOR

 **James Ryan** is an addict in recovery. He is an assistant professor of writing at the University of Alaska Southeast. James holds a PhD in Composition and Rhetoric, a master's in Theology, and a bachelor's in Creative Writing. This book is the result of his experiences in recovery, as well as his dissertation research into the writing experiences of addicts in Twelve-Step recovery programs.

ABOUT THE PUBLISHER

Lantern Publishing & Media was founded in 2020 to follow and expand on the legacy of Lantern Books—a publishing company started in 1999 on the principles of living with a greater depth and commitment to the preservation of the natural world. Like its predecessor, Lantern Publishing & Media produces books on animal advocacy, veganism, religion, social justice, humane education, psychology, family therapy, and recovery. Lantern is dedicated to printing in the United States on recycled paper and saving resources in our day-to-day operations. Our titles are also available as ebooks and audiobooks.

To catch up on Lantern's publishing program, visit us at www.lanternpm.org.

facebook.com/lanternpm
instagram.com/lanternpm
twitter.com/lanternpm